# INSIDE DESIGN NOW

DUDE!
SHAKA
CHAMPION
DUDE!

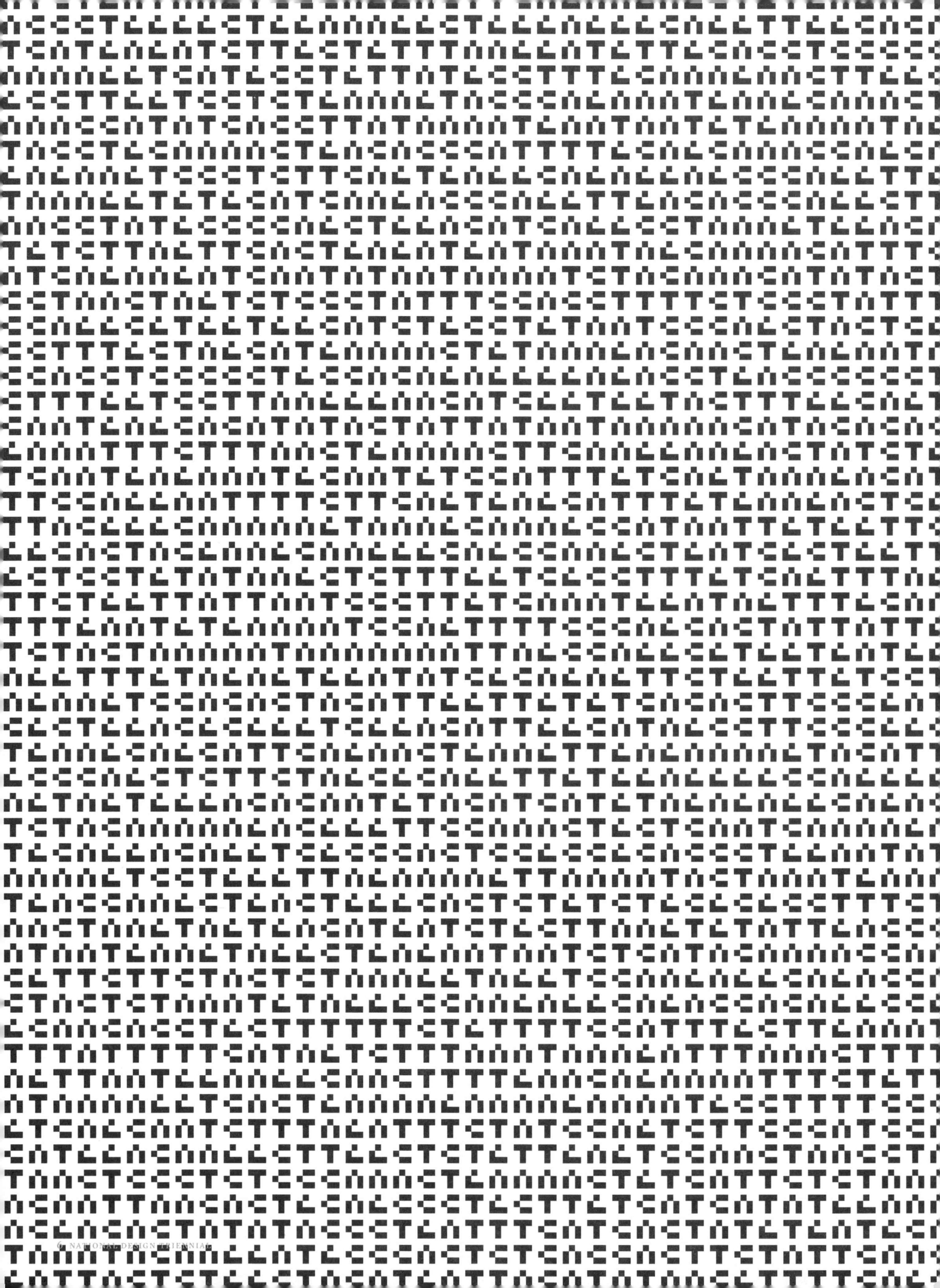

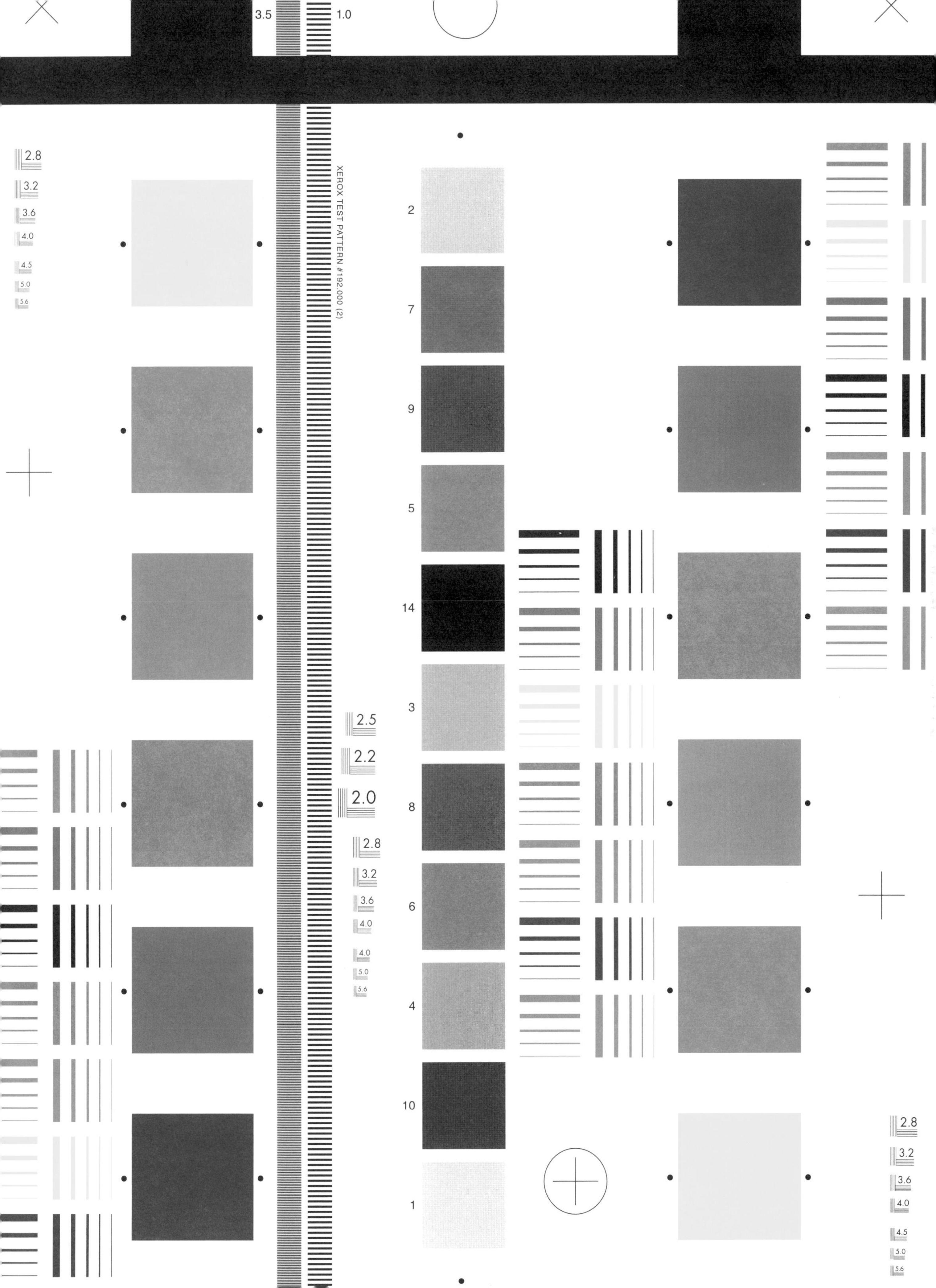
3.5
1.0
XEROX TEST PATTERN #192.000 (2)
2.8
3.2
3.6
4.0
4.5
5.0
5.6
2
7
9
5
14
3
8
6
4
10
1
2.5
2.2
2.0
2.8
3.2
3.6
4.0
4.0
5.0
5.6
2.8
3.2
3.6
4.0
4.5
5.0
5.6

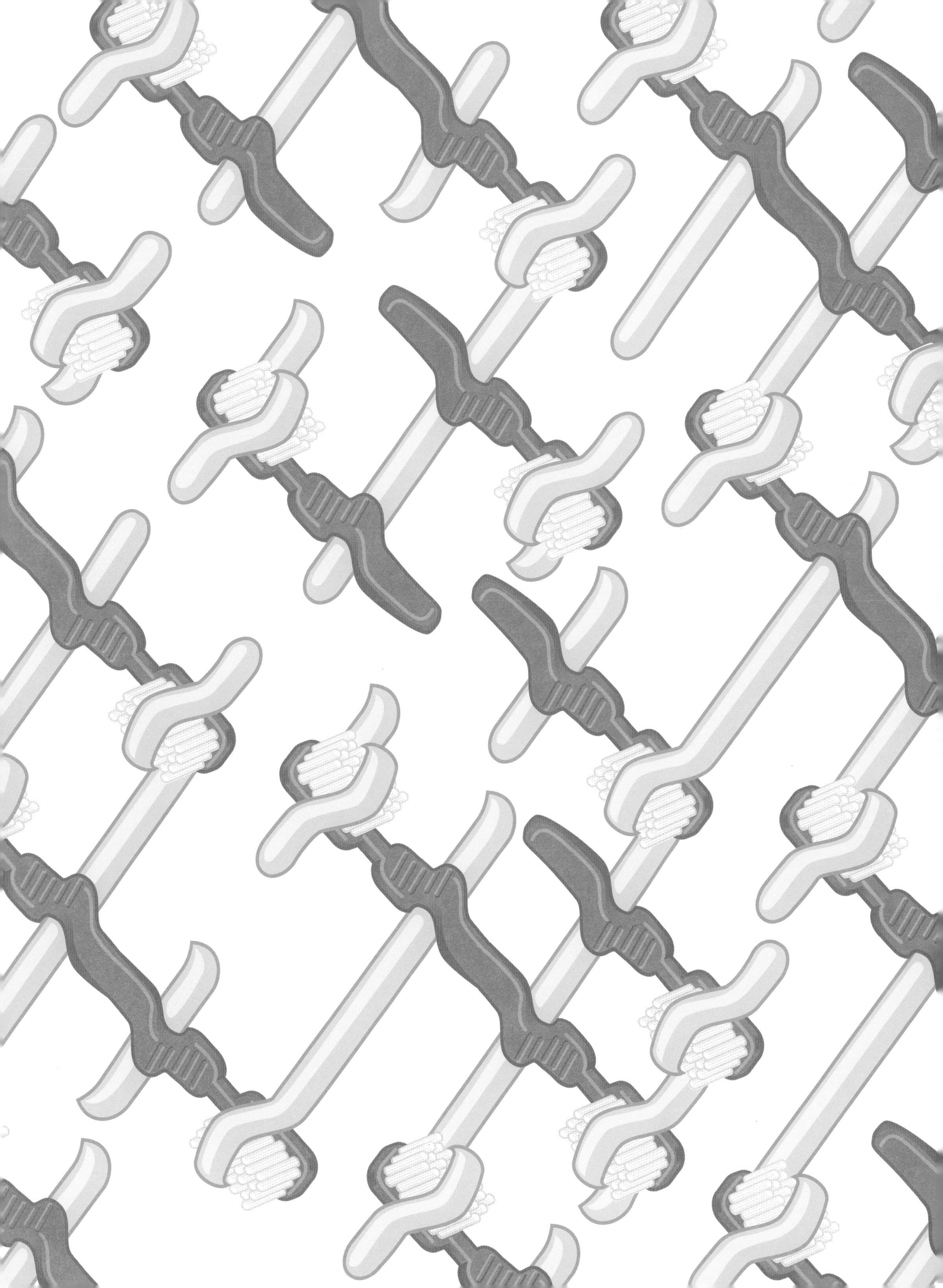

SASKATCHEWAN
SASKATOON
REGINA
CALGARY
RED DEER
LETHBRIDGE
KELOWNA
THE UNITED STATES
WASHINGTON
SEATTLE
TACOMA
OLYMPIA
SPOKANE
YAKIMA
OREGON
PORTLAND
SALEM
EUGENE
IDAHO
BOISE
IDAHO FALLS
POCATELLO
TWIN FALLS
MONTANA
MISSOULA
HELENA
GREAT FALLS
BILLINGS
BOZEMAN
NORTH DAKOTA
BISMARCK
SOUTH DAKOTA
PIERRE
RAPID CITY
WYOMING
CASPAR
CHEYENNE
LARAMIE
NEBRASKA
CALIFORNIA
SACRAMENTO
SAN FRANCISCO
SAN JOSE
LOS ANGELES
SAN DIEGO
BAKERSFIELD
NEVADA
RENO
CARSON CITY
LAS VEGAS
UTAH
SALT LAKE CITY
OGDEN
PROVO
COLORADO
DENVER
BOULDER
COLORADO SPRINGS
ARIZONA
PHOENIX
FLAGSTAFF
TUCSON
YUMA
NEW MEXICO
SANTA FE
ALBUQUERQUE
LAS CRUCES
TEXAS
EL PASO
AMARILLO
LUBBOCK
PACIFIC OCEAN
ALASKA
ANCHORAGE
FAIRBANKS
JUNEAU
ARCTIC OCEAN
BERING SEA
GULF OF ALASKA
BEAUFORT SEA
YUKON
CANADA
MEXICO
BAJA CALIFORNIA
GULF OF CALIFORNIA
TIJUANA
MEXICALI
CHIHUAHUA
SONORA
DURANGO
COAHUILA

ONTARIO
QUEBEC
MAINE
MINNESOTA
WISCONSIN
MICHIGAN
LAKE SUPERIOR
LAKE HURON
LAKE MICHIGAN
LAKE ONTARIO
LAKE ERIE
OTTAWA
MONTREAL
TORONTO
NEW YORK
VERMONT
NEW HAMPSHIRE
MASSACHUSETTS
RHODE ISLAND
CONN.
BOSTON
NEW YORK CITY
PENNSYLVANIA
PHILADELPHIA
NEW JERSEY
IOWA
ILLINOIS
CHICAGO
INDIANA
OHIO
MD.
BALTIMORE
DELAWARE
WASHINGTON D.C.
W.VA.
MISSOURI
KENTUCKY
VIRGINIA
TENNESSEE
MEMPHIS
NASHVILLE
N.CAROLINA
S.CAROLINA
ARKANSAS
MISSISSIPPI
ALABAMA
GEORGIA
ATLANTA
LOUISIANA
NEW ORLEANS
FLORIDA
MIAMI
HOUSTON
GULF OF MEXICO
HAWAII
OAHU
HONOLULU
ATLANTIC OCEAN

NATIONAL DESIGN TRIENNIAL

# INSIDE DESIGN NOW

ELLEN LUPTON DONALD ALBRECHT SUSAN YELAVICH MITCHELL OWENS

COOPER-HEWITT, NATIONAL DESIGN MUSEUM

SMITHSONIAN INSTITUTION

PRINCETON ARCHITECTURAL PRESS

Published by
**Princeton Architectural Press**
37 East Seventh Street
New York, New York 10003

For a free catalog of books, call 1.800.722.6657.
Visit our web site at www.papress.com.

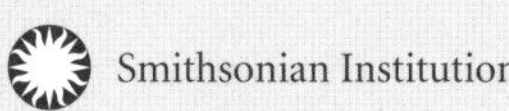



Printed and bound in China
06 05 04 03 5 4 3 2 1 First edition

Printed on Mohawk Superfine softwhite eggshell and Lumi matt papers.



Project coordinator: Mark Lamster

Special thanks: Nettie Aljian, Ann Alter, Nicola Bednarek, Janet Behning, Megan Carey, Penny Chu, Russell Fernandez, Clare Jacobson, Nancy Eklund Later, Linda Lee, Jane Sheinman, Katharine Smalley, Scott Tennent, Jennifer Thompson, Joe Weston, and Deb Wood of Princeton Architectural Press—
Kevin C. Lippert, publisher

ISBN: 1-56898-394-8

Library of Congress
Cataloging-in-Publication Data

Inside design now: National Design Triennial / Ellen Lupton ... [et al.].
p. cm.
Catalog of an exhibition held at Cooper-Hewitt, National Design Museum, Smithsonian Institution, New York.
Includes bibliographical references and index.
ISBN 1-56898-394-8 (alk. paper) —
ISBN 1-56898-395-6 (pbk. : alk. paper)
1. Design—History—20th century—Exhibitions.
I. Lupton, Ellen. II. Cooper-Hewitt, National Design Museum.
NK1390.I54 2003
745.4'074'7471—dc21

2002015746

## PREFACE





## ESSAYS



## DESIGNERS

# contents

# preface

PAUL WARWICK THOMPSON

DIRECTOR

*Cooper-Hewitt*

*National Design Museum*

*Smithsonian Institution*

The *National Design Triennial* was inaugurated by Cooper-Hewitt, National Design Museum to study and celebrate contemporary design in the United States. Interdisciplinary in nature, the *Triennial* reviews cutting-edge trends and future horizons across the fields of design practice, from architecture, interiors, and landscape design to product design, graphic design, fashion, film, and new media. It is the only exhibition program of its kind in the United States. Great thanks go to our founding sponsor, BP, as well as to Birkenstock, Agnes Bourne, the Lily Auchincloss Foundation, Inc., and Joel and Anne Ehrenkranz for their essential support in making this exhibition a reality.

The first *National Design Triennial* opened in the spring of 2000. It placed a strong emphasis on technology, from consumer devices for work, play, and communication to the software applications that were transforming the design disciplines. The second *Triennial*, subtitled *Inside Design Now*, pays special attention to the realm of the interior, both at home and in the workplace. Understood psychologically as well as physically, the concept of the interior is explored at the scale of objects, garments, and printed matter as well as buildings, cities, and landscapes.

An interior can be as private as a bedroom or as public as a subway car, as tiny as the chambers of an artificial heart or as expansive as an urban development. As cultures become increasingly global and nomadic, new technologies and social shifts are changing our understanding of interior spaces. Contemporary design enables the exchange of data, the flow of goods, and the communication of ideas, as well as providing settings for work, rest, and contemplation. Technology is still at constant play in contemporary design, but now it has been internalized.

Many of the works selected for *Inside Design Now* reveal a fascination with beauty and decoration, expressed from a distinctly contemporary point of view. Sensuous materials, lush patterns, and exquisite production details come together with new technologies, pop culture imagery, and fresh approaches to scale, color, and construction.

*Inside Design Now* presents the work of eighty emerging and established designers and firms operating at the most innovative and provocative level in design today. The curatorial team of Donald Albrecht, Ellen Lupton, Mitchell Owens, and Susan Yelavich have worked together to create an exhibition and book that reflect the energy and diversity of design today in the United States.

DICKSTEIN RESIDENCE
New York City, 1999
Detail, custom upholstered chair
Designers: William Diamond and Anthony Baratta, Diamond + Baratta
Photography: Melanie Acevedo

# acknowledgments


ELLEN LUPTON

DONALD ALBRECHT

SUSAN YELAVICH

MITCHELL OWENS

CURATORS

*National Design Triennial*

Many people and institutions helped create this book and the exhibition it accompanies. Thanks goes to all the designers, photographers, firms, and manufacturers who shared their work and ideas. Their talents and resources made this project possible.

We are particularly grateful to BP, the founding sponsor of the *National Design Triennial*. We also extend our thanks to Birkenstock, Agnes Bourne, the Lily Auchincloss Foundation, Inc., and Joel and Anne Ehrenkranz for their invaluable assistance, as well as to the Andrew W. Mellon Foundation for their support of this book.

The exhibition was designed by Sandra Wheeler and Alfred Zollinger, of Matter Practice, who have brought a special sensitivity to the museum's historic building, the Andrew Carnegie Mansion. Working with lighting designer Anita Jorgensen, they allow it to come alive as an interior furnished with contemporary objects and surfaces.

The entire staff of Cooper-Hewitt, National Design Museum helped create the *Triennial*. Appreciation goes to everyone who contributed to the project's content, design, production, administration, development, marketing, maintenance, security, and educational programming. We are particularly grateful to Paul Warwick Thompson, who has enthusiastically supported the project as he develops his new vision for the museum.

Special thanks are directed to several key people at the museum: Allison Henriksen, Curatorial Assistant, for collecting and communicating information among all the project's participants and editing the book's captions; Elizabeth Johnson, Editor, for refining the content of this book; Caroline Baumann, Development Director, for her impassioned support of the exhibition's development; Steven Langehough, Associate Registrar, for organizing the shipping of objects; Jennifer Northrop, Communications Director, and Stephen Malmberg, Public Affairs Specialist, for promoting the exhibition to the press and public; Matt Flynn for photographing many of the objects; Jill Bloomer for arranging the photo shoots; and Dorothy Dunn, Head of Education, for her oversight of the project's relationship to all the Museum's audiences; and Jennifer Brundage, Monica Hampton, and Mei Mah, for conceiving and implementing an exciting array of educational programs. Finally, extreme gratitude is owed to Lindsay Stamm Shapiro, Head of Exhibitions; Jen Roos and Alicia Cheng, Co-Directors of Design; and Jocelyn Groom, Scott Wilhelme, and the museum's full exhibitions and design staff, whose skills and talents helped create a safe, beautiful, and functional environment for the *Triennial*.

This publication reflects the museum's ongoing collaboration with Princeton Architectural Press. Special thanks go to our editor, Mark Lamster, and to Kevin Lippert, publisher.

The best part about working on the *National Design Triennial* is collaborating with an amazing team of curators, as well as meeting new designers and reconnecting with people whose careers I have followed for a long time. I am grateful to all the creative people who produced the *Triennial*, but above all, I thank my friend and colleague Susan Yelavich for her beauty, intelligence, and dedication to design studies.

The heavy labor of producing this book was lightened by the consistent efforts and good humor of our editors, Elizabeth Johnson and Mark Lamster, and our managing editor, Allison Henriksen.

Elke Gasselseder contributed her visual talent and technical expertise to the production of this book in my home office in Baltimore.

My friends are a huge part of my life; I thank Claudia Matzko and Jennifer Tobias for their love, wit, and constancy.

My family is a constant source of pleasure and inspiration. My love goes out to Jay, Ruby, and Abbott; to Mary Jane and Ken; to Bill and Shirley; to Michelle, Anwar, and Layla; and to Julia, Ken, and all their children. **EL**

I am eager to thank many people who made curating this second *National Design Triennial* an enjoyable and rewarding experience. My wonderful cocurators, the exhibition's designers, and the museum's exhibition management and construction team, led with tremendous effort and grace by Lindsay Shapiro, have been essential to this collaborative effort. Searching for—and having colleagues suggest—participants is the most enjoyable part of the process, equaled by working with the participants themselves to shape their presentations. My great friend and collaborator Natalie Shivers has provided essential guidance in writing the texts, probing me to think more clearly about the work of the participating designers and architects. Cooper-Hewitt editor Elizabeth Johnson shaped the final manuscripts with great care and thoughtfulness. Randi Mates, Chelsea Grogan, and especially Allison Henriksen were essential to the team, anticipating every task and doing so with humor and grace. My friends and family are of great importance to me. These exhibitions would not happen without them. **DA**

My thanks to Susan Yelavich, who asked me to be a part of the *Triennial* band of cocurators, and to Allison Henriksen and Elizabeth Johnson, whose patience and fortitude never wavered and whose demeanors never betrayed the daily pressures and frustrations. And for putting up with my computer-hogging, wee-hours writing, and occasional fit of temper, I owe a debt of gratitude to my partner, Matthew Zwissler, and our daughter, Catherine. **MO**

I want to thank my fellow curators for making this collaboration as enjoyable as it was fruitful. And while each of us brought our specific vantage points to the *Triennial*, Ellen Lupton contributed something more. She brought the project full circle and made this book a work of design itself, a mirror of the ideas that the *Triennial* designers cultivate in their work and the ideas we curators extrapolate from it.

Thanks also to Allison Henriksen, my treasured colleague before the *Triennial* and indispensable curatorial assistant during it. Allison provided essential support to the book and exhibition, serving both as sounding board and one-person search engine. I am very grateful to Elizabeth Johnson for her care in editing this catalog. And special thanks are owed to Lucy Commoner and Emily Miller, both of whom offered ideas and introductions to designers that shaped my selections. Indeed, I am indebted to all of my colleagues at Cooper-Hewitt over the years for the remarkable education they have afforded me.

Finally, my deepest love and gratitude to my husband, Michael, and son, Henry, for their patience and always insightful behind-the-scenes critiques. **SY**

*National Design Triennial: Inside Design Now* is sponsored by BP. 

Additional funding is provided by Birkenstock, Agnes Bourne, the Lily Auchincloss Foundation, Inc., and Joel and Anne Ehrenkranz.

DUDE!
SHAKA
CHAMPION
DUDE!

DUDE!
SHAKA
CHAMPION
DUDE!

# the producers

# ellen lupton

Curated by
Ellen Lupton
Donald Albrecht
Susan Yelavich
Mitchell Owens

2x4
ABIOMED, Inc.
Charles S. Anderson
Antenna Design
As Four
Asymptote
Rick Baker
Bryan Bell
Blu Dot
Cynthia Breazeal
Bureau Betak
Stephen Burks
Critz Campbell
The Chopping Block
Kelly Christy
co-lab
Collaborative
Laurie DeMartino
Demeter Fragrance Library
Diamond + Baratta
Dave Eggers
Peter Eisenman
Paul Elliman
Escher + GuneWardena Architecture
Ford Motor Company
Benjamin Fry
Fuseproject
Futurefarmers
Tess Giberson
Green Lady + HunterGatherer
The Hoefler Type Foundry
David Hoey
Joseph Holtzman
House Industries
Viktor Jondal
Maira Kalman
KW:a
LoyandFord
Lutz + Patmos
Tod Machover
Maharam
Geoff McFetridge
Stephen McKay
Gene Meyer
J. Abbott Miller
Mike Mills
Isaac Mizrahi
Ted Muehling
Christoph Niemann
Frank Nuovo
Yusuke Obuchi
Michele Oka Doner
Gaetano Pesce
Picture Projects
Mark Pollack
Michael Rakowitz
Bob Sabiston
Stanley Saitowitz
Paula Scher
Jennifer Siegal
Smart Design
Paige Stahl
Christopher Streng
Daniel Streng
SuperHappyBunny
Target Corporation
Jennifer Tipton
Isabel Toledo
Troika Design Group
Andrea Valentini
Gabriela Valenzuela-Hirsch
Jhonen Vasquez
Cesar Vergara
Kiki Wallace + Mark Sofield
David + Sandy Wasco
Dennis Wedlick
David Weeks Lighting + Butter
Lorraine Wild
Stephen Wolfram
Jim Zivic

# "I'm rocking on your dime," says the panda bear.

The bear is sitting at a bar, a beer and a cigarette in front of him. His flat silhouette appears on a t-shirt by Geoff McFetridge, a young designer based in Los Angeles. McFetridge and his slouchy, working-class panda convey the attitude of an increasingly influential set of designers who want to shape the content and conditions of the work they do. "I'm rocking on your dime," says the designer who sees the client as a source of capital for creating inventive work equipped with a cultural life.

Graphic design is, among the design professions, the area most at blame for visual waste and overload in modern society. Graphic design often serves as a lubricant for other disciplines (product design, architecture, fashion) and as the gloss and glitter of the media industries (publishing, film, television, the Internet). Typically, graphic designers provide the spit and polish but not the shoe.

Not so for some of the most interesting designers working today. They are writing books as well as designing them. They are creating products, furniture, garments, textiles, typefaces, databases, magazines, novels, music, critical essays, films, and videos. They have become *producers*, working to initiate ideas and make them happen.

The phrase "designer as author" appeared in the 1990s to describe new aspirations for the practice of graphic design. The word *author* suggests agency and creation, as opposed to the more passive functions of consulting, styling, and formatting. As an author, the designer could create books, exhibitions, posters, or publications whose outcome was not dictated by a client. Furthermore, a designer could develop a "signature style," a uniquely recognizable visual penmanship.

In his 1996 essay "The Designer as Author," Michael Rock described the contradictions as well as the freedoms suggested by authorship.[1] The concept of the lone creator had long been attacked within literary studies. In 1968 the French theorist Roland Barthes had proclaimed the "death of the author," the end of the writer as a singular, self-contained voice. Barthes described the circulation of signs, styles, and genres within the vast social system that constitutes literature. Meaning is made by readers as well as writers.[2]

1. Michael Rock, "The Designer as Author," in *Looking Closer Four: Critical Writings on Graphic Design*, ed. Michael Bieruit, William Drenttel, and Steven Heller (New York: Allworth Press, 2002), 237–44. Originally published in *Eye*, no. 20 (Spring 1996).
2. Roland Barthes, "The Death of the Author," in *Image/Music/Text*, trans. Stephen Heath (New York: Hill and Wang, 1977), 142–48.

I'M ROCKING ON YOUR DIME
Silkscreened t-shirt, 1999
Designer: Geoff McFetridge, Champion Graphics
Produced for exhibition at George's Gallery, Los Angeles

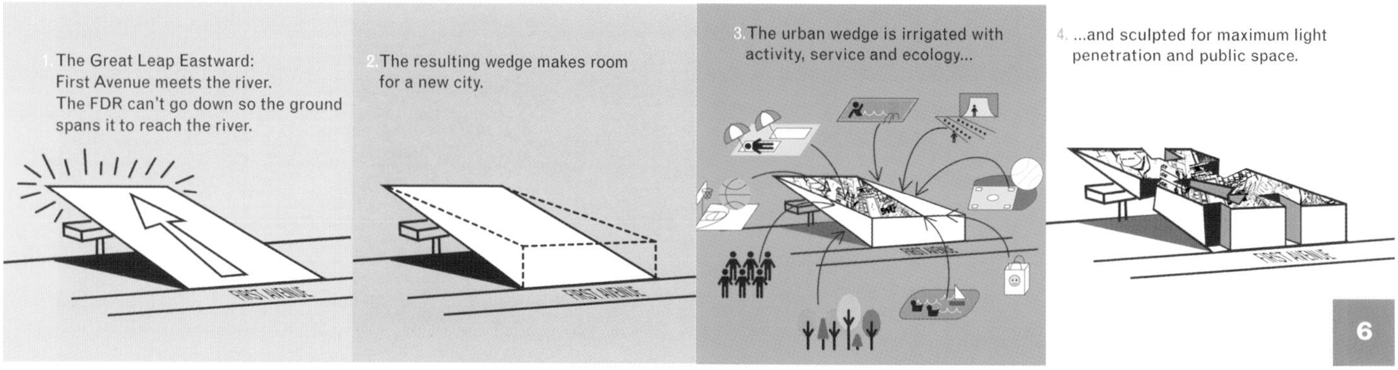

1. The Great Leap Eastward:
First Avenue meets the river.
The FDR can't go down so the ground spans it to reach the river.

2. The resulting wedge makes room for a new city.

3. The urban wedge is irrigated with activity, service and ecology...

4. ...and sculpted for maximum light penetration and public space.

6

UNCITY
Detail from accordian book produced for an architectural competition, 2001
Designers: Michael Rock, Karen Hsu, Alice Chung, Dan Wood, and Amale Andraos, 2x4; with OMA, KPF, Davis Brody Bond, Toyo Ito, DIRT Studio, and Ove Arup

In the early 1990s, Michael Rock became prominent within the graphic design field as a critic and educator. He founded the firm 2x4 with Susan Sellers and Georgie Stout in 1993, where he and his colleagues were able to fold ideas developed as writers, teachers, and students into an influential design practice. Many of the studio's projects are based in research; the outcomes promote flexible use by clients and audiences. In place of forging a "signature style," 2x4 works to uncover visual forms from popular culture or from a client's own history. In Rock's words, "Ultimately the author equals authority.... We may have to imagine a time when we can ask, 'What difference does it make who designed it?'... The primary concern of both the viewer and critic is not who made it, but rather *what* it does and *how* it does it."[3]

While the author may be a solitary originator of content, the producer is part of a system of making. In the context of contemporary media, a producer is, typically, someone who puts together a team, builds a budget, and secures access to distribution networks. In music and television, a producer is in charge of the technical aspects of a project. A producer—whether functioning in an executive capacity or a technical one—belongs to a network of creative and economic collaborators.

The German critic Walter Benjamin attacked the traditional definition of authorship in his essay "The Author as Producer" (1934). He exclaimed that new forms of communication—film, radio, advertising, newspapers, the illustrated press—were melting down traditional artistic genres and corroding the borders between writing and reading. Benjamin wrote:

> What we require of the photographer is the ability to give his picture the caption that wrenches it from modish commerce and gives it a revolutionary useful value. But we shall make this demand most emphatically when we—the writers—take up photography. Here, too, therefore, technical progress is for the author as producer the foundation of political progress.[4]

Benjamin claimed that to bridge the divide between author and publisher, reader and writer, poet and popularizer, is a revolutionary act that challenges the social institutions of literature and art.

Benjamin celebrated the proletarian ring of production—as opposed to the bourgeois solitude implied by authorship. Within graphic design practice, production refers to the preparation of artwork for manufacture. Production is design's blue-collar, hourly-wage base. It is the traditional domain of the paste-up artist, the film stripper, the hand-letterer, and the typesetter.

3. Rock, "Designer as Author," 244.
4. Walter Benjamin, "The Author as Producer," in *Reflections: Essays, Aphorisms, Autobiographical Writings*, ed. Peter Demetz (New York: Schocken Books, 1978), 230. See also Ellen Lupton, "The Designer as Producer," in *The Education of a Graphic Designer*, ed. Steven Heller (New York: Allworth Press, 1998), 159–62.

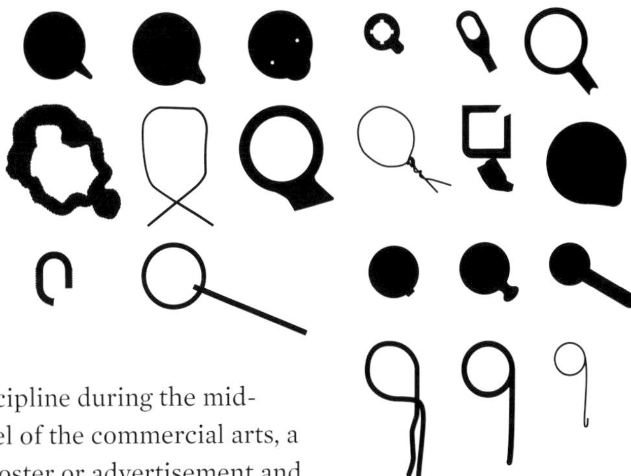

BITS
Digital typeface (letter q)
Designer: Paul Elliman

Graphic design emerged as a distinct discipline during the mid-twentieth century. In the old-fashioned model of the commercial arts, a printing company determined the look of a poster or advertisement and then physically produced it. The printing firm often set the type, laid it out on the page, and provided illustrations. As these services split apart, the designer became the provider of ideas and director of production.

The "desktop" revolution that began in the mid-1980s merged many production activities back into the process of design. Today, a designer sitting at a computer workstation can set copy, correct text, and retouch photographs, as well as create and manipulate sound, video, animations, and interfaces. The result is both a proletarianization of design and new access to creating and manipulating content. Such changes have enabled a small company such as HunterGatherer to produce print graphics, films, and Websites as well as designs for textiles, t-shirts, and furniture.

Independent entrepreneurs are now leaders of the typeface industry, once dominated by large manufacturers who could finance the creative development, tooling, manufacture, and distribution of fonts. House Industries aims to infuse digital typography with the qualities of hand-lettering and sign painting. The Hoefler Typefoundry creates fonts commissioned by clients or offered directly to designers via mail-order and the Internet. Paul Elliman creates typefaces that are exploratory and experimental rather than commercial.

Like these font producers, Charles S. Anderson creates raw material for use by other designers. CSA Archives is a collection of digital illustrations and photographs. Anderson conceives his enterprise as a direct challenge to the huge stock houses that dominate the business and sell clichéd, leftover images at prices that undercut independent photographers and illustrators. Many of his images poke fun at the depictions of wholesome "professionals" that fill standard stock catalogs.

Dave Eggers has built a unique practice out of the convergence of design, production, and authorship. A self-described "hack designer and Macintosh temp," Eggers founded the journal *Timothy McSweeney's Quarterly Concern*, in 1998, at age 28. He used his basic production skills to publish the journal himself. *McSweeney's* quickly drew attention from the literary world, in part because of its brazenly bookish design. Resisting the corporate control of bookstores, Eggers makes McSweeney's publications available only online or through independent booksellers, not through large chains.

CELLULAR AUTOMATON
Digital image, 2002
Designer: Stephen Wolfram
From *A New Kind of Science* by Stephen Wolfram
Publisher: Wolfram Media, Champaign, Illinois

Although his early work included menial forms of production, Eggers is now an editor, publisher, and author—a producer in the executive sense. In 2000 Simon & Schuster published the memoir *A Heartbreaking Work of Staggering Genius*, about how Eggers, at age 22, lost his parents and became the guardian of his eight-year-old brother, Toph. Designed by Eggers, the book became a bestseller.[5]

As Eggers proves, the author isn't dead, he has just learned how to set type. The book isn't dead, either, despite frequent warnings of its imminent demise. The 1,376-page tome *S, M, L, XL,* coauthored by architect Rem Koolhaas and graphic designer Bruce Mau in 1996, spurred the publication of other big books, including Mau's own *Life Style* (626 pages) and John Maeda's *Maeda@Media* (480 pages). An editor of design and architecture books was quoted in the *New York Times* about how contemporary architects are rushing to publish their own big volumes. "We get lots of fat-book proposals," he said. Technology allows architects—for better or worse—to control the design, editing, and writing of their own books. "And they understand the book as a physical object, one that should take up a great deal of space."[6]

Perhaps the biggest book of 2002 is *A New Kind of Science*, by Stephen Wolfram. The book, more than 1,200 pages long, provides a new theory of nature that aims to rewrite nearly every field of scientific study.[7] Wolfram executed his research on a computer in his home office, using a software program (Mathematica) of his own design. Wolfram chose to present his research in a single printed volume, edited and designed by his own private company, Wolfram Media. He thus rejected the academic protocol of submitting articles to peer-reviewed journals in favor of what might be called "vanity publishing" were it not for the importance of what he has created.

Wolfram insists that no conventional publisher could have adequately produced his huge book, which is filled with detailed computer-generated illustrations. Furthermore, the magnitude of his ideas demands presentation in a single bound volume—a book holding the key to life itself. Dribbling out his research in a series of separate articles would have lacked the impact of one sweeping text, the culmination of ten years of work. This scientist has become author and entrepreneur, an academic outsider who has made his research into products for his own use and distribution.

Although Wolfram's *New Kind of Science* is the work of a single author, it nonetheless represents the labors of many people—graphic designers, font designers, layout assistants, proofreaders, program testers, and a manufacturing manager—but, curiously enough, no editor.[8] Traditionally,

5. Dave Eggers, *A Heartbreaking Work of Staggering Genius* (New York: Simon & Schuster, 2000).
6. Rem Koolhaas and Bruce Mau, *S, M, L, XL* (New York: Monacelli Press, 1996); Bruce Mau, *Life Style* (London: Phaidon Press, 2000). John Maeda, *Maeda@Media* (New York: Rizzoli, 2000).
6. Eve M. Kahn, "Architecture Books With the Heft of Blocks and Bricks," *New York Times* (February 8, 2001).
7. Stephen Wolfram, *A New Kind of Science* (Champaign, Illinois, 2002).
8. On Wolfram and his book, see Steven Levy, "The Man Who Cracked the Code to Everything," *Wired* (June 2002): 132–37, 146. Levy points out the book's lack of an editor.
9. Lauren Oliver, "Private Industry," *Surface*, no. 32 (2001): 114–20, 221. Oliver notes the importance of McFetridge's "rocking on your dime" t-shirt to designer/producers in Los Angeles.

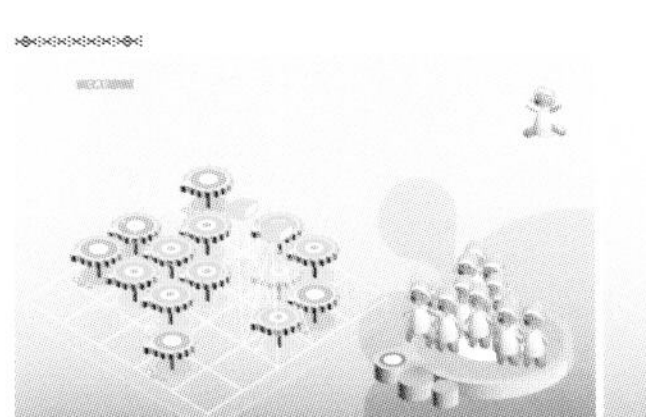
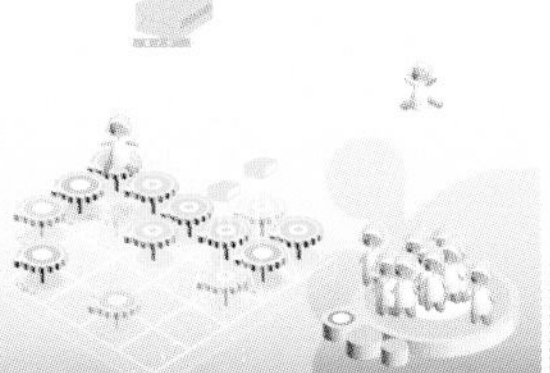
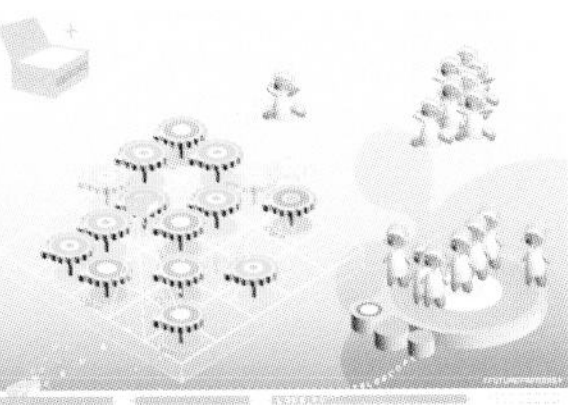

an editor mediates between intellectual authorship and material production. Indeed, many publishing houses refuse to let authors meddle with the physical realization of their works. In the book designs of J. Abbott Miller, Lorraine Wild, and Bruce Mau, the graphic designer becomes an editor, actively shaping the organization, content, and even the basic conception of a book.

Graphic designers also have become editors of magazines. Miller edits and art directs the journal *2wice*; Joseph Holtzman is editor, art director, and publisher of the quarterly *nest*. Holtzman, who sees himself first as an interior designer, brings the skewed perspective of an outsider to the medium of print. Working with an almost amateur sense of typography and layout, he brings the decorative intensity of a room to his strange and elaborate pages.

The Internet has allowed people of all manner of obsession and prior training to try on the roles of editor and publisher. Although the pornography business survived the collapse of the dot-com bubble better than literary magazines did, the Web remains a place where serious content can be developed and distributed. At Picture Projects, Alison Cornyn and Sue Johnson produce Websites that document issues such as abuse and overpopulation in the U.S. penal system, using clean, elegant interfaces to weave together visual and verbal content. Futurefarmers, founded by Amy Franceschini, reflects on issues of ecology and community by building interactive landscapes inhabited by candy-colored animated characters—Hello Kitty meets the rain forest.

Mike Mills is a graphic designer who has become a filmmaker. Mills directs television commercials for corporations such as Nike, Volkswagen, and The Gap as well as independent films and music videos. As pointed out in the pop culture journal *Surface*, Geoff McFetridge's slogan "I'm rocking on your dime" describes Mills's attitude toward the film business. He sees real opportunities for creativity in mass-media work, and, furthermore, such projects help him pursue his own independent films.[9]

Whereas the term *author*, like *designer*, suggests the cerebral workings of the mind, *producer* privileges the activity of the body. Production values things over ideas, making over imagining, practice over theory. Graphic designers today have opportunities to bring these spheres together, to actively mediate between form and content. By understanding the tools of physical production, they are achieving greater intellectual and economic control of their work.

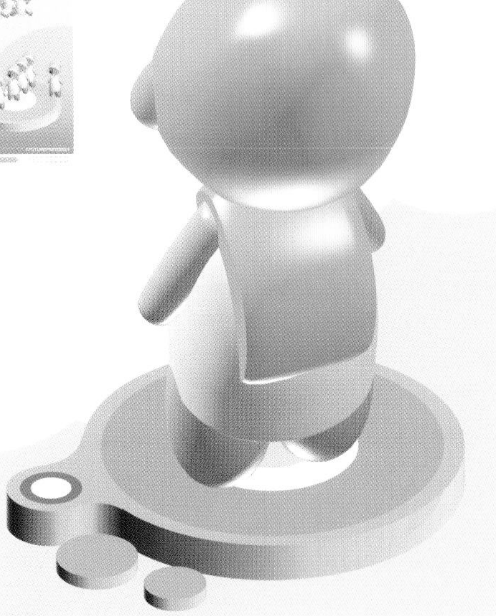

MIND THE BANNER
Website, 2000
Designer: Amy Franceschini, Futurefarmers
Client: NTT Data, Japan

# the show people

## donald albrecht

Curated by
Ellen Lupton
Donald Albrecht
Susan Yelavich
Mitchell Owens

2x4
ABIOMED, Inc.
Charles S. Anderson
Antenna Design
As Four
Asymptote
Rick Baker
Bryan Bell
Blu Dot
Cynthia Breazeal
Bureau Betak
Stephen Burks
Critz Campbell
The Chopping Block
Kelly Christy
co-lab
Collaborative
Laurie DeMartino
Demeter Fragrance Library
Diamond + Baratta
Dave Eggers
Peter Eisenman
Paul Elliman
Escher + GuneWardena Architecture
Ford Motor Company
Benjamin Fry
Fuseproject
Futurefarmers
Tess Giberson
Green Lady + HunterGatherer
The Hoefler Type Foundry
David Hoey
Joseph Holtzman
House Industries
Viktor Jondal
Maira Kalman
KW:a

LoyandFord
Lutz + Patmos
Tod Machover
Maharam
Geoff McFetridge
Stephen McKay
Gene Meyer
J. Abbott Miller
Mike Mills
Isaac Mizrahi
Ted Muehling
Christoph Niemann
Frank Nuovo
Yusuke Obuchi
Michele Oka Doner
Gaetano Pesce
Picture Projects
Mark Pollack
Michael Rakowitz
Bob Sabiston
Stanley Saitowitz
Paula Scher
Jennifer Siegal
Smart Design
Paige Stahl
Christopher Streng
Daniel Streng
SuperHappyBunny
Target Corporation
Jennifer Tipton
Isabel Toledo
Troika Design Group
Andrea Valentini
Gabriela Valenzuela-Hirsch
Jhonen Vasquez
Cesar Vergara
Kiki Wallace + Mark Sofield
David + Sandy Wasco
Dennis Wedlick
David Weeks Lighting + Butter
Lorraine Wild
Stephen Wolfram
Jim Zivic

# Mask makers. Set designers. Illuminators of ordinary things.

The 2003 *National Design Triennial* participants treat design as theater. Some dominate the stages and screens where they visually interpret the fictional worlds conceived by writers and directors. Others turn their vivid imaginations to unexpected places like city streets and exhibition galleries, transforming them into arenas for performing their ideas. Still others dramatize the normally invisible forces of science, society, and culture. They critique the status quo and address issues as diverse as migration, homelessness, and gentrification in contemporary America.

These designers believe in the transformative power of their work. Stage lighting designer Jennifer Tipton's description of her medium applies equally well to a number of projects featured in this volume: "Light is visual music with the same mystical power to transport an audience—a viewer or group of viewers—effortlessly from one place, one time, one idea to another without having to make the individual steps along the way." Like Tipton, many participants use light transcendently, imbuing ordinary objects with extraordinary dimension. In her own work, Tipton illuminates life itself with her stagecraft, weaving design and narrative into a seamless whole. Light turns product design into translucent sculpture in the chandeliers of Stephen McKay and architecture into film set in Frank Escher and Ravi GuneWardena's Electric Sun tanning salons, where light from tanning beds casts shifting veils of colored illumination onto walls and dramatically silhouettes staff and customers.

Lighting also shades the meaning of objects. By turning a vintage dress and armchair into lamps, Critz Campbell infuses them with a bittersweet nostalgia. They pull us back to the past, yet remind us by their modernity that we can't go home again. With backlighting, the meaning of everyday domestic things is elevated by Paul Kariouk and Mabel Wilson, partners in KW:a, in their exhibition on the plight of migrants, *(a)way station*. Ford Motor Company's GloCar, designed by Laurens van

**HOUSE/LIGHTS**
Theater production, 1999
Wooster Group, New York City
Lighting designer: Jennifer Tipton
Director: Elizabeth LeCompte
Photography: Mary Gearheart

SPECIAL #8
Lighting/table, 2001
Milk acrylic, stainless steel, lightbulb
Designers: SuperHappyBunny with Dino Alzadon
Manufacturer: SuperHappyBunny
Photography: SuperHappyBunny

den Ackers, is a full-scale roadside semaphore with illuminated plastic LED panels that change colors, intensity, and frequency to communicate to surrounding drivers. And fast food becomes props for mobile lifestyles in the hands of SuperHappyBunny. They pump up the scale of a standard Chinese food takeout box into a glowing, Pop art table.

No longer is ornament crime, despite Austrian architect Adolf Loos's famous declaration to the contrary. Today's designers are embracing decoration, but refracting it through the lens of modernism. It has become a state of mind and a medium of many moods: contemplative in the hands of Critz Campbell, magically insane in the settings created by David Wasco and Sandy Reynolds-Wasco for *The Royal Tenenbaums*. And consider David Hoey's store windows for New York's Bergdorf Goodman department store, where fashion and interior design meet 1930s screwball comedy. Hoey creates ironic tableaux of banal materials like toasted Wonder Bread and wigs that serve as backdrops for couture clothes.

In our entertainment-driven world, theatricality has colonized nearly every realm of public life, including the street. The fashions of LoyandFord and Kelly Christy are more costume than clothing. LoyandFord's stylish designs started out in the performance-centered club world of Berlin and today clothe the performance-centered world of city streets. Christy has designed hats for Broadway, giving a modern *Sex and the City* skew to the all-female sexual hijinks in a recent revival of Clare Booth Luce's famous late 1930s play, *The Women*. Christy's original hats for nontheatrical patrons boost their wearers' show-stopping quotients with whimsical miniature scenes and names like "Veronica Lake" and "Let's Skate." On a more cerebral level, sculptor Michael Rakowitz acts as a street-smart provocateur. His tents made of inflated garbage bags fill a dual function: while housing the homeless they also serve as posters for this seemingly intractable urban problem.

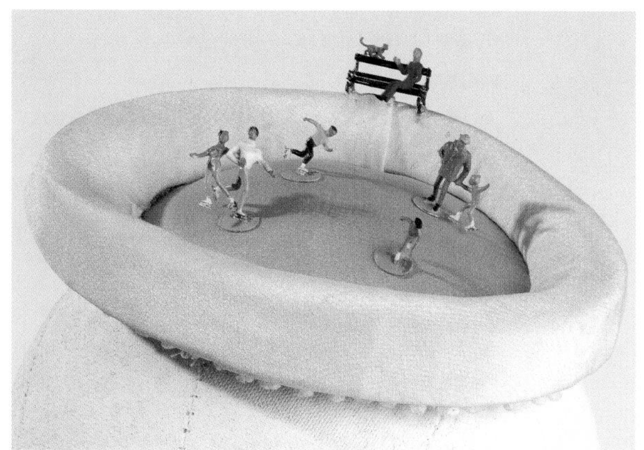

LET'S SKATE
Hat, 1999
Buckram, silk crepe, miniatures
Designer: Kelly Christy

VOID CHESS SET
Porcelain, 2002
Designer: Anton Ginzburg, Collaborative
Manufacturer: Haasprojekt, USA
Photography: Nigel Cox

Dramatizing the remarkable fusion that can occur at the intersection of art and science is the goal of other *Triennial* designers. Yusuke Obuchi's Wave Garden off the coast of Southern California promotes energy conservation while it fluidly maps in three dimensions the rise and fall of energy use in the region, making architecture a metaphor for flux and transformation. ABIOMED's AbioCor heart is a genuine scientific breakthrough on par with recent achievements in cloning. It is also a potent symbol of the permeable boundary between man and machine. Its launch in 2001 represented the culmination of a period of intense collaboration between doctors, engineers, and designers—a sure sign that blurring the boundaries between disciplines cross-pollinates ideas and fosters innovation. Many *Triennial* participants celebrate this combustible energy in their firms' names, such as Collaborative, co-lab, and fuseproject, as well as in the composition of their practices.

Stretching the boundaries of contemporary science into the realms of rhetoric and imagination also fascinates modern designers, especially when they're dealing with current ethical debates. In the hands of the Collaborative group, science becomes metaphor. Their F&M drinking glasses, inspired by recent scares about foot-and-mouth disease, queasily unite farm animal imagery and the ritual of eating. Science turns into extravagant spectacle in Rick Baker's makeup designs for the recent remake of the film *Planet of the Apes*. Baker's transformations, which also include the 1980s film *An American Werewolf in London*, have greatly advanced Hollywood's relentless quest to visualize human-into-animal metamorphoses. If nothing else, *Planet of the Apes* is a pop-culture manifestation of contemporary anxieties about horrific mutations that have become all the more persuasive with the scientific mapping of the human genome.

Whether they are designing cars, landscapes, or movie sets, the work of those included in this book suggest the potency of design as a medium of communication and commentary. These designers are show people, creating visual tours de force, performing on the stage of design.

# the new iconoclasts

## susan yelavich

Curated by
Ellen Lupton
Donald Albrecht
Susan Yelavich
Mitchell Owens

2x4
ABIOMED, Inc.
Charles S. Anderson
Antenna Design
As Four
Asymptote
Rick Baker
Bryan Bell
Blu Dot
Cynthia Breazeal
Bureau Betak
Stephen Burks
Critz Campbell
The Chopping Block
Kelly Christy
co-lab
Collaborative
Laurie DeMartino
Demeter Fragrance Library
Diamond + Baratta
Dave Eggers
Peter Eisenman
Paul Elliman
Escher + GuneWardena Architecture
Ford Motor Company
Benjamin Fry
Fuseproject
Futurefarmers
Tess Giberson
Green Lady + HunterGatherer
The Hoefler Type Foundry
David Hoey
Joseph Holtzman
House Industries
Viktor Jondal
Maira Kalman
KW:a
LoyandFord
Lutz + Patmos
Tod Machover
Maharam
Geoff McFetridge
Stephen McKay
Gene Meyer
J. Abbott Miller
Mike Mills
Isaac Mizrahi
Ted Muehling
Christoph Niemann
Frank Nuovo
Yusuke Obuchi
Michele Oka Doner
Gaetano Pesce
Picture Projects
Mark Pollack
Michael Rakowitz
Bob Sabiston
Stanley Saitowitz
Paula Scher
Jennifer Siegal
Smart Design
Paige Stahl
Christopher Strong
Daniel Streng
SuperHappyBunny
Target Corporation
Jennifer Tipton
Isabel Toledo
Troika Design Group
Andrea Valentini
Gabriela Valenzuela-Hirsch
Jhonen Vasquez
Cesar Vergara
Kiki Wallace + Mark Sofield
David + Sandy Wasco
Dennis Wedlick
David Weeks Lighting + Butter
Lorraine Wild
Stephen Wolfram
Jim Zivic

# 2003. We are in the infancy of a new century,

still feeling the reverberations of millenarian tremors that refused to neatly confine themselves to the nonsectarian Y2K bug. Global unrest and economic turbulence have exerted a strong undertow during the past three years—the years that are the scope of this *National Design Triennial*—charging, if not exactly changing, the currents of contemporary thought and practice. For no matter how cataclysmic the news or how dire the warnings—at least at this writing—we have not seen a fundamental behavioral shift. Americans still create and consume with characteristic faith in a better future. Anxiety nibbles at the edge of good feeling in our largely affluent society.

However, since ideas in gestation often coalesce under the added impetus of events, it is tempting to view the collective unconscious of design as a subset of the psyche of the nascent twenty-first century. Within this curatorial conceit, we can discern some parallels between our everyday responses to the new uncertainty and their material expression. At least three directions seem to flourish in this climate. There is a cadre of designers who have taken their futures, and their work, literally into their own hands with a latter-day do-it-yourself ethos and vestigial communitarian spirit. Then there are those who seem to be girding themselves (and us) for what's ahead by developing variously animate creatures to hold our hands on this side of the millennial threshold. And there is another loose confederation whose work holds up a mirror to our condition of instability, reinventing the baroque in all its surreal theatricality.

The work featured in *Inside Design Now* will ultimately resist convenient behavioral parallels with society's instincts to retreat, advance, or freeze in the face of change. Such a strictly sociological take would ignore its very existence as a discrete practice with conventions that predate any exhibition's timeframe. Indeed, the most common phenomenon across the board was the reemergence of craft and decorative arts within a richer and expanded understanding of design. (Hence this book's title.) But a closer look at the individuals and work featured will reveal a portrait of an extremely complex environment where there is, indeed, a finely nuanced relationship between design and culture, a relationship that guarantees the products of design their meaning.

THE WORLD FROM HERE
Illustrated book, 2001
Offset lithography
Designer: Lorraine Wild
Photography: Paula Goldman
Publisher: UCLA Grunwald Center for the Graphic Arts and the Armand Hammer Museum of Art and Cultural Center, Los Angeles

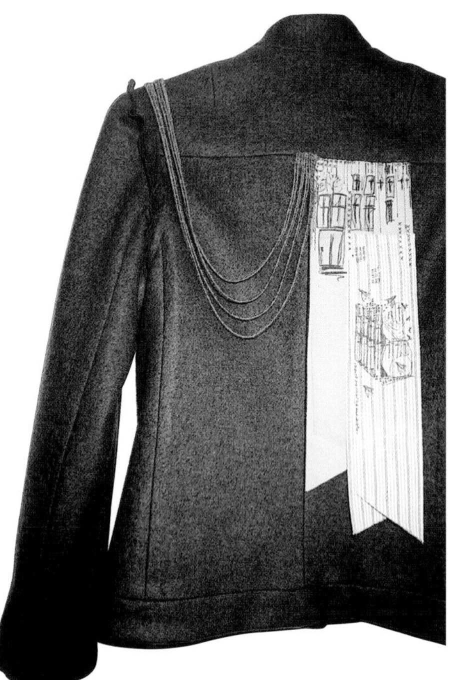

CHARCOAL JACKET
Wool, wool cording, cotton lining, fabric ink, ribbon, 2002
Designers: Tess Giberson in collaboration with Ambriel Floyd
Photography: Leeta Harding, Courtesy *Index Magazine*

Among those designers who keep the production of their work close at hand, the perennial Luddite suspicion of disenfranchisement and desire for control has been overtaken by a deeper grasp of design history and the platform it offers for invention. No Post Modern rehash here, no facile adaptations of stylistic precedents. Rather, there is a new comfort with the processes and materials of handwork that stems from a palpable desire to participate in the making of things in ways that may be direct and simple, but decidedly not simplistic.

Clothing designer Tess Giberson uses the sewing machine like a calligrapher's pen. Handmade, her garments draw on the rarified world of couture, but owe an aesthetic debt to its opposite—the homemade, self-styled counterculture she grew up in. Her clothes are personal but not precious.

The authenticity of touch intrinsic to the artisanal is risky territory, fraught with sentimentality and prey to the irrelevance of one-offs. But it is increasingly the means through which a generation of iconoclasts are forging a new ecumenical practice, drawing on the long-buried inheritance of the decorative arts. Ted Muehling taps directly into that legacy with his jewelry and porcelain pieces—exercises in pure form infused with eighteenth-century romanticism. Furniture designer Jim Zivic strips raw materials of their overt Industrial Revolution associations, leaving just enough residual memory to dissipate the strangeness of a coffee table carved out of coal or a leather rug clamped with steel staples.

Lorraine Wild, herself a pioneer in the writing of twentieth-century design history, embodies the transitional nature of graphic design in a practice where the physical nature of print informs the virtual space of digital production. Similarly straddling two modes of making, David Weeks fabricates custom-designed lighting fixtures in his studio, and, with Lindsey Adelman, his partner in Butter, designs low-cost lamps for mass production.

The same paradigm operates in Jennifer Siegal's work, but with a significant shift in scale. A proponent of design-build architecture, she champions manufactured housing. Just as Siegal's handsome alternatives to trailers don't condescend to their prospective owners, Kiki Wallace and Mark Sofield's Prospect Newtown—a subdivision in suburban Colorado—celebrates individuality, even eccentricity, through a radically different set of design codes. The valorization of idiosyncrasy reaches its apotheosis in Gaetano Pesce's cult of the flaw. Pesce designs furniture to be made variously by the workers who pour its resin forms. The accidental is built-in, resulting in a kind of humanism by default.

WAKING LIFE
Animation still, 2000
Designer: Bob Sabiston
Photography: Richard Linklater

Accidents are not traditionally welcomed in the realm of technology, but increasingly the unpredictability of human behavior is. As a matter of fact, we are so enamored with the possibilities of lifelike avatars, that simulated bodies have become a matter of jurisprudence.

Consider that on 16 April 2002, the Supreme Court struck down a ban on virtual child pornography—pornography rendered accurately yet digitally, raising the question of who or what was being violated. We've reached the point where the highest court in the land is being asked to determine if there is a difference between human reality and digital reality. For now, at least, they have upheld the distinction. This just happens to be an extremely sensitive example of the ethical questions that are arising out of artificial lifeforms that we are now used to in more mundane circumstances. On airplanes, safety instructions offered by computer-animated characters command more attention than those given by flight attendants. Gorillaz is a cult band that appears as animated characters (the musicians show up only as silhouettes behind a scrim on stage) whose songs warn, "The digital won't let me go... I'll pay when tomorrow becomes today." In Tom Tykwer's 1999 film *Run Lola Run*, Lola disconcertingly morphs into a cartoon character and back again.

We are beginning to accept the veracity of a parallel universe, and designer/scientists like Cynthia Breazeal are raising the prospect that we'll have new companions to accompany us into the future. Breazeal prefers a blatant falsity in her robotic flora and fauna that look artificial but behave naturally. Likewise, Bob Sabiston, animator of the film *Waking Life*, creates characters that move just like humans but look like cartoons. Breazeal and Sabiston have in common the ability to elicit the uncanny from computation. They up the ante on the suspension of disbelief that we all knowingly participate in every time we read a novel, or see a play or film. And in the long run, they raise larger theological questions about our responsibility to technology that makes us feel differently or behave differently, come the day when we can't turn it off.

Tod Machover's digital instruments don't offer companionship, but they do alter learning behavior by making sound physical and music intuitive. Unlike Breazeal's independent robots, Machover's Beatbugs and Music Shapers are closer to the tradition of industrial design since their success depends on objects we manipulate. For Masamichi Udagawa and Sigi Moeslinger of Antenna Design interactive design is practiced equally in the hardware of the New York City subway car and the software that sends virtual cherry blossoms spiraling up through the Great Hall of Cooper-Hewitt, National Design Museum during the 2003 *Triennial*.

CYBERFLORA
Concept rendering, 2002
Design team: Cynthia Breazeal, project lead; Jeff Lieberman, design lead; Dan Steihl
Rendering: Ryan Kavanaugh

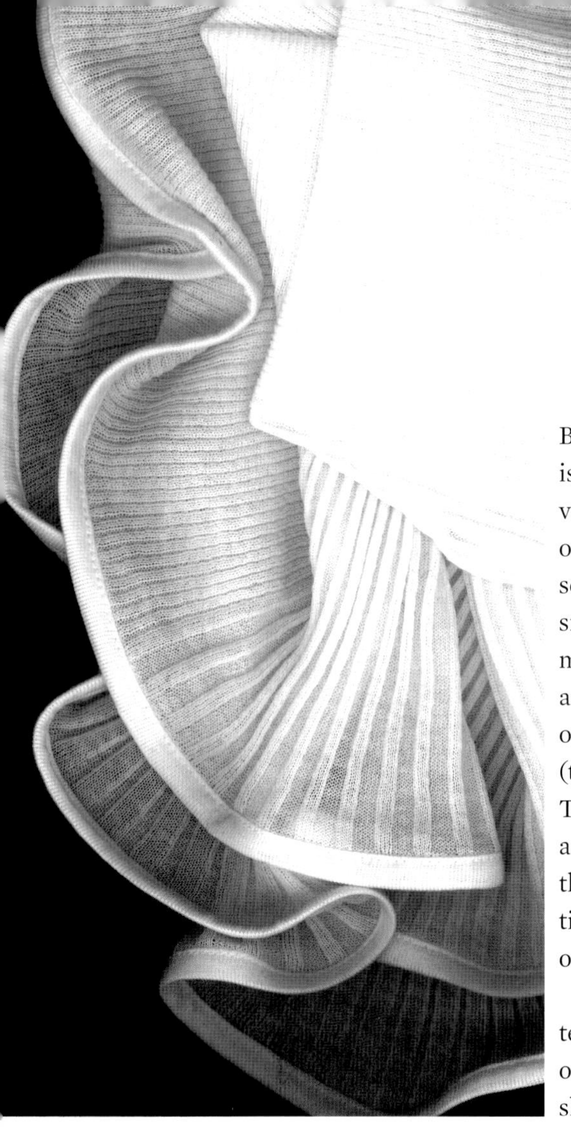

T-SHIRT WEDDING GOWN
Fabric detail, 2000
Cotton lisle
Designer: Isabel Toledo
Photography: Goran Vejvoda

Beyond our quest for wired and pixeled surrogates, design culture today is rich with analog demonstrations of animation. Indeed, this is a vanguard with a long tradition. Proving that design ideas follow a pattern of loops not timelines, we can find echoes of our own ambitions in the late seventeenth-century Baroque. In Vienna, Wolfgang von Kempelen's life-size automaton, the Turk, was winning chess games, while in Rome, marble sculpture all but danced out of churches.[1] The goal was the same as it is today: entertainment—immersive, erotic, determined to capture our distracted attentions, be it through dynamic manipulation of space (think Borromini) or elaborate articulation of surface (think Bernini). Then and now beauty was re-legitimized in a period of unabashed aestheticism, confident enough to place pleasure ahead of theory. Just as the High Baroque flowered after an era of Jesuitical austerity, in our own time a generation of architects and designers are rethinking strictures of the twentieth-century orthodoxy.

Peter Eisenman's architecture has always been animated by a spatial tension that stems from his continual critique of the parent ideology of modernism. Over the last decade, computer software has seismically shifted that dynamic, allowing him to imbed the Cartesian grid within the terrain of geography and patterns of social behavior. He alerts us to our surroundings, making the experience of being in his spaces usefully disorienting. Fashion designer Isabel Toledo has an even more pronounced schizophrenic relationship with structure and surface. Sometimes her geometries create architecture for the body to live in; sometimes they implode around the human form. The design quartet As Four may be the most explicit reincarnation of the theatrical hysteria of the baroque. Clothes that start out as geometry problems gather into rapturous volumes of folds and curves.

In much of this work there is a delightfully perverse satisfaction that comes from using the precision of structure to yield the appearance of wanton excess or sheer beauty. That alchemy is intrinsic to Mark Pollack's textiles, whose rigors of construction are invisible yet wholly essential. Designed to cover windows not bodies, his fabrics have the complexity and depth of stained glass, woven in layers with flaps and flanges variously anchored to manipulate light and offer shade.

Joseph Holtzman's affinity to the baroque is less about the physics of push and pull than the hyper-narrative of layered surfaces and their composite beauty. The idea that environments are like books that can be read is once again enjoying credence among designers. Holtzman offers treatises on proportion and ornament; J. Abbott Miller tells more literal stories. He uses the space of exhibitions as the space of propaganda unapologetically, even honestly, in our own era of counter-reformation. Miller's strategies of storytelling grow organically from his practice as a writer and graphic designer. The formal elegance of his exposition distinguishes it from the more prosaic tactics of theming.

It's not that storytelling has become less important in recommending products and places to our attention; but designers have found that they can be less explicit. Today's consumers read visual subtexts like religious allegories. Maharam demonstrates the power of inference with textiles that are infused with news from the sports and fashion pages. Covered in mesh and microfiber, ordinary office furniture takes on the mantle of power and style, and a heightened sense of drama is conferred on the everyday space of work.

The use of spectacle to evoke spiritual ecstasy may have been the essence of the baroque ideal. Today we can find spectacle delivered nightly on CNN, or what passes for it on reality TV shows, but we have to look elsewhere for transcendence. Isaac Mizrahi's costume designs for Mark Morris, American Ballet Theater, and Twyla Tharp make the theater one of those places we can find it for a few hours. His acute sensitivity to the innuendo of fashion cues the audience to respond more keenly to the performance by drawing on the reservoir of memory held in the tip of a hat or length of a skirt.

HARLEY-DAVIDSON OPEN ROAD TOUR
Touring exhibition, 2002
Designer: J. Abbott Miller
Photography: Timothy Hursley

The idea that design can evoke states of mind is finally what distinguishes the work cited above. Without forsaking its reality, its defining functionality, this is design that seeks to acknowledge, and sometimes heighten, the reality of our emotional and psychological selves. We see it in the deliberate imperfection of the crafted; we seek it in the calculated chance behaviors of digital creatures; we experience it in the fluctuations of sensibility built into a single artifact. The design of uncertainty, iconoclasm, and restless energy are momentarily codifiable, but they are thankfully unpredictable.

1. The Turk was actually a manned, life-size figure, according to Tom Standage ("Monster in a Box," *Wired*, March 2002), but it duped audiences across Europe in the seventeenth century.

# design to desire

## mitchell owens

Curated by
Ellen Lupton
Donald Albrecht
Susan Yelavich
Mitchell Owens

2x4
ABIOMED, Inc.
Charles S. Anderson
Antenna Design
As Four
Asymptote
Rick Baker
Bryan Bell
Blu Dot
Cynthia Breazeal
Bureau Betak
Stephen Burks
Critz Campbell
The Chopping Block
Kelly Christy
co-lab
Collaborative
Laurie DeMartino
Demeter Fragrance Library
Diamond + Baratta
Dave Eggers
Peter Eisenman
Paul Elliman
Escher + GuneWardena Architecture
Ford Motor Company
Benjamin Fry
Fuseproject
Futurefarmers
Tess Giberson
Green Lady + HunterGatherer
The Hoefler Type Foundry
David Hoey
Joseph Holtzman
House Industries
Viktor Jondal
Maira Kalman
KW:a
LoyandFord
Lutz + Patmos
Tod Machover
Maharam
Geoff McFetridge
Stephen McKay
Gene Meyer
J. Abbott Miller
Mike Mills
Isaac Mizrahi
Ted Muehling
Christoph Niemann
Frank Nuovo
Yusuke Obuchi
Michele Oka Doner
Gaetano Pesce
Picture Projects
Mark Pollack
Michael Rakowitz
Bob Sabiston
Stanley Saitowitz
Paula Scher
Jennifer Siegal
Smart Design
Paige Stahl
Christopher Streng
Daniel Streng
SuperHappyBunny
Target Corporation
Jennifer Tipton
Isabel Toledo
Troika Design Group
Andrea Valentini
Gabriela Valenzuela-Hirsch
Jhonen Vasquez
Cesar Vergara
Kiki Wallace + Mark Sofield
David + Sandy Wasco
Dennis Wedlick
David Weeks Lighting + Butter
Lorraine Wild
Stephen Wolfram
Jim Zivic

# Simple or complex, sublime or ridiculous,

design at its best feeds our wildest dreams, sparks emotional surges, inspires one's hand to reach out and touch something, anything. (Surely it's no coincidence that design and desire sound alike.) Good design involves us completely, whether it's a why-didn't-I-think-of-that measuring cup by Smart Design or a newfangled house that architect Bryan Bell created exclusively for fruit pickers but whose concepts of livability (and stylistic panache) cross every socioeconomic boundary. Shortsighted design, on the other hand, makes life more difficult, or at the very least, exasperating.

The humanization and democratization of design was paramount to the Arts and Crafts movement of the late nineteenth century, when the power of design was held up as a beacon of hope, inspiration, and spiritual fulfillment in an increasingly mechanized Victorian world. Skylines now littered with smokestacks and nuclear reactors bear all-too-eloquent witness that the Industrial Revolution triumphed. But over the last few years, a significant murmur of protest has been heard. Multitudes of talented architects, fashion and product designers, and graphic artists are rediscovering the possibilities of design as the quickest way to improve lives, inspire joy, and jumpstart sluggish minds.

In the new millennium, it is obvious that defining the future means increasingly turning back to embrace the basics, whatever the medium. The murals, children's books, and theatrical sets of Maira Kalman, for instance, shrug a collective shoulder at highbrow sophistication and instead choose to revel in the freedom and charm inherent in imperfection and naiveté, however calculated its effects. Even when smoothly translated to the small screen by the artists of Nickelodeon, *Invader Zim*, an edgy comic book by the reclusive young Bay Area artist Jhonen Vasquez, retains a subversive adolescent whimsy and black humor that recalls the often apocalyptic ballpoint doodles that probably still decorate the margins of math books in high school classrooms around the country.

**COUTURE VOYEUR**
Magazine illustrations, cover and spreads, 2000
Offset lithography
Artist: Maira Kalman
Publisher: *The New York Times Magazine*

SELF-HELP HOUSING:
SOSNA HOUSE
Digital rendering, 2001
Design team: Bryan Bell, Kristine Wade, Ryan Gilbin, Ethan Cohen, Meredith Kelly, Lisa McClellan, Gary Shaffer, Hubert Snyder, David Rentsel, Oscar Sanchez, Cristina Chang
Rendering: Brian King

FORESTBURG HOUSE
Forestburg, New York, 1997
Designer: Dennis Wedlick, Dennis Wedlick Architect
Photography: Jeff Goldberg/ESTO

Architects, too, are retrenching, eschewing the market-driven impulse to build big, bland, and baronial in favor of addressing the needs of the rest of the world community, a marginalized majority that's been called "the other 98 percent." Though their audiences are markedly different, both Bryan Bell and Dennis Wedlick exploit overlooked, often denigrated building materials while sensitively and stylishly addressing the needs of the underprivileged (Bell's clients range from migrant farm workers to first-generation immigrants) as well as the just plain underfinanced (Wedlick's award-winning houses often cost less than $150,000).

Adaptive reuse of natural resources is part of the twenty-first-century design agenda, too, but without the earnestness of the 1960s granola-and-macramé set. Product designer Gabriela Valenzuela-Hirsch, for instance, utilizes literal refuse—albeit exotic-wood leftovers scavenged from Central American beaches and jungles—to create earthy but elegant home products whose sale also supports reforestation programs and social services for the rural poor in her native Costa Rica. Sculptor Michele Oka Doner collects fallen branches, seed pods, leaves, and thorns, then magically reinterprets them into diamond-bedecked gold and bronze jewelry, serving pieces, and ornamental vessels. And young product designer Paige Stahl, barely out of school, melds nature with technology through her creation of a floor lamp that illuminates a room while nurturing a pocket-size forest of housebound greenery.

Minimalism continues to be a design-world constant, of course, but lately the clichéd school of reductivism has been rendered increasingly warm to the eye, at times leavened with welcome comic relief. Christopher Brosius and Christopher Gable, cofounders of Demeter Fragrance Library, have turned the perfume world on its head by capturing and bottling basic aromas (tar, waffles, tomatoes, snow) that many of us take for granted or have entirely forgotten. Fashion designers Tina Lutz and Marcia Patmos have carved out an individualistic niche as well, knitting cashmere sweaters, scarves, and coats in collaboration with modern artists and thought-provoking product designers, a rare and refreshing cross-pollination not seen since haute couturière Elsa Schiaparelli and agent provocateur Salvador Dalí decided to join forces back in the 1930s.

Classics are being reinterpreted, too, instead of dismissed as hopelessly old-hat. Familiar motifs and everyday applications are blown out of context or enthusiastically rejiggered to become suddenly, refreshingly new. Industrial designer Cesar Vergara's locomotives are turning heads and increasing ridership in the West and Pacific Northwest, the design of his hurtling vehicles mesmerizing enough to force naysayers to revisit the continuing debate over the economic viability of rail travel in the United States. Fashion and home-product designer Gene Meyer has been consistently producing forward-thinking clothes and accessories by refracting 1960s lifestyle icons like college gridiron stars and Elvis Presley in *Blue Hawaii* through his thoroughly modernist prism. Interior designers William Diamond and Anthony Baratta rummage through history's closet with equal enthusiasm, surfacing with traditional patterns and objects—tartan, neoclassical swags, braided rugs—that they then pump up to epic proportions.

It isn't all backward glances and inspired nostalgia trips, of course. Frank Nuovo, a jazz musician turned product designer for the cell-phone manufacturer Nokia, has literally redefined personal communication, as youths around the globe text-message their way through life. Andrea Valentini uses high-tech plastics to create furniture and housewares that seduce even the most reluctant passerby, while Lise Anne Couture and Hani Rashid of Asymptote dream up future-shock structures that wrap, subsume, envelop, and coerce. Viktor Jondal, a young product designer with a brief but notable track record, embraces new materials, learns their structural tricks, then teaches them to do more, whether for a bent plywood chair with a magical lack of visible support or paper-pulp used in his concept for modular hotel rooms. Through his firm, Bureau Betak, Alexandre de Betak, an impresario of image-making, devises high-tech, high-concept productions for fashion designers that cram all the grandeur and glory of grand opera into about fifteen minutes of now-you-see-it-now-you-don't extravaganza. And the brothers Streng, Christopher and Daniel, together and separately, turn out intense, innovative, daring modern home furnishings and accessories: a ceiling light that's little more than a bulb and a plastic bag, a fluorescent tray, a bar stool with the gravitas of a intergalactic altar.

It's all about design putting an enjoyable spin on mundane activities. The minds at Smart Design, for instance, put as much energy into developing the perfect ergonomic spatula as other designers expend fashioning a space shuttle—and with more measurable universal impact. Their Victorian predecessors would be proud.

**JURICK RESIDENCE**
Manhasset, New York, 1999
Detail of custom patchwork chair and Portuguese needlepoint rug
Designers: William Diamond and Anthony Baratta, Diamond + Baratta
Photography: William Diamond

**LOW CHAIR**
Composite resins, 2001
Designer: Daniel Streng
Photography: Nate Estanson

MICHAEL ROCK b. 1959

SUSAN SELLERS b. 1967

GEORGIE STOUT b. 1967

**2x4**

*New York City*

1, 2

A 200-foot-long wall carries you back through the deep, narrow space of Prada's flagship store in New York City. Overscaled flowers cover the wall, each filled with strange fragments of pixellated imagery.

The wallpaper, conceived by the graphic design consultancy 2x4, is part of the site's elaborate media component. Throughout the store, flat-screened monitors tucked among the merchandise display short films on subjects linked—directly or spuriously—to the high-end Italian fashion house: clothing, factories, sex, Italianism. The floral shapes on the wallpaper contain stills from the films, some of which were also produced by 2x4. The wallpaper and films will change every eight months.

2x4 was founded in 1993 by Michael Rock, Susan Sellers, and Georgie Stout. The group is known for its critical, research-based approach to graphic design. 2x4 has collaborated on several projects with architect Rem Koolhaas, including the flagship Prada store in New York City and the Guggenheim museums in Las Vegas.

At the Guggenheim Hermitage Museum in Las Vegas, the architect has penetrated the casino's faux-Venetian facade with a massive Cor-Ten steel box. Signage, designed by 2x4, consists of enormous letters rusted into the steel, providing a potential background for more informal graphics, such as posters or graffiti. Such "urban operations" would break up the huge letters and provide opportunities to announce temporary exhibitions. Signage for the Guggenheim Las Vegas consists of 17-foot-tall letters that extend from the wall onto the ceiling.

2x4 has produced graphic design that is both visually arresting and intellectually compelling, creating a rhythm of change and ephemerality that undercuts the presumed authority and permanence of the built environment and the corporate brand. **EL**

**1, 2**
**PRADA WALLPAPER**
New York City, 2002
Digital print on coated fabric
Designers: Karen Hsu and Michael Rock, 2x4 (with OMA/AMO architects: Rem Koolhaas, Ole Scheren, Eric Chang, Tim Archambault)
Client: Prada
Photography: Courtesy Prada

**3, 4**
**THE GUGGENHEIM HERMITAGE MUSEUM**
Las Vegas, Nevada, 2001
Architectural graphics, corten steel
Designers: Karen Hsu, Michael Rock, and Georgie Stout, 2x4 (with OMA/AMO architects: Rem Koolhaas, Joshua Ramus, Christian Bandi)
Client: Guggenheim Museum

**5, 6**
**THE GUGGENHEIM LAS VEGAS**
Las Vegas, Nevada, 2001
Architectural graphics, anodized aluminum, glass, automotive paint
Designers: Karen Hsu, Michael Rock, and Georgie Stout, 2x4 (with OMA/AMO architects: Rem Koolhaas, Joshua Ramus, Christian Bandi)
Client: Guggenheim Museum

Guggenheim photography courtesy 2x4

GUGGENHEIM HERMITAGE MUSEUM
LOREM IPSUM

3

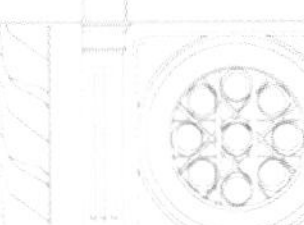
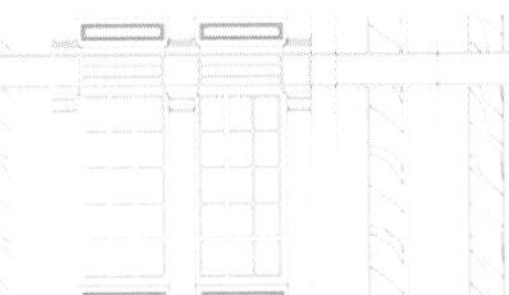
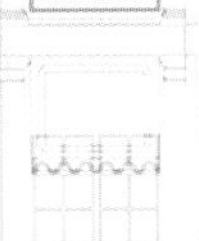
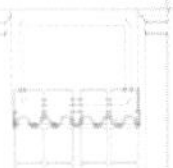
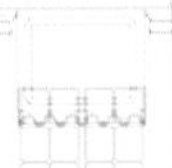
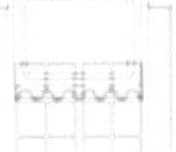
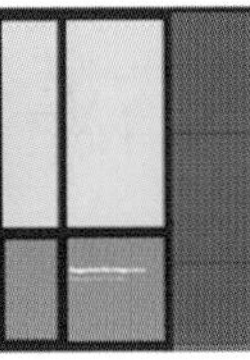
GUGGENHEIM HERMITAGE MUSEUM

4

5, 6

## ABIOMED, INC.

*Danvers, Massachusetts*

1

Inventors have dreamed for decades of creating an artificial heart, but a truly epochal moment in their search came on 2 July 2001, when surgeons in Louisville, Kentucky, placed the first fully implantable artificial heart within the body of 58-year-old Robert Tools. ABIOMED's plastic-and-titanium AbioCor™ Implantable Replacement Heart is revolutionary. Unlike earlier versions of artificial hearts, which required hooking recipients to refrigerator-sized power units, the AbioCor heart can facilitate the freedom and mobility of a productive life. This 4-pound marvel of miniaturization, no bigger than a grapefruit, fits within the patient's chest. No wires or tubes pierce the skin, but an external battery-operated transmitter is attached to a waist belt and charges an internal transmitter that operates the heart. And, although AbioCor costs about $70,000, it eliminates the $10,000 that heart transplant patients would spend each year on anti-rejection drugs.

AbioCor's launch capped an intensive, two-decade development process involving doctors and aerospace engineers, who took full advantage of previously unavailable microchips and software. In 1995 ABIOMED engaged Fitch, the industrial design giant, to help turn their concept into a physical product. During their year on the project, Fitch helped ABIOMED to give a more human shape to the artificial heart and aided in improving the design of the unisex power belt. Much more work was required before the launch, however, and Jim Couch, senior vice president and general manager at the time in Fitch's office in Columbus, Ohio, has described today's AbioCor as "the great grandson" of the 1995 version. Today ABIOMED is working hard to make the heart smaller and to enable patients to survive longer—living testaments to this contemporary wonder of design and technology. **DA**

1
**ABIOCOR™**
Artificial heart, 2001
Designer: ABIOMED, Inc.
Photography: Courtesy ABIOMED

2
**ABIOCOR™**
Artificial heart, 2001
Designer: ABIOMED, Inc.
Illustrations based on graphics from *The New York Times*
Redrawn by Elke Gasselseder

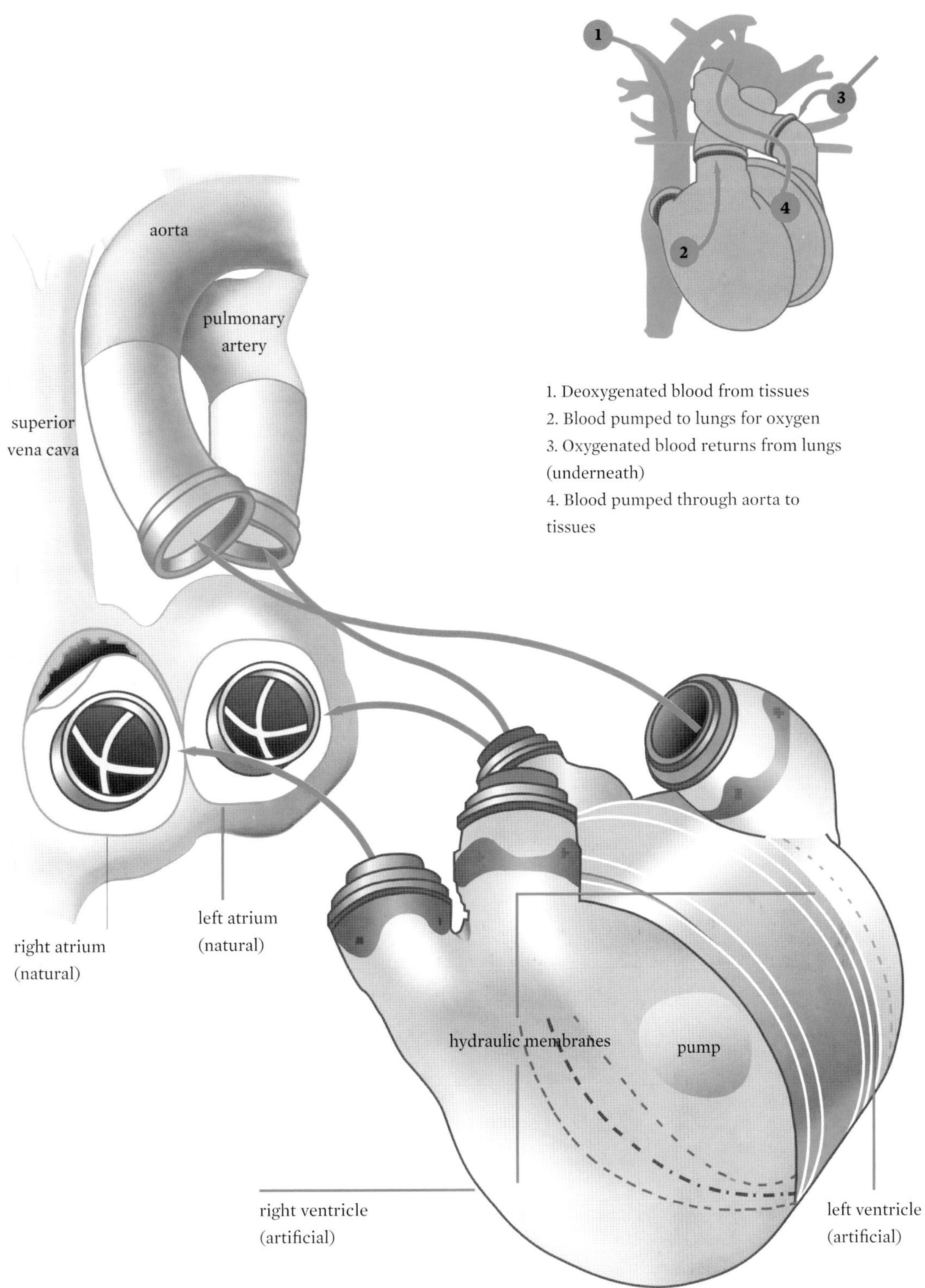


Inside the device, an electric pump forces the hydraulic membranes to expand and contract to pump blood through the body.

2

## CHARLES S. ANDERSON b. 1958

CSA IMAGES

*Minneapolis*

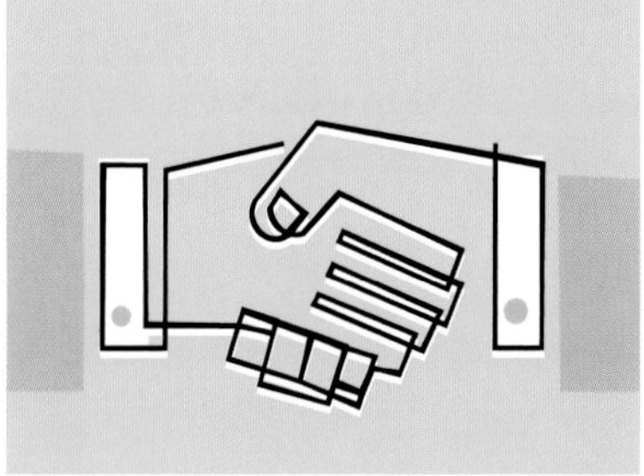

Charles S. Anderson has reinvented the stock image business by building a vast virtual warehouse of original pictures, created in-house by his own team of designers, illustrators, and photographers.

The picture industry is an expanding element of the design world's economic food chain. Conventional "stock" consists of discarded outtakes from commissioned projects or speculative work produced to meet the anticipated, generally banal, needs of business—anything from sunsets to smokestacks. Stock is often viewed as a dumping ground for pictures.

Aiming to create a new kind of stock house, Charles S. Anderson founded CSA Images in 1989, which operates alongside his full-service design studio. CSA Images has produced tens of thousands of digital illustrations, drawn from an enormous library of clip-art books, magazines, catalogs, and other ephemera; thousands of additional images are built entirely from scratch. A photographic series called Plastock revolves around Anderson's encylopedic collection of plastic objects. Anderson and his staff tease this found material into a second life, making it modern and relevant to contemporary designers by re-drawing it, shifting its scale, or breaking it into layers of color and line. Every image is in digital form, yet many evoke the physical techniques of printing.

CSA makes fun of the visual clichés endlessly recycled by the big stock houses, such as business people shaking hands or salesmen high-fiving. A new CSA category, "By the Numbers," offers original paint-by-number-style illustrations of businessmen. Anderson says, "The dusty painting technique casts the shadow of Enron on these pictures. Maybe they won't sell, but we like the social commentary."

Charles S. Anderson has changed the way designers think about stock by attacking the conventions of this ubiquitous medium. **EL**

**CSA IMAGES**
Illustrations and design elements
Art director: Charles S. Anderson,
Designers, illustrators and photographers: Charles S. Anderson, Todd Piper-Hauswirth, Erik Johnson, Aaron Dimmel, Kyle Hames, Sheraton Green, Jovaney Hollingsworth, Vashmour Campbell, Jason Schulte, Tim White

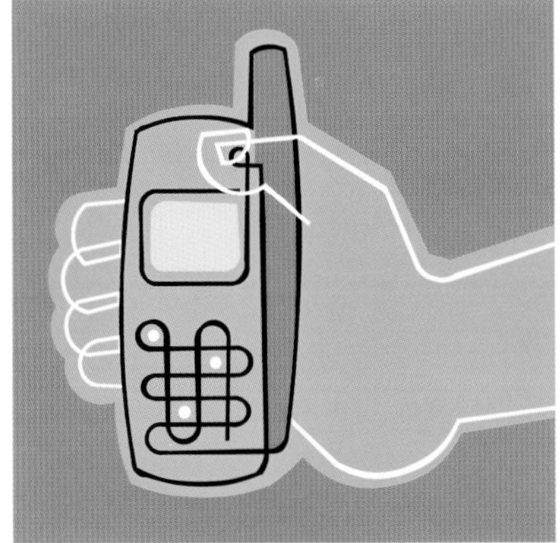

Tobacco kills

MASAMICHI UDAGAWA b. 1964

SIGI MOESLINGER b. 1968

## ANTENNA DESIGN

*New York City*

1

An antenna is a sensory appendage, a conductor of information. Industrial designers Masamichi Udagawa and Sigi Moeslinger are Antenna. Conductors in both the literal and figurative sense, Udagawa and Moeslinger create highly functional products for complex social situations, and, amazingly, in this age of mediation, they do it without an army of marketing gurus behind them.

In 2000 the duo integrated their informal studies with institutional research to transform nothing less than the New York City subway car with their R142A model. While the technical challenges of the project are not to be underestimated, it's the design's behavioral cues that make the R142A work. The periwinkle blue of the seating looks fresh, clean, and calm; the hand railings curve elegantly while serving as barriers to would-be pickpockets; LED screens and audio recordings announce train stops with welcome clarity. Together with Antenna's MetroCard vending machines, the trains have generated a sense of safety, order, and pleasure for the system's millions of riders, and, in the process, have been a boon to mass transit and the city's image. Antenna's work in this realm continues with a proposal for a new indoor Commuter Rail Bench with slats that create interesting shadow play, day or night.

Shadow play is also fundamental to the experimental side of their work, where the interaction of people and light create microcosms of cause and effect. For the *Triennial,* Antenna created a shower of cherry blossoms. Petals float and cluster in relation to the number of visitors traversing the Museum's grand staircase, creating a satisfying symmetry between the electrodes that trigger the blooms and the nerve endings they touch in us. **SY**

1

**CHERRY BLOSSOMS**
Design for installation, 2002
Digital rendering
Designers: Masamichi Udagawa, Sigi Moeslinger
Commissioned by Cooper-Hewitt, National Design Museum, New York City
Rendering: Bruce Pringle

2, 3

**NEW YORK CITY TRANSIT R142A SUBWAY CAR, INTERIOR AND EXTERIOR VIEWS**
Stainless steel, stainless steel tubing, FRP, rubber, melamine, 2000
Designers: Masamichi Udagawa and Sigi Moeslinger, in collaboration with Sandra Bloodworth, MTA Arts for Transit
Manufacturer: Kawasaki Rail Car
Photography: Ryuzo Masunaga

4

**NEW YORK CITY TRANSIT METROCARD VENDING MACHINE**
Stainless steel housing, porcelain enamel-coated steel, 1999
Design team: Masamichi Udagawa, Sigi Moeslinger, David Reinfurt, Kathleen Holman
Manufacturer: Cubic Transporation Systems, USA
Photography: Masamichi Udagawa

5

**COMMUTER RAIL BENCH**
Design for transit bench, 2001
Digital rendering
Designers: Masamichi Udagawa, Sigi Moeslinger
Rendering: Bruce Pringle

2

3

4

5

## AS FOUR

*New York City*

1

GABi + ADi + ANGE + K.A.i. = the iconoclasts of As Four. Nothing else adds up so neatly about this quartet whose clothing design is the incarnation of the modern baroque. Gesture + extravagance + asymmetry + intelligence = the more accurate sum of their collaboration.

Hailing respectively from Lebanon, Israel, Tajikistan, and Germany, the foursome met in New York and started making clothing in the mid-1990s, *making* being the operative word here. As Four creates its clothing by spontaneously cutting the fabric themselves. Patterns follow later in GABi + ADi + ANGE + K.A.i. sizes instead of the usual numbers.

The designers have made an art of immediacy that can be felt in the very act of putting on their clothing. Often, there are no buttons or fasteners of any kind. The precision of the cut and the gravity of the fabric work in taut relation to the architecture of the body. Planes of fabric are punctuated with circular voids that become sleeves and pantlegs when engaged with human limbs. If the rhetoric has the ring of sci-fi, it's not accidental. As Four anthropomorphizes their clothing, sometimes putting the skeletal veins of seams on the outside, designing knee and elbow joints with vents that expand and contract with robotic movement, creating second skins that can adapt to different bodies.

Their practice swings on a pendulum of extremes. Their Mustache pants, flat as steamrolled cartoon characters, are animated into three dimensions by a zipper. Their petaled Hair Do is as voluptuous as their cut-out Snow Man Wrap is restrained: plane geometry gives way to an ecstasy of diagonals, folds, and curves. With ET, Call Home, a flat paisley shape edged with a 144-inch zipper, mutates into a sinuously angled cocktail dress in one breathtaking gesture. As Four submits definitive proof that geometry doesn't have to be plain. **SY**

1
**AS FOUR GRAFFITI**
Display of Fall 2001 line
at Purple Institute, Paris
Designer: As Four
Photography: As Four

2
**HAIR DO**
Garment, 2001
Silk organza
Designer: As Four
Photography: As Four

3–6
**ET, CALL HOME**
Dress, 2002
Duchess silk with hand-embroidered
silver sequins and pearls
Designer: As Four
Model: So Young
Photography: As Four

2

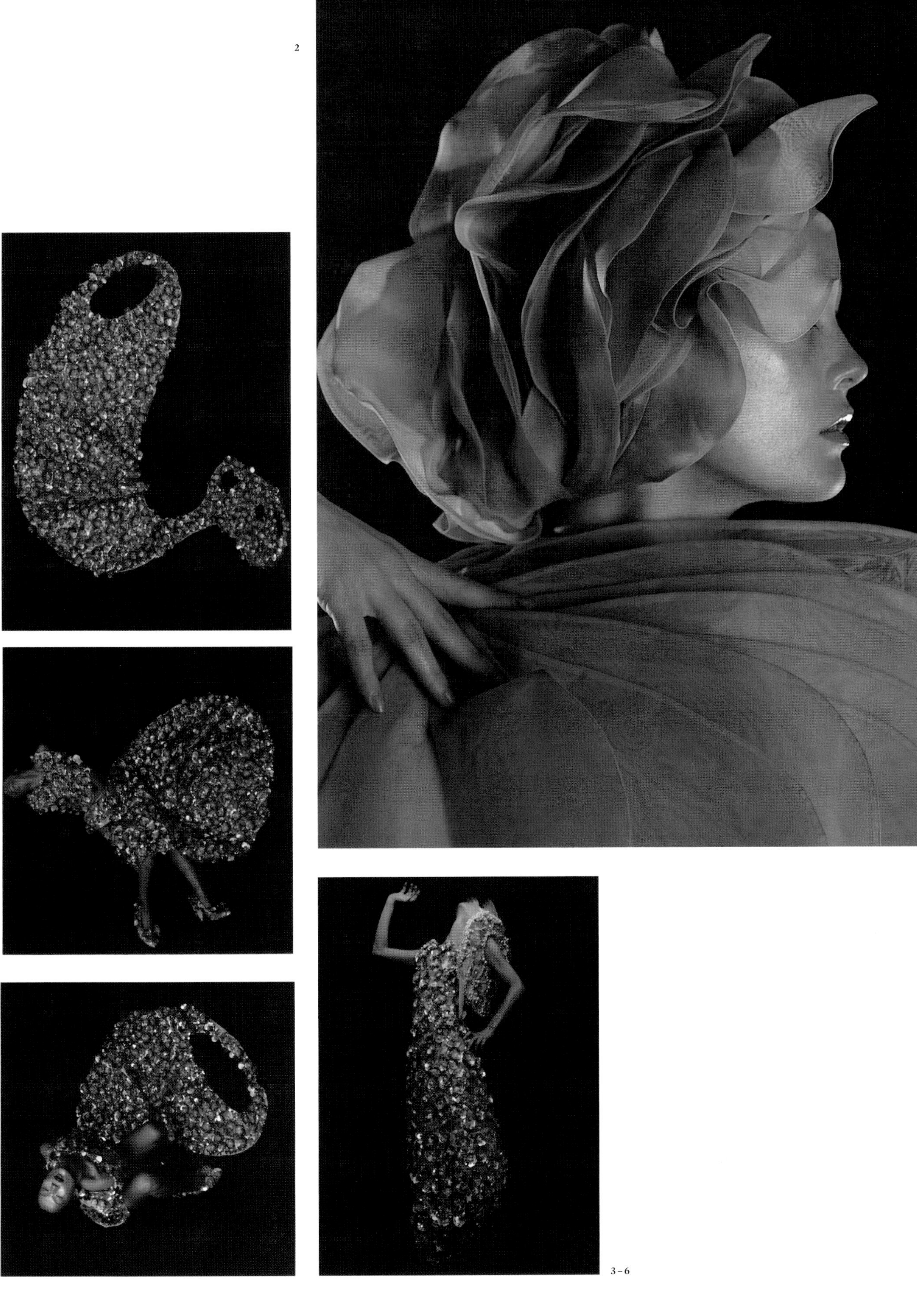

3–6

LISE ANNE COUTURE b. 1959

HANI RASHID b. 1958

## ASYMPTOTE

*New York City*

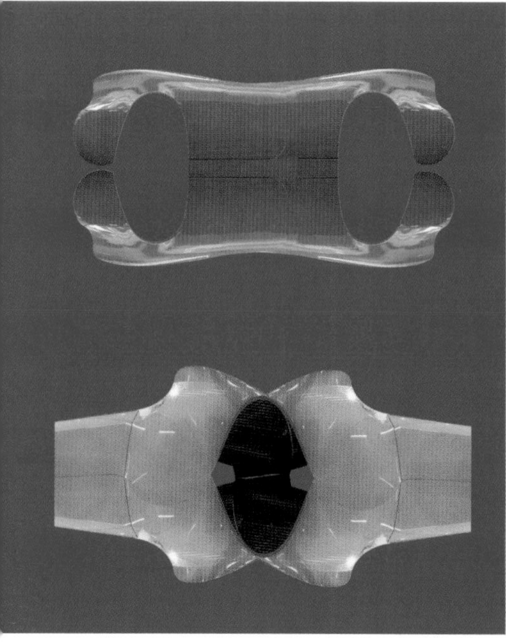

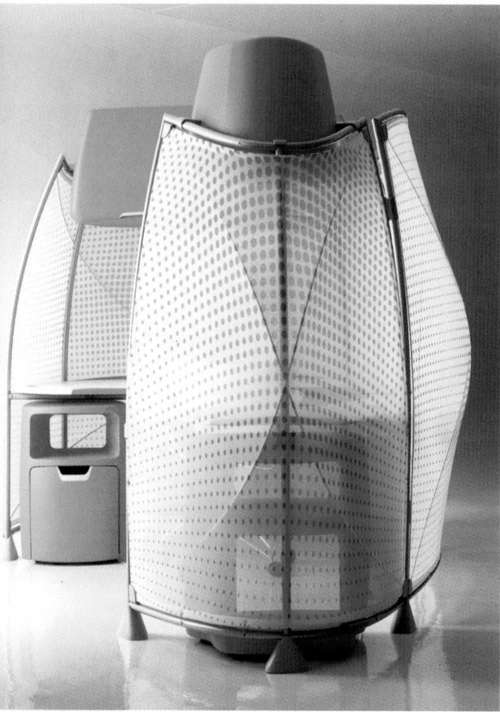

1, 2

Since 1989, Asymptote, headed by Lise Anne Couture and Hani Rashid, has eschewed conventional concepts of architecture and design. Its buildings, workspaces, museums, furniture, and interiors seem designed to question the very notion of solidity itself.

While other architectural firms produce buildings that celebrate permanence, Couture and Rashid seem to construct their creations out of clean air and elegant membranes rather than bricks and mortar. As their mission statement explains, the principals "draw inspiration from a wide range of sources not traditionally associated with architecture, among them the phenomena of information, tectonics of dynamic systems, and contemporary city-space, and organic systems of transportation." In other words, their work is thoughtfully defiant and spiritually challenging. Apparently weightless while also seeming to react to some mysterious gravitational pull, Asymptote's designs bulge and swell, attract and repel, reveling in the sensuality of their curvaceous silhouettes and built-in transparency while broadcasting the promise of comfort and safety. The firm's A3 furniture system for Knoll, for example, wraps around the office worker like a protective membrane, the corners and angles of the traditional cubicle banished for something more spiritual, more forgiving.

That same sense of serenity infuses Asymptote's design for the Mercedes-Benz Museum of the Automobile in Stuttgart, Germany. There, white walls flex under a rippling roof, while inside lies a multilevel display area whose silhouette recalls a collection of mesas. And the firm's recently completed HydraPier, an award-winning municipal pavilion in Haarlemmermeer, the Netherlands, juts into its watery site like a futuristic boomerang, all swoosh and sizzle, an eyecatcher that flings the idea of an eighteenth-century folly somewhere to the edge of the Milky Way. **MO**

1
**MOTIONSCAPES**
Spatial studies, 2002
Digital rendering
Designers: Lise Anne Couture, Hani Rashid
Client: Documenta XI

2
**KNOLL A3 FURNITURE SYSTEM**
2001
Principal desigers: Lise Anne Couture, Hani Rashid
Design team: Noboru Ota, Jose Salinas, Birgit Schoenbrodt, Renate Weissenboeck, Hannah Yampolsky with Karen Stone and Douglas Reuter, Knoll
Client: Knoll
Photography: Ramak Fazel

3
**HYDRAPIER**
Haarlemmermeer, The Netherlands, 2002
Principal designers: Lise Anne Couture, Hani Rashid
Design team: Elaine Didyk, Birgit Schoenbrodt, Jose Salinas, John Cleater
Client: City of Haarlemmermeer, Floriade Festival
Photography: Courtesy Asymptote

4
**EYE BEAM MUSEUM OF ART AND TECHNOLOGY**
Concept rendering for competition, 2001
Principal designers: Lise Anne Couture, Hani Rashid
Client: Eyebeam Atelier/John Johnson
Rendering: Asymptote

3

4

## RICK BAKER b. 1950

*Cinovation Studio*

*Glendale, California*

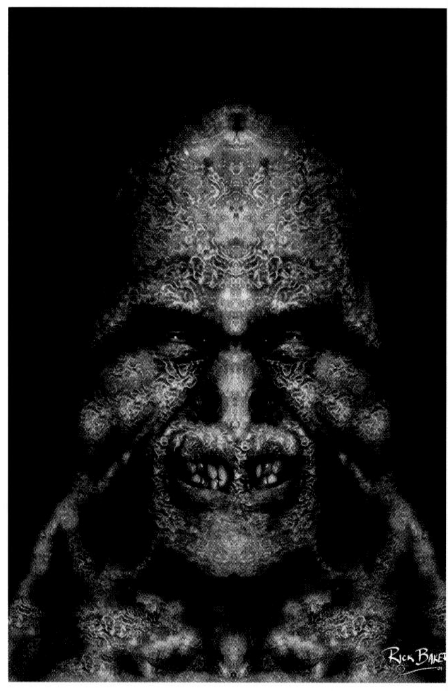

1, 2

Makeup designers are essential to film's storytelling powers. They shape character, alter time by changing actors' ages, and put faces on our greatest fears with their monsters and aliens. Winner of the first annual Academy Award for makeup in 1981 for *An American Werewolf in London*, Rick Baker has demonstrated his mastery of every dimension of his craft. In *How the Grinch Stole Christmas* (2000) he turned Dr. Seuss's storybook creatures into flesh, and in *Men in Black 2* (2002) added several new species to Hollywood's creature kingdom.

Baker achieved these cinematic fantasies through a process begun in the 1930s with the development of liquid foam-rubber latex, a revolutionary substance that mimics the suppleness of human skin, and new techniques that mold it into prosthetics applied directly to an actor's face.

*Planet of the Apes* (2001), for which Baker masterminded 400 human-to-simian metamorphoses, is the most persuasive example of his adaptation of these techniques. Watching the film's original 1968 version, Baker noticed that thick makeup pieces kept actors from moving their lips. "That's a shame," Baker observed, "because apes are very expressive with their mouths as they bare their teeth." Baker avoided the problem in the remake with a two-pronged solution. Custom dentures pushed the actors' faces into the muzzle-like profiles of apes, and thin prosthetic faces completed the transformation while still allowing the subtlest expressions to be captured on screen. By designing many different masks, each with its own hand-sewn hairs, Baker created a realistically diverse simian population.

Such small design details create large effects. Rick Baker aids actors in realizing their craft, advances the magic illusionism at the heart of filmmaking, and multiplies alternative realities in the popular imagination. **DA**

1

**HOW THE GRINCH STOLE CHRISTMAS**
Concept art for Grinch character makeup, ca. 2000
Special makeup effects designer: Rick Baker, Cinovation Studio
Director: Ron Howard
Studio: Universal Studios
Photography: Courtesy Rick Baker

2

**MEN IN BLACK 2**
Concept art for Helmet Head character make up, ca. 2002
Special makeup effects designer: Rick Baker, Cinovation Studio
Director: Barry Sonnenfeld
Copyright: 2002 Columbia Pictures, Industries, Inc. All rights reserved.
Photography: Courtesy Columbia Pictures

3–6

**PLANET OF THE APES**
Film stills, 2001
Special makeup effects designer: Rick Baker
Studio: 20th Century Fox Film Corporation
Director: Tim Burton
Photography: Courtesy PhotoFest

3–6

## BRYAN BELL b. 1959

DESIGN CORPS

*Raleigh, North Carolina*

1–3

Great architecture isn't cheap. Or is it? Bryan Bell has proved—handily, repeatedly, bouyantly—that custom housing is within reach of everyone. And he means that quite literally. Troubled by the disequilibrium between the popularity of architecture and the number of people who actually have any contact with an architect, Bell sees his role as curiously selfless. He is the anti-Roark. "The greater public, the 98 percent without access to architects, certainly does not understand what we do and what we can do for them," he says. "Presenting the reasons that design can help is our task, not theirs." As a result, Bell's architecture is focused, in many cases, on improving the lives of the poor and the disenfranchised. Architecture as a social solution rather than an exercise in social advancement is his message.

For migrant apple pickers in Pennsylvania, Bell and his nonprofit company, Design Corps, which employs recent architecture graduates as part of the AmeriCorps program, devised an inexpensive but chic corrugated steel mobile home. Moveable from job to job and hooked up to water, sewage, and power lines, it provides a solid, welcoming, but temporary residence that is larger and infinitely more comfortable than the typical cramped migrant housing. The Pink House is another of Bell's delightful and engaging domestic experiments: a handsome barnlike house whose cheery pink panels of insulation are in full view through walls sheathed in clear, corrugated fiberglass siding.

What makes Bell's work a joy to behold is its inventive practicality, not to mention its respect for the human condition. A talent that would otherwise be spent erecting yet another skyscraper or adding another McMansion to the surburban landscape is here spent on the common good. And Bell does it with style, grace, and ingenuity. **MO**

1, 2

**SELF-HELP HOUSING:**
**DILLON HOUSE AND SOSNA HOUSE**
Digital renderings, 2001
Design team: Bryan Bell, Kristine Wade, Ryan Gilbin, Ethan Cohen, Meredith Kelly, Lisa McClellan, Gary Shaffer, Hubert Snyder, David Rentsel, Oscar Sanchez, Cristina Chang
Project funding: U.S. Department of Agriculture Rural Housing Service
Clients: Theresa Dillon and Robert & Sajal Sosna
Renderings: Brian King

3

**MANUFACTURED MIGRANT HOUSING**
Adams County, Pennsylvania, 2002
Design team: Bryan Bell, Kindra Welch, Melissa Tello, Lesli Stinger, Vicente Sauceda, Kristztina Tokes, Andrea Dietz, Justin Staley, Anne Thomas
Funded by the Pennsylvania Department of Community and Economic Affairs and the National Endowment for the Arts
Photography: Kindra Welch

4–6

**GUEST WORKER HOUSING (PINK HOUSE)**
Sunnyside Farms, Virginia
Concept renderings, 2002
Design team: Bryan Bell, Victoria Ballard Bell, Brian King, Ginger Watkins, Jeff Evans, Seth Peterson, Kersten Harries
Renderings: Brian King, Seth Peterson

4–6

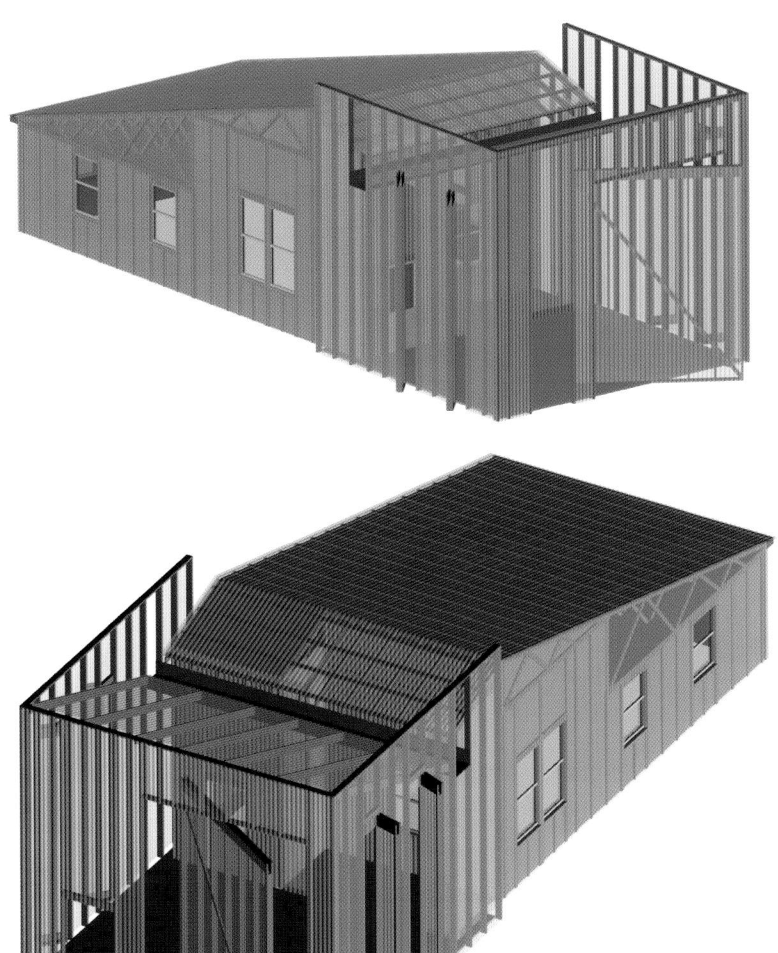

MAURICE BLANKS b. 1964

JOHN CHRISTAKOS b. 1964

CHARLIE LAZOR b. 1964

## BLU DOT

*Minneapolis*

1, 2

Minneapolis-based Blu Dot confounds the cultural prejudices that favor America's coasts as the seedbeds of all things cool. Their affordable furniture is as elegantly designed and easy-to-assemble as their products' names are light-hearted. The Felt-Up Chair, made of felt and metal tubes, reveals their penchant for double entendres, while Droopy, designed for Target, conjures Disney. Its soft panels of rip-stock nylon become taut walls when hung over the table's steel-rod frame. Other forays into everyday products include Flip Me, a beautiful Parson-style table with a top that converts from plastic laminate (able to withstand the wear-and-tear of children) to oak (the perfect host for stylish adult parties) and Strata, a storage unit that's purchased by the layer and assembled into shelves and cabinets without hardware or tools. Strata's cabinet doors are rubber, a sensuous, delightful surprise.

Founded in 1996 by Maurice Blanks, John Christakos, and Charlie Lazor, friends schooled in architecture and art at Williams College, Blu Dot has produced about forty furniture pieces. "What makes our furniture different and affordable," Christakos says, "is that we approach design from the inside out, with production, packaging, and shipping in mind. The forms of our furniture bubble up from these issues." Blu Dot's partners enjoy working within technical and economic constraints. Like Charles and Ray Eames before them, the firm was commissioned by Herman Miller to design a new line of furniture. Created recently for the company's Red line, Blu-Dot's Plug and Play is an erector set of filing units, shelves, and other components "plugged" into freestanding pegboard screens. Although this project didn't reach the marketplace, Blu Dot still pursues the holy grail of good design—design that is, Lazor says, "useful and delightful to ordinary people, everyday." **DA**

**1, 2**
**DROOPY**
Table, 2001
Polyethylene, ripstop nylon, chromed steel rod
Designers: Charlie Lazor, John Christakos, and Maurice Blanks
Manufacturer: Blu Dot, Minneapolis
Photography: Charlie Lazor

**3**
**FLIP ME**
Table, 2001
Rift-sawn white oak, laminate, stainless steel
Designers: Charlie Lazor, John Christakos, and Maurice Blanks
Manufacturer: Blu Dot, Minneapolis
Photography: Paul James

**4**
**STRATA**
Storage system, 2002
Bent birch plywood, rubber, stainless steel
Designers: Charlie Lazor, John Christakos, and Maurice Blanks
Manufacturer: Blu Dot, Minneapolis
Photography: Kris Clover

**5**
**PLUG AND PLAY SCREEN**
Prototype, 2001
Polyethylene, powder-coated steel,rubber
Designers: Charlie Lazor, John Christakos, and Maurice Blanks
Client: Herman Miller, Zeeland, Michigan
Photography: Peter Madson, Charlie Lazor

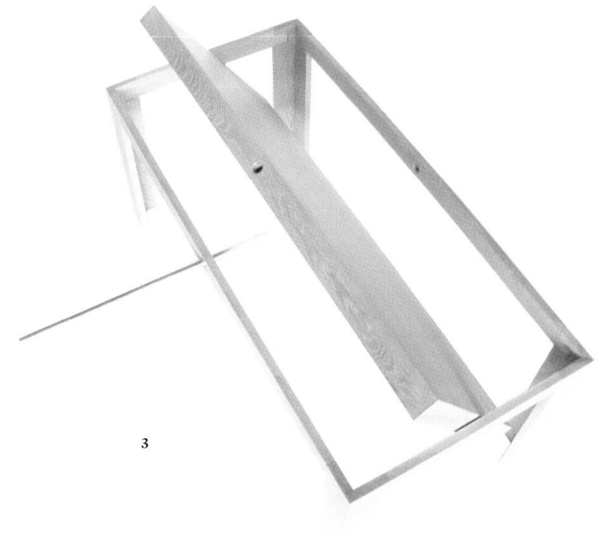

3

4

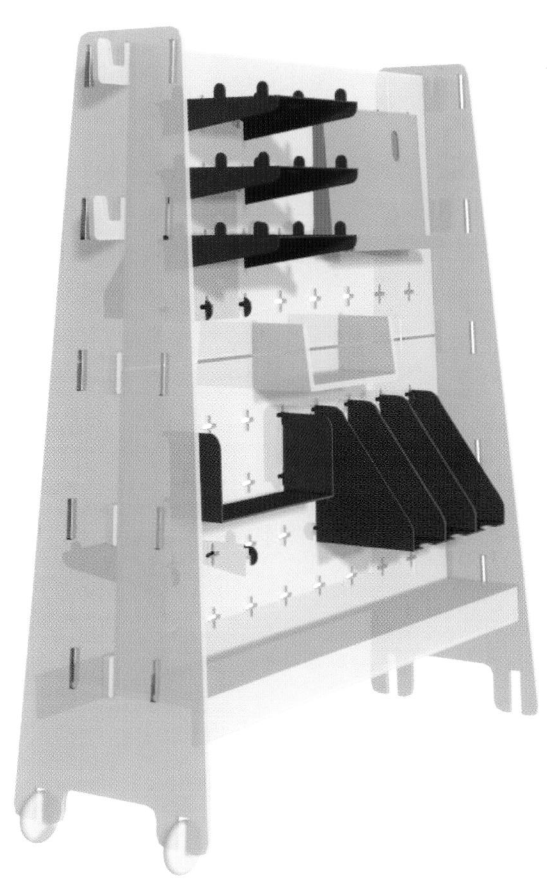

5

## CYNTHIA BREAZEAL b. 1967

MIT MEDIA LAB

*Cambridge, Massachusetts*

1

In the Steven Speilberg movie *A.I.*, an adopted robotic child—a futuristic Pinocchio—is abandoned, not because he can never be made into a real boy, but because he is already so very "real." Cynthia Breazeal served as a consultant for *A.I.*, but she is decidedly not interested in robots we can't distinguish from ourselves. For over a decade Breazeal has been making creatures that look adamantly different from us but behave uncannily like us.

Breazeal sees the potential of artificial intelligence to go beyond drones that defuse bombs, deliver specimens in hospitals, and work on assembly lines. With Anima Machina, a novel entry into the nature vs. nurture debates, she explores emotional intelligence in a generation of robots that blend plant and animal traits. Here are artificial flowers of a whole new order. Synthetic but far from dead, this species shows interest in us. Their vivid, hard, shiny shells contain sophisticated electro-mechanical systems that allow petals to open or close, tentacles to reach or retreat in response to our movements, whether coaxing or aggressive.

Developed in tandem with Breazeal's virtual flora is a new breed of fauna. Building on the success of Kismet, a responsive robot that even had a theological adviser, Breazeal has fashioned elfin offspring with expressive, exaggerated eyes and ears as part of her ongoing research into the ways humans and robots interact physically and emotionally.

*A.I.* was a tale of the deception of appearances, which some might say is the definition of art. Breazeal's creatures, while playful and familiar, announce their fakery with truth to materials, which some might say is the definition of design. They are no less powerful for being metaphors: her alien world's ecology is changed by our presence as surely as the real world is every day. **SY**

1
**CYBERFLORA**
Concept rendering, 2002
Design team: Cynthia Breazeal, project lead; Jeff Lieberman, design lead; Dan Steihl
Rendering: Ryan Kavanaugh

2
**CYBERFAUNA**
Concept rendering, 2002
Design team: Cynthia Breazeal, project lead; Jeff Lieberman, design lead; Jesse Gray, Ryan Kavanaugh, Bill Tomlinson
Rendering: Ryan Kavanaugh

2

ALEXANDRE DE BETAK b. 1968

## BUREAU BETAK

*New York City*

1

In the beginning, fashion shows were relatively modest affairs—a handful of poker-faced mannequins walking through a close-packed room or down a runway, holding numbers that corresponded to their ensemble's position in the program. Today, fashion and its related products have become as much about the presentation as about the couture clothes and the sylphs who wear them. And no company has had a more profound impact on the way fashion designers present themselves to the press, and therefore to the world, than Bureau Betak.

Of the company, founder Alexandre de Betak has written, "Our mission . . . consists of transmitting the message and the image of a collection, product, or event by choosing and elaborating on the theme, the design of the space and the set, the choice of the models, the music, the hair, the makeup, [and] the styling." In short, Bureau Betak, which was founded in Paris in 1988 and has been based in New York City since 1994, is an impresario of the evanescent, masterminding to the last mousse-drenched curl how a corporate brand is perceived through epic theatrical productions that hue to Andy Warhol's fifteen-minute dictum of the measure of fame in the modern world.

For designer Hussein Chalayan, Bureau Betak created a claustrophobic runway of tilted planes straight from the cabinet of Dr. Caligari, part space-age temple, part padded-wall asylum. For John Bartlett, giant wood frames approximated prison cells. And when Emmanuel Ungaro launched his perfume Desnuda, the company choreographed an exquisite, hypnotic desert fantasia composed of pink glitter, rosy lights, whirling dervishes, and glistening pools. Bureau Betak's provocative presentations are the mirages of the new millennium, devised to instantly seduce before vanishing without a single trace. **MO**

1
**CHRISTIAN DIOR HAUTE COUTURE**
Fall 2001 show
Scaffold, glass, red lucite, lights
Designer: Alexandre de Betak
Client: Christian Dior
Photography: Alexandre de Betak

2
**JOHN BARTLETT**
Design for Fall 2001 show
Digital rendering
Designer: Alexandre de Betak
Client: John Bartlett
Rendering: Phillip Speakes

3
**JIL SANDER SUN**
Fragrance launch, 2002
Detail, orange neon
Designer: Alexandre de Betak
Client: Jil Sander, Lancaster
Photography: Alexandre de Betak

4
**JIL SANDER SUN**
Fragrance launch, 2002
Table, laquered wood, steel beam, orange neon
Designer: Alexandre de Betak
Client: Jil Sander, Lancaster
Photography: Alexandre de Betak

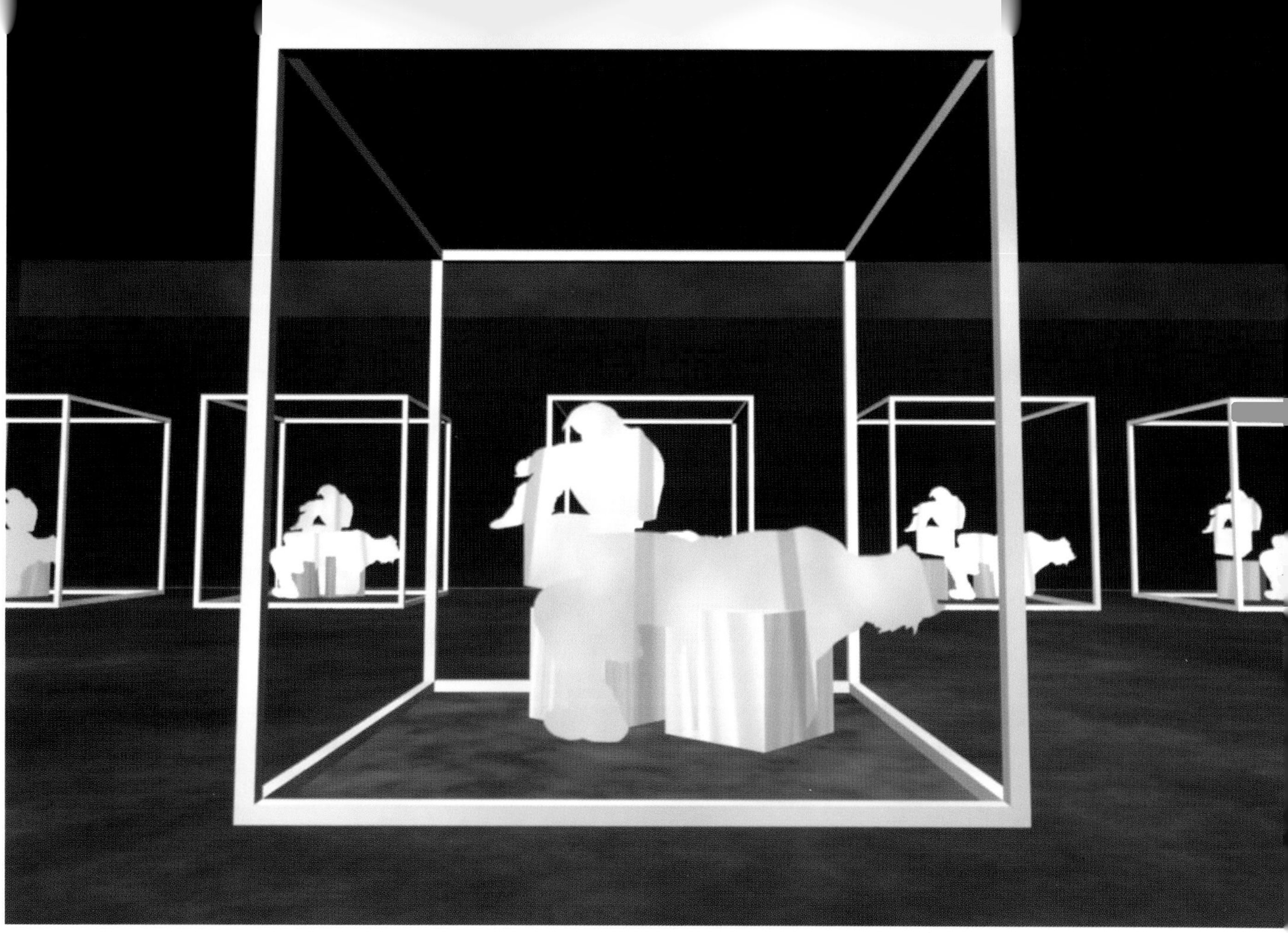

2–4

**STEPHEN BURKS** b. 1969

READYMADE PROJECTS

*New York City*

1, 2

Stephen Burks wants to bring awareness of furniture and interiors to a new market of international youth, whose appetites have profoundly altered music, fashion, and graphics over the past fifteen years. From his studio Readymade Projects, he reinterprets "street style"—with its associations of personal mobility and do-it-yourself technology—and moves it from "the active city to the interactive interior."

Burks's Plank of Wood project consists of narrow sheets of plywood that lean against a wall. Each, with a slotted handle along its side, has a different function—storing CDs, hanging coats, displaying messages. One, fitted with a single lightbulb, underscores the readymade humor of a project that uses minimal means to create informal, portable furnishings.

In a shelving system produced by Cappellini, thin planes of varnished steel are supported by cross-braces of satined stainless steel. The shelving appears poised for transformation, its crisscrossed members suggesting potential expansion or contraction.

Burks's tabletop objects also imply flexibility and change. His Serving Vases for Cappellini have tall, narrow cylinders for stem flowers inside, and long, wide-base vessels, designed to hold floating blossoms. A system of objects called Crown, part of Covo's Smash collection, consists of a glass bowl and two larger, bottomless glass collars. These pieces can take several configurations, with the bowl resting inside or near the open rings of glass.

A writer and critic as well as designer, Burks is keyed into the international design scene, yet is influenced by the local vocabulary of downtown New York, itself a set of attitudes more truly international than that of the modern furniture showroom. Burks brings these worlds together in his global, mobile objects and environments. **EL**

1
**SERVING VASES COLLECTION**
Ceramic, 2001
Designer: Stephen Burks
Manufacturer: Cappellini Progetto Oggetto, Italy
Photography: Courtesy Cappellini

2
**CROWN CENTERPIECE/ SMASH COLLECTION**
Glass, 2001
Designer: Stephen Burks
Manufacturer: Covo, Italy
Photography: Carlo Lavatori

3
**DISPLAY SHELVING SYSTEM**
Varnished steel and satined steel, 2000
Designer: Stephen Burks
Manufacturer: Cappellini Progetto Oggetto, Italy
Photography: Courtesy Cappellini

4
**PLANK OF WOOD**
Furnishings, 2002
Plywood, laminate, assorted hardware
Designer: Stephen Burks,
Additional design help for
Plank of Wood speakers: Camella Ehlke
Photography: Stephen Burks

3

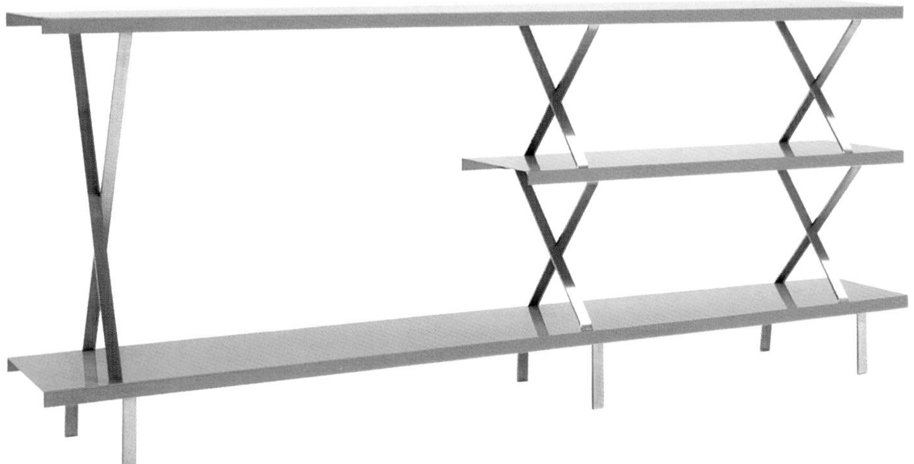

4

## CRITZ CAMPBELL b. 1967

b9

*Chicago*

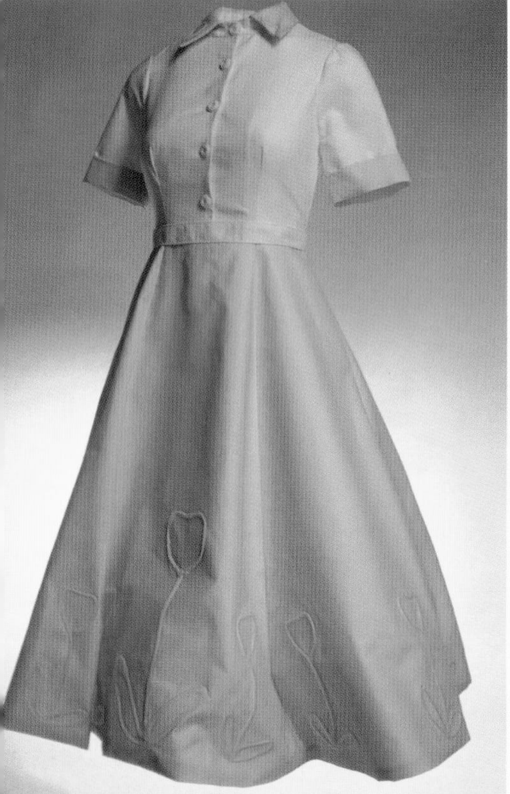

1, 2

Critz Campbell's Eudora chair, named after his fellow Mississippian, author Eudora Welty, is the design equivalent of a steel magnolia. Seemingly the archetypal 1930s armchair in grandmother's living room, Eudora is upholstered in charming vintage fabrics. Emanating coziness, the chair glows from within. These nostalgic associations draw people toward Eudora, only to discover that the chair is made of fiberglass, its fabric is encased in resin, and its source of light is fluorescent tubes. Some people thrill to its novel materials. Some make the connection to such design icons as Shiro Kuramata's Miss Blanche chair (1988), in which flowers are suspended in clear acrylic resin. Still others are disappointed, even disquieted, as their sentimental memories are turned on end.

Part art object, part commercial product, the Eudora chair embodies the dual nature of Campbell's sensibility. (This duality was reinforced by his education at the School of the Art Institute of Chicago and at England's Parnham College, where he learned traditional furniture-making.) While Campbell has designed inexpensive shelving and furniture for a mass market, the custom-made Eudora chair and the more recent Luna Dress lamp are his quirkiest reinterpretations of American icons. Inspired by 1950s Simplicity dress patterns, Luna, fabricated by Cindy Schilder, uses a familiar fashion silhouette to demonstrate an experimental lighting process. Luna's two layers of cotton are woven with phosphorescent copper wires that glow in embroiderylike tulip patterns.

The pun behind the name of Campbell's studio—b9—suggests his work's double edge. Like Campbell himself, his designs initially appear sweetly "benign." But closer inspection reveals a serious core, one that layers technical innovation, fine craftsmanship, design history, and an understanding of the meaning of objects in contemporary culture. **DA**

1, 2
**LUNA DRESS**
Lighting fixture, 2002
Cotton, crinoline, phosphorescent cable
Designers: Critz Campbell, Cindy Schilder
Photography: Critz Campbell

3–5
**EUDORA CHAIRS**
Fiberglass, cotton fabric, polyester resin, fluorescent lights, 2001
Designer: Critz Campbell
Fabrics: "Norfolk Rose" by Waverly Fabrics (3); "Geo Magic Jewels" by Kings Road (4); "Robot Man" by Alexander Henry (5)
Photography: Critz Campbell

3

4, 5

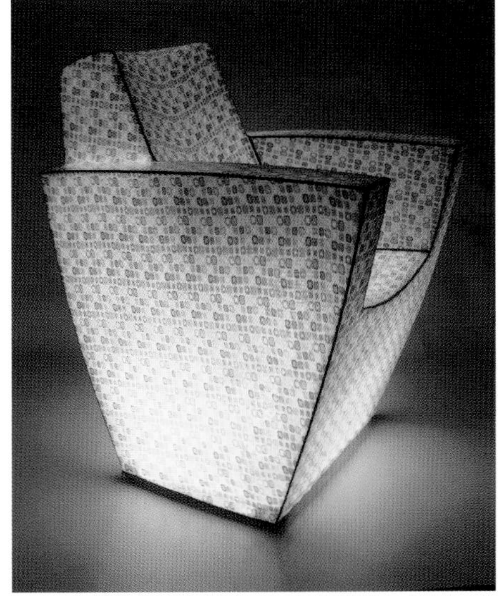

MATTHEW RICHMOND b. 1975

THOMAS ROMER b. 1969

ROBERT REED b. 1974

## THE CHOPPING BLOCK

*New York City*

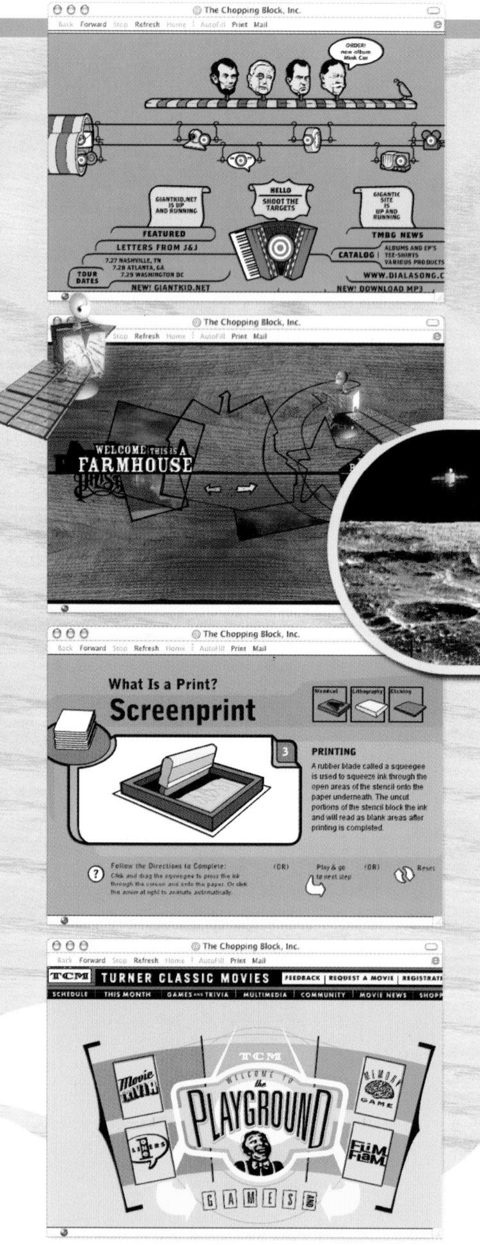

1–5

The designers at The Chopping Block treat their work like a game. They create Websites and other interactive media that are not only rich in content and functionality but are also lots of fun. "Welcome to the Playground," announces the 2001 homepage for turnerclassicmovies.com, a site that indexes 50,000 classic film titles.

The Chopping Block was founded in 1996 by Matthew Richmond, Thomas Romer, Robert Reed, and Mike Essl, four designers who had just graduated from The Cooper Union in New York City. (Essl is no longer a partner.) One of their first projects was a Website for the band They Might Be Giants, produced in collaboration with their teacher and mentor from Cooper Union, Barbara Glauber. The band has continued to be a dedicated client; a recent interface is based on a carnival-style shooting gallery.

Many of The Chopping Block's clients come from the music and entertainment industries. A Website for Phish's "Farmhouse" album centers on the old barn that houses the band's recording studio. A site for Francis Ford Coppola's *Apocalypse Now Redux* uses film grabs and audio clips to weave an interactive narrative. In each project, typography, illustration, and animation are used to build distinctive on-screen brands.

Understanding the Web as a place where identity is easily manipulated, The Chopping Block team constantly transforms the firm's own image. A changing parade of pop culture themes has animated their Websites, from Nascar and NASA to the Boy Scouts. An illustration of eight kids dressed as grown-ups sums up the spirit of The Chopping Block: a team of young designers amazed and delighted to be shaping the course of a new medium. **EL**

1
**TMBG.COM**
Website, 2000
Designers: Thomas Romer and Jay Hillyer
Client: They Might Be Giants

2
**PHISH FARMHOUSE**
Website, 2000
Designers: Matthew Richmond and Thomas Romer
Client: Phish

3
**MOMA: WHAT IS A PRINT**
Interactive kiosk and Website, 2001
Designers: Thomas Romer, Haik Hoisington, and Chandler McWilliams
Client: Museum of Modern Art

4
**TURNERCLASSICMOVIES.COM**
Website, 2001
Designers: Robert Reed and Charles Michelet
Client: Turner Classic Movies

5
**APOCALYPSENOW.COM**
Website, 2001
Designers: Robert Reed, Chandler McWilliams, and Steve Bowden
Client: Miramax Films

6
**CHOPPING BLOCK THEMES: NASCAR, HORROR, NASA, SCOUTS, ORANGES, NO! KIDS**
Website identities, 1997–2002
Designers: Thomas Romer, Mike Essl, Jason Hillyer, Charles Michelet, Robert Reed, and Matthew Richmond

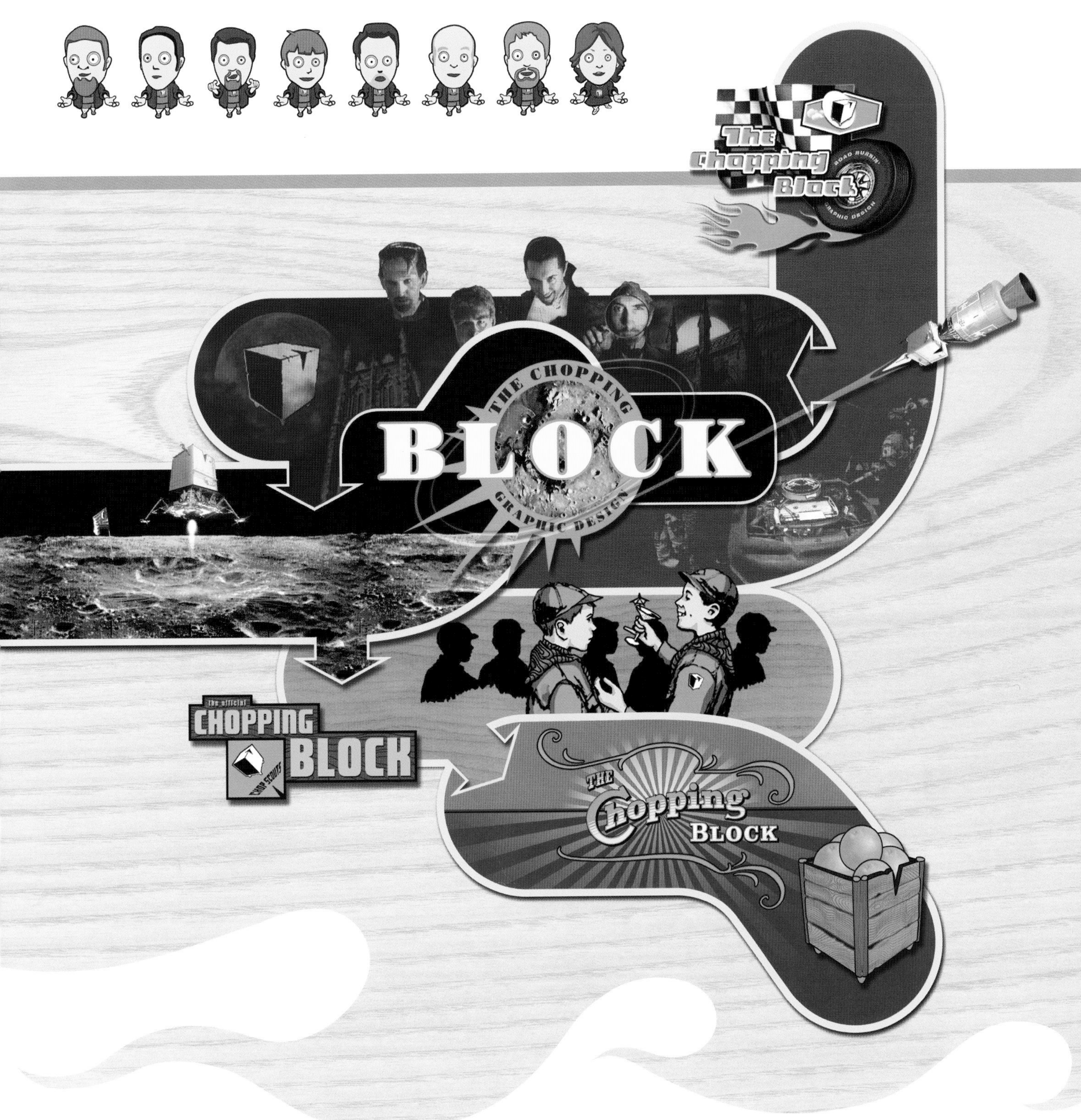
The Chopping Block
ROAD BURNIN'
GRAPHIC DESIGN
THE CHOPPING
BLOCK
GRAPHIC DESIGN
the official
CHOPPING
BLOCK
CHOP SCOUTS
THE
Chopping
BLOCK

6

## KELLY CHRISTY b. 1960

*New York City*

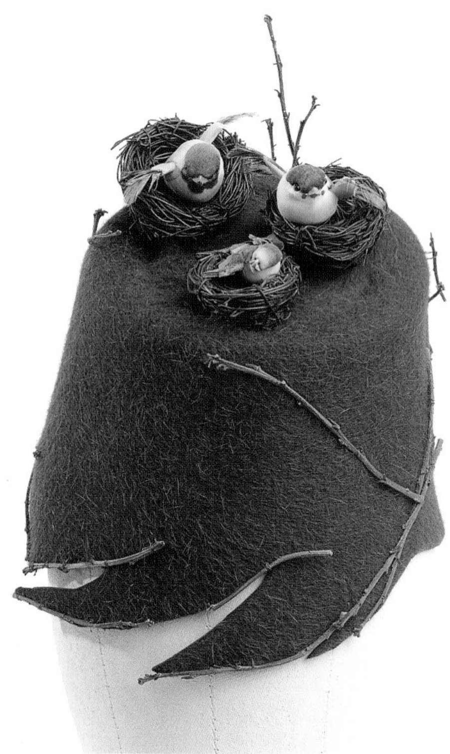

1, 2

Ever since President John F. Kennedy went hatless in the 1960s as a sign of youthful vigor and disregard for traditional formalities, millinery has become more costume than convention. Designer Kelly Christy revels in this sartorial evolution, giving each of her unique hats a name to reflect a specific mood or character, like "Let's Skate" or "Veronica Lake." Christy has a theatrical flair that made her the ideal choice to design hats for the recent Broadway revival of Clare Booth Luce's play *The Women* (costumes were done by Isaac Mizrahi). "For a classic milliner," Christy says, "that was a dream. The play is set in the late thirties, a perfect period, because that's when hats were frivolous." Inspired by French couturière Elsa Schiaparelli and Adrian, who costumed the play's 1939 Hollywood adaptation, Christy created eighteen fantasy hats that mined the era's penchant for toylike dimensions and exotic materials while visually portraying each character's distinct personality.

Christy helps her clientele achieve similar distinction. Working out of a small shop in the fashionable Manhattan neighborhood of Nolita, she designs and fabricates her own hats, hoping to keep her craft "personal and detailed." Recently she has focused her dramatic aesthetic on a series of designs that put miniature landscapes on people's heads. Combining cloth and miniatures, this new generation of hats represents snow scenes, complete with skiers and trees, as well as ice skating rinks and picnics. An Iowa native and nature lover, Christy sees analogies between her designs and the canopied silhouettes created by groves of trees. Birds' nests inspired a series of hats made of twigs, artificial birds, and eggs. In an age of mass-produced fashion, Kelly Christy holds out for customization, transforming her clients into eccentric actors in the drama of city life. **DA**

1
**BIRD'S NEST**
Hat, 2000
Rabbit fur felt, twigs, bird's nest, birds
Designer: Kelly Christy

2
**BASKET-O-CHICKS**
Hat, 2002
Antique straw, straw braid, twigs, chicks
Designer: Kelly Christy

3
**SNOW SCENE**
Hat, 2002
Rabbit fur felt, miniatures
Designer: Kelly Christy

4
**LET'S SKATE**
Hat, 1999
Buckram, silk crepe, miniatures
Designer: Kelly Christy

Photography: Matt Flynn

3

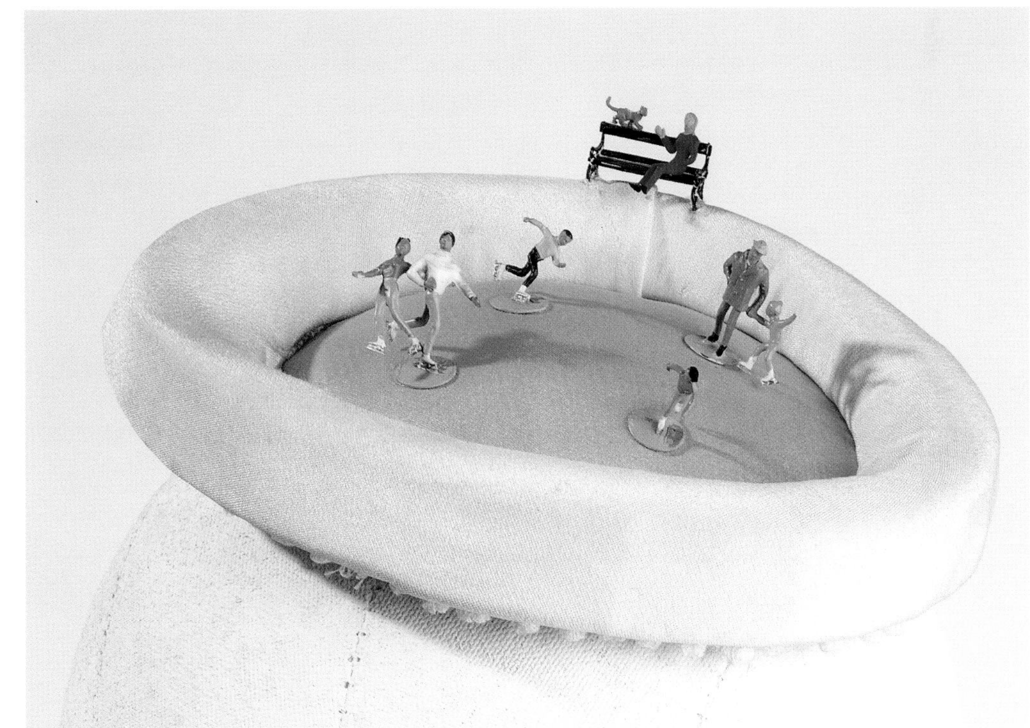

4

GREG VENDENA b. 1969

## CO-LAB

*Detroit*

1–3

Greg Vendena works in the city that symbolizes postindustrial America—Detroit. Substandard housing and dilapidated public spaces are among the troubles addressed by Vendena and his architecture and design practice, co-lab. Established in 2001, co-lab—a contraction of collaborative, labor, and laboratory—includes Vendena, a graduate in architecture from the local Cranbrook Academy of Art; Christine Dunn, an architect and artist; and Fabio Fernandez, an artist, teacher, and community organizer. (Others often join them as well.) Fusing social commitment and environmentalism, co-lab makes a "progressive response to the conditions around us."

Co-lab's major design strategy is a clever recycling of everyday materials. Abandoned tires, plentiful detritus of Detroit's car culture, have been converted into outdoor plant holders and shingles that keep rain and wind out of houses. Global automaking, however, doesn't always reach local residents. Only one in four city dwellers owns a car. The others often rely on Detroit's inadequate mass transportation, so co-lab has proposed recycling thrift-store suitcases into colorful bus shelters. Co-lab also renovates abandoned houses using renewable energy systems and recycling materials such as wood scraps into tiles for floors, walls, and tabletops.

In the future co-lab wants to improve the furniture in local parks by capitalizing on an ad-hoc process in which residents have traditionally gathered discarded household chairs to create meeting spaces. Working with the community, co-lab will transform scrap metal into 250-pound replicas of these vernacular ancestors.

"Thinking ecologically," Vendena says, "reasserts our organic reality and the evanescence and interconnection of all things." Co-lab's approach to specific local issues responds to problems vexing all post-industrial cities. "Detroit," Greg Vendena says, "is everywhere." **DA**

1
**TIRE SHINGLES**
Salvaged tires, 2001
Designer: Greg Vendena
Photography: Robert Herrick

2
**TIRE PLANTER**
Salvaged tire, 2000
Designer: Greg Vendena
Photography: Robert Herrick

3
**TIRE SIGN**
Detroit context study, 1999
Photography: Greg Vendena

4, 5
**SUITCASE BENCH AND ARC DE VALISE BUS SHELTER**
Watercolor concept drawings, 2001
Designers: Greg Vendena, Fabio Fernandez, and Christine Dunn
Photography: Tim Thayer

6
**GATHERING SPACE**
Detroit context study, 1999
Photography: Greg Vendena

7
**IRON CHAIR**
Cast scrap iron, 1999
Designer: Greg Vendena
Photography: Robert Herrick

4

5

6, 7

JESSICA CORR b. 1973

WILLIAM DOLL b. 1969

ANTON GINZBURG b. 1974

JOE SERRINS b. 1970

## COLLABORATIVE

*New York City*

Design meets science on the level of metaphor in the work of Collaborative, a group who joined forces in 2000 to "shed our professional skins and experiment collectively." Product designer Jessica Corr, decorator William Doll, architect Joe Serrins, and decorative artist and graphic designer Anton Ginzburg are inspired by such phenomena as cloning and mutation. They have created floor tiles that mate carpet and rubber, drinking glasses shaped like animal hooves, and a lamp that morphs from a flat sheet into a luminous sphere, resembling a glowing coil of DNA.

Eternal Carpet Tiles solves the problem of keeping white carpeting clean by encasing rug samples in clear rubber. In their organic process, the designers submerge carpet squares in a shallow tray of liquid rubber. As the rubber hardens, each square is frozen in a different orientation, making each product unique.

Eternal Carpet Tiles was conceived by all four partners. Other projects have been created by individual members and draw on the group's intellectual support. Corr designed the electroluminescent Kirilume lamp, and Ginzburg spawned the F&M series of shaded glasses in the shape of cow and deer hooves, giving zoological meaning to the term "stemware." These were designed during recent scares about foot-and-mouth and mad cow diseases, which the group believes suggested "a new relationship between man and animal." Collaborative's interest in updating traditional materials and processes is given exquisite form in Ginzburg's 2002 "void" chess set, whose hollow, hand-cast porcelain pieces have matte exteriors and glossy glazed interiors. (The chessboard is a basketweave of two shades of Ultrasuede ribbon.) Science even influences how Collaborative works. Working alone or together, they form and reform like a molecular structure. **DA**

**1, 2**

1
**KIRILUME**
Pendant light fixture, 2001
Die-cut electroluminescent film
Designer: Jessica Corr
Manufacturer: Collaborative
Photography: Annie Schlechter

2
**ETERNAL CARPET TILES AND MAT**
Clear rubber and carpet, 2001
Designers: Jessica Corr, William Doll, Anton Ginzburg, Joe Serrins
Manufacturer: Collaborative
Photography: Annie Schlechter

3
**F&M GLASSES**
Mold-blown glass, 2001
Designer: Anton Ginzburg
Manufacturer: Collaborative
Photography: Nigel Cox

4
**VOID CHESS SET**
Porcelain, 2002
Designer: Anton Ginzburg
Manufacturer: Haasprojekt, USA
Photography: Nigel Cox

3

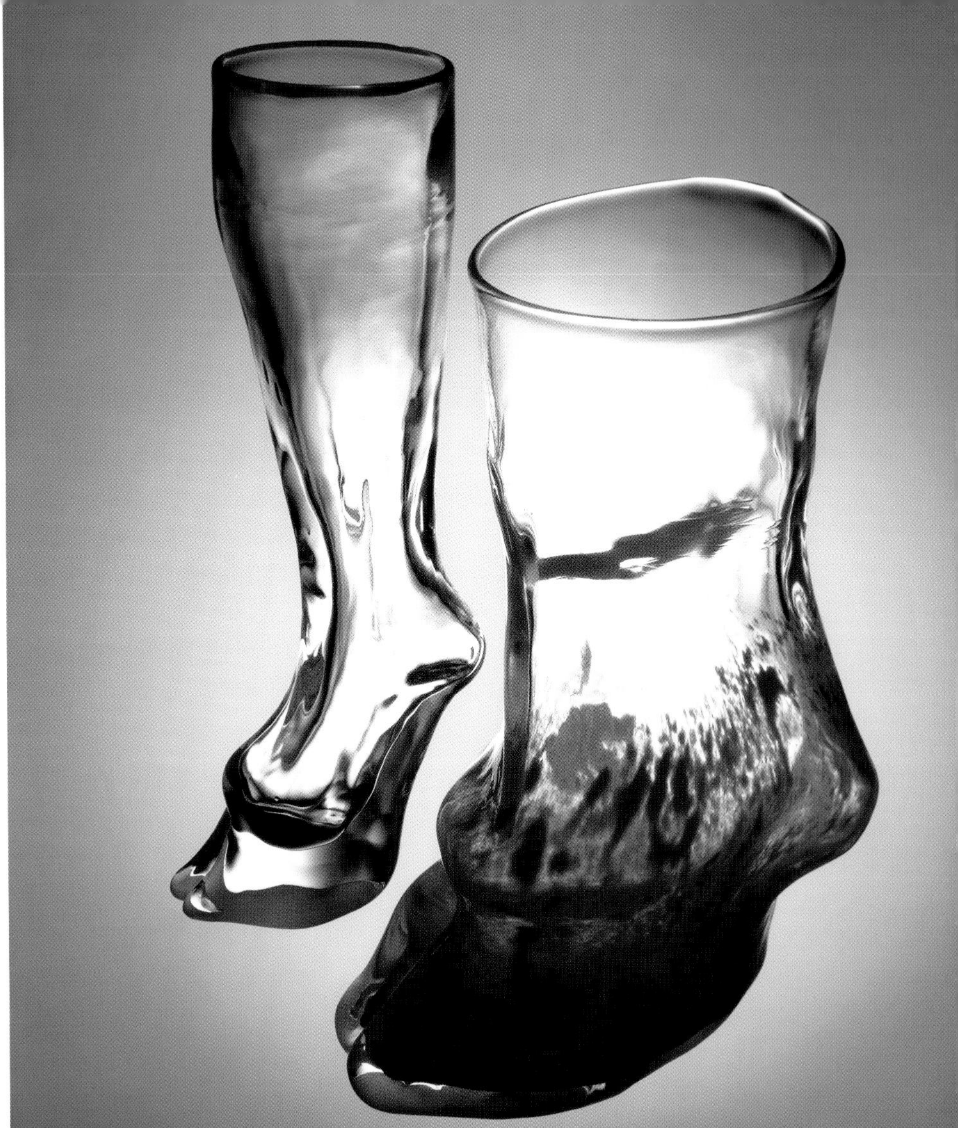

4

## LAURIE DEMARTINO b. 1964

LAURIE DEMARTINO DESIGN

(STUDIO D)

*Minneapolis*

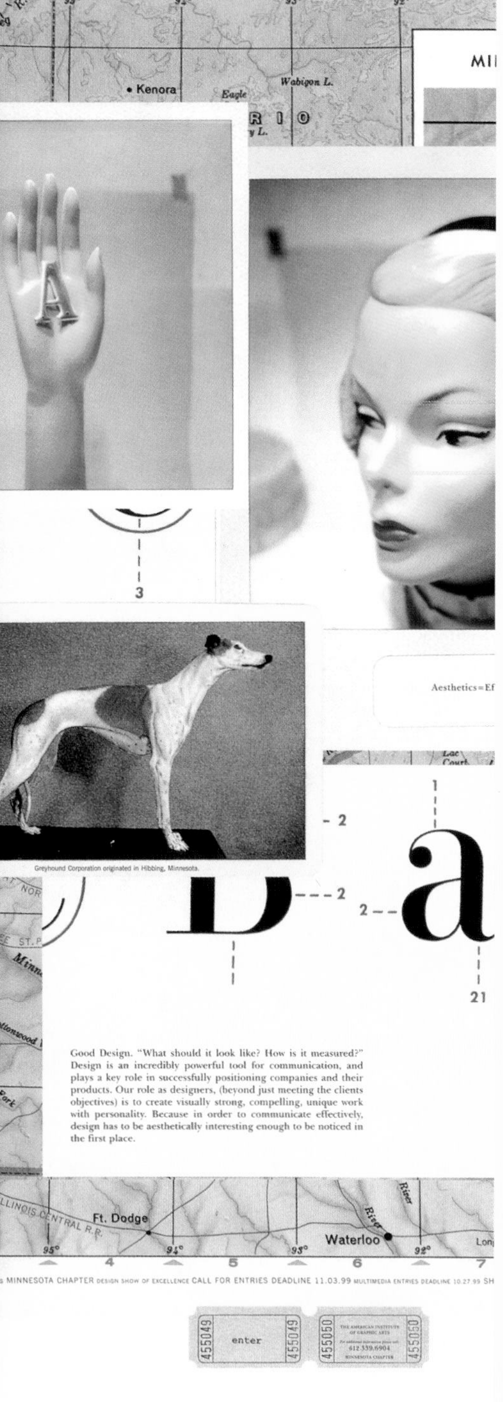


1

A decorative yet documentary sensuality infuses the work of Laurie DeMartino, who orchestrates layers of image, pattern, and text into rich surfaces. A poster for a Minnesota design competition is a collage of elements spread out like evidence from a scientific inquiry or a police dossier. *Twelve Identities,* a promotional publication for French Paper, features letterheads designed by DeMartino's students. Opposite each design, she created a portrait of the student by nesting a deadpan mugshot within an assembly of decorated papers, unfolded packages, and official documents, each element selected to express the individual's personality.

DeMartino's approach to typography also merges blunt observation and subtle interpretation. Small, sharp letterforms occupy orderly frames and boxes that articulate information into precise and legible hierarchies. These structures of containment are at once delicate and extreme, like Victorian undergarments, becoming decoration in their own right. In *Twelve Identities,* gridded boxes of text slip off the page or pass under and over the book's perforated cover.

Frango Chocolates are produced for the Marshall Field's department store in Chicago. DeMartino's new Frango box combines crisp stripes of color with soft layers of typographic ornament to create an updated package that still hints at the candies' dowdy, old-fashioned appeal. Not all of her work is so luxuriously decorated—disposable beverage cups covered with a two-color pattern of simple line drawings were designed to be printed on a limited budget.

With each project, Laurie DeMartino expresses her contemporary sense of surface. The page or package is both physical matter and conveyor of illusion, a fragment clipped from a larger continuum whose boundaries are unknown. **EL**

1

**AIGA MINNESOTA DESIGN SHOW**
Poster, 1999
Offset lithography
Designer: Laurie DeMartino
Client: AIGA Minnesota Chapter
Photography: Laurie DeMartino

2, 3

**TWELVE IDENTITIES**
Publication, cover and interior spread, 1999
Offset lithography
Designer: Laurie DeMartino
Copywriter: Lisa Pemrick
Client: French Paper Company
Photographer: Steve Belkowitz

4

**TARGET STORES**
Beverage cups, 1999
Flexography on Styrofoam
Designers: Laurie DeMartino
Illustrator: Paulina Reyes
Client: Target Stores
Photography: Steve Belkowitz

5

**FRANGO CHOCOLATES**
Packaging, 2000
Offset lithography
Designers: Laurie DeMartino and Paulina Reyes
Client: Marshall Field's
Photography: Steve Belkowitz

2, 3

Twelve Identities.
12


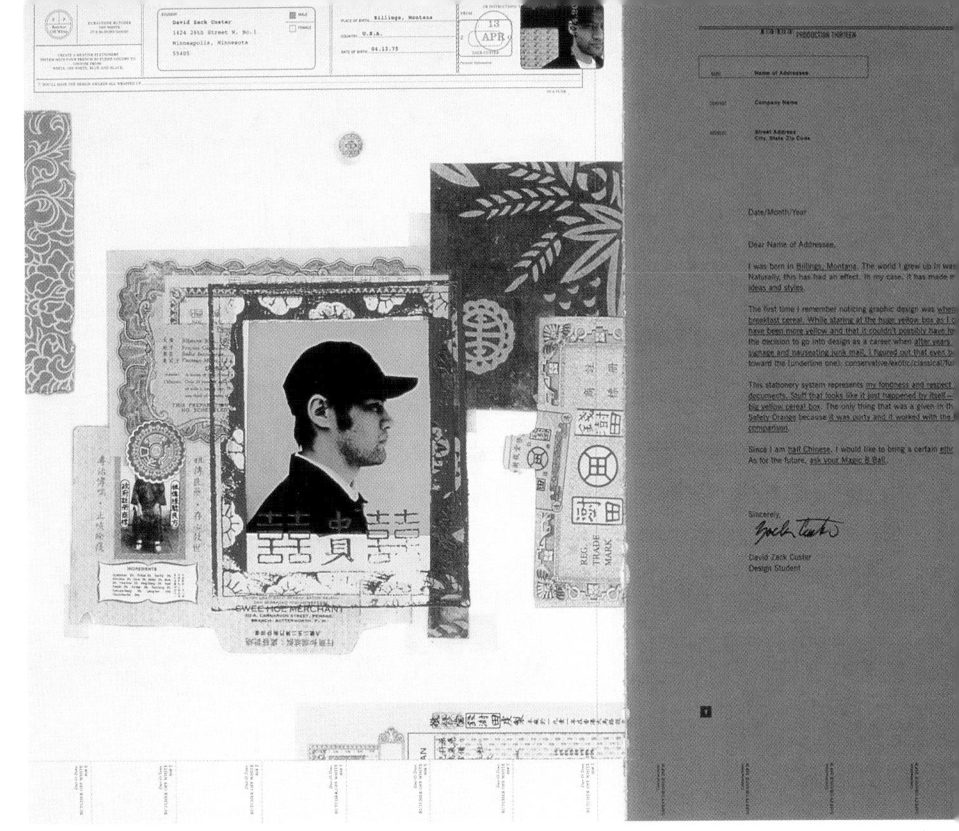

David Zack Custer
1624 29th Street W. No.1
Minneapolis, Minnesota
55405
Billings, Montana
U.S.A.
04.13.75
13 APR
SWEE HOE MERCHANT
REG. TRADE MARK
PRODUCTION THIRTEEN
Name of Addressee
Company Name
Street Address
City, State Zip Code
Date/Month/Year
Dear Name of Addressee,
I was born in Billings, Montana. The world I grew up in wa
Naturally, this has had an effect. In my case, it has made
ideas and styles.
The first time I remember noticing graphic design was whe
breakfast cereal. While staring at the huge yellow box as I
have been more yellow and that it couldn't possibly have
the decision to go into design as a career when after years
signage and nauseating junk mail, I figured out that even
toward the (underline one): conservative/exotic/classical/fu
This stationery system represents my fondness and respect
documents. Stuff that looks like it just happened by itself—
big yellow cereal box. The only thing that was a given in th
Safety Orange because it was purty and it worked with the
comparison.
Since I am half Chinese, I would like to bring a certain eth
As for the future, ask your Magic 8 Ball.
Sincerely,
David Zack Custer
Design Student

4

Frango
Frango
Frango
TOFFEE CRUNCH CHOCOLATES


5

CHRISTOPHER BROSIUS b. 1962

CHRISTOPHER GABLE b. 1963

## DEMETER FRAGRANCE LIBRARY

*New York City*

Throughout the history of manufactured scents, the goal of the master perfumer has always been a simple one: to create fragrances that allure, romance, make dizzy with desire, or simply mask a less desirable odor. Demeter Fragrance Library, an award-winning indie perfumer, creates scents with altogether edgier raisons d'etre. Its cofounders ransack the communal olfactory memory for ingredients and combinations that provide alternative answers to a fundamental question: What exactly is a perfume?

The contents of Demeter's library of more than 1,300 exotic, esoteric, even purposefully noxious scents are as raw and recognizable as their elemental names imply: Dirt, Tomato, Funeral Home, Waffle, Steam Room, Crust of Bread, Snow (winner of two 2000 U.S. Fragrance Star of the Year awards from the Fragrance Foundation), Sugar Cane (a 2001 Fragrance Foundation award winner), and more. Since forming the company in 1993, Christopher Brosius, the company's creative director and perfumer, and Christopher Gable, Demeter's president, have been distilling and recreating everyday scents at their factory in Sunbury, Pennsylvania, and then packaging them inside clear, basic bottles that belie the baroque experience within.

Pull off the bottle's silver cap, however, and Demeter's subversive intentions become instantly clear: some of its creations are fragrances, some are definitely odors. The scents lurking in this little company's archive are not all meant to be worn. Many are concocted as gentle Proustian reminders, while others are strictly atmospheric hand grenades, each spritz a startlingly vivid reminder that one man's perfume is another man's poison. **MO**

**DIRT, TOMATO, GINGERALE, SNOW**
Scent in glass containers, 2002
Designers: Christopher Gable and Christopher Brosius
Manufacturer: Demeter Fragrance Library
Photography: Sharon Pincus

DEMETER
Tomato
Pick-Me-Up
Cologne Spray
1 oz/30 ml
Simple, subtle
singular scents
each day, everywhere.
Contains: Ethanol Denatured (SD Alcohol 39C),
Parfum (Fragrance), Aqua (Water).
Demeter Fragrances, Red Cross, PA 17823 USA

DEMETER
Gingerale
Pick-Me-Up
Cologne Spray
1 oz/30 ml
Simple, subtle
singular scents
each day, everywhere.
Contains: Ethanol Denatured (SD Alcohol 39C),
Parfum (Fragrance), Aqua (Water).
Demeter Fragrances, Red Cross, PA 17823 USA

DEMETER
Snow
Pick-Me-Up
Cologne Spray
1 oz/30 ml
Simple, subtle
singular scents
each day, everywhere.
Contains: Ethanol Denatured (SD Alcohol 39C),
Parfum (Fragrance), Aqua (Water).
Demeter Fragrances, Red Cross, PA 17823 USA

WILLIAM DIAMOND b. 1952

ANTHONY BARATTA b. 1959

## DIAMOND + BARATTA

*New York City*

1, 2

In the 1940s the American decorator Dorothy Draper famously proclaimed, "The wider the stripe, the smarter the effect." Sixty-odd years later, New York interior designers William Diamond and Anthony Baratta, business partners and longtime Draper devotés, have taken their idol's obsession with the overscale to illogical extremes, concocting a witty range of fabrics and floorcoverings in which Americana and Surrealism meet in one grand graphic collision.

Founders of the SoHo residential interior design firm of Diamond + Baratta, the duo has made a specialty of traditionalist decors imbued with the flair of an old-fashioned carnival funhouse, as if Mount Vernon was made over for Pee-Wee Herman. In a woven cotton fabric that is part of the pair's collection for the American textile manufacturer Lee Jofa, houndstooth checks are blown up to 100 times their normal size. Seventeeth-century Delft tiles depicting jaunty sailboats are transmuted into giant octagonal panels in a floorcovering design for Stark Carpet. And for a private client's apartment in New York City, braided rugs—the stuff of middlebrow Colonial Revival interiors since the days of Wallace Nutting—are deftly recolored in candy-bright hues like lime green, ice blue, and shocking pink, then handcrafted to outlandish 60-foot lengths.

Curiously, Diamond + Baratta's tongue-in-chic creations have the strange effect of emphasizing the eternal rightness of their traditional underpinnings rather than undermining them for satirical gain. Comical and reverential, playful and patriotic, the designers' bold, brash works give true-blue motifs a life-affirming effervescence. **MO**

1
**FELDMAN RESIDENCE**
New York City, 1997
Designers: William Diamond and Anthony Baratta
Photography: Antoine Bootz

2
**JURICK RESIDENCE**
Manhasset, New York, 1999
Detail of custom patchwork chair and Portuguese needlepoint rug
Designers: William Diamond and Anthony Baratta
Photography: William Diamond

3
**GLEACHER RESIDENCE**
Palm Beach, Florida, 2000
Detail of custom designed "Delft" rug
Designers: William Diamond and Anthony Baratta
Photography: William Diamond

4
**BLANK RESIDENCE**
Rumson, New Jersey, 1999
Designers: William Diamond and Anthony Baratta
Photography: Francois Dischinger

5
**DICKSTEIN RESIDENCE**
New York City, 1999
Detail of custom braided rug
Designers: William Diamond and Anthony Baratta
Photography: Melanie Acevedo

3

4

5

## DAVE EGGERS b. 1970

MCSWEENEY'S

*San Francisco*

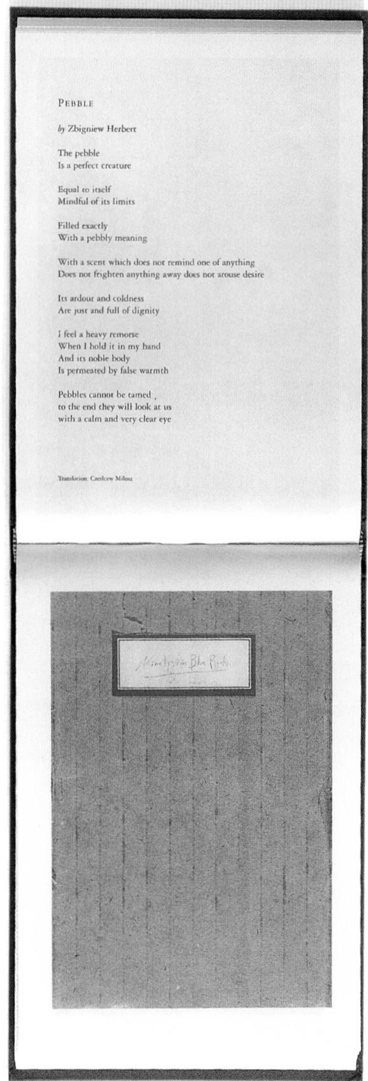

PEBBLE

*by* Zbigniew Herbert

The pebble
Is a perfect creature

Equal to itself
Mindful of its limits

Filled exactly
With a pebbly meaning

With a scent which does not remind one of anything
Does not frighten anything away does not arouse desire

Its ardour and coldness
Are just and full of dignity

I feel a heavy remorse
When I hold it in my hand
And its noble body
Is permeated by false warmth

Pebbles cannot be tamed
to the end they will look at us
with a calm and very clear eye

1

Dave Eggers is an author, editor, and publisher who designs his own pages. As creator of *Timothy McSweeney's Quarterly Concern*, founded in 1998, Eggers immediately attracted attention with his journal's physical appearance as well as its content.

A typical page from *McSweeney's* is calm and symmetrical, its text set in the subdued Renaissance typeface Garamond 3. Titles and headlines are centered. Margins and columns are often fortified with crisp rules. Eggers rebels against the visual rebelliousness we have come to expect—routinely—from young designers. Even the *McSweeney's* Website (mcsweeneys.net), designed by Elizabeth Kairys, features centered lines of type on a white screen; for emphasis the site employs brown, one of the most infrequently used colors on the Internet.

*McSweeney's* has no fixed format. Some issues are collections of separate pamphlets. One issue has four different covers; another has a completely blank front with all the cover information hidden on the back. Issue 6 is a single hardcover volume whose orientation can shift from vertical to horizontal in response to the flow of content.

McSweeney's also publishes books, including Stephen Dixon's *I.*, whose die-cut cover exposes a portrait printed inside. *English as She Is Spoke* is a soberly presented edition of an absurdly erroneous Portuguese-to-English phrase book from 1855. *The New Sins*, produced with David Byrne, resembles a pocket-sized Bible charting contemporary desires.

Each McSweeney's publication conveys a serene yet unsettled bookishness. Dave Eggers, a former Macintosh temp and "reformed hack designer," seems to enjoy writing subscription notices and copyright pages as much as editorials. He appears to observe himself fondly as he wears the publisher's cloak of seriousness and authority. **EL**

**1**
**MCSWEENEY'S NO. 6**
Magazine, interior spread, 2001
Offset lithography
Designer and editor: Dave Eggers
Design associate: Peter Kaplan
Publisher: McSweeney's

**2, 3**
**STEPHEN DIXON: I**
Book, binding and fly-leaf, 2002
Die-cut case binding with letterpress text; offset lithography
Designers: Dave Eggers, Elizabeth Kairys
Cover art: Daniel Clowes
Publisher: McSweeney's Books

**4, 5**
**DAVID BYRNE: THE NEW SINS**
Book, interior spreads, 2002
Offset lithography
Designers: Dave Eggers and David Byrne
Author and photographer: David Byrne
Publisher: McSweeney's Books

**6**
**JOSÉ DA FONSECA AND PEDRO CAROLINO:**
**ENGLISH AS SHE IS SPOKE**
Book binding, 2002
Case binding with letterpress text
Cover designer: Elizabeth Kairys
Interior book design: Dave Eggers and Jennifer Broughton
Publisher: McSweeney's Books

Photography: Matt Flynn

2, 3

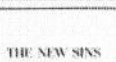
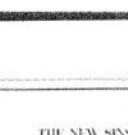

THE NEW SINS

SWEETNESS

The voice of Sweetness is the snake that offered the apple. The soft murmurs, the whispered nothings, the gentle words—they still the heart and cover poison with sugar. Sweetness dwells in the heart.

The Heart is like the Sea, wherein dwells the Leviathan, and creeping things innumerable. The Heart is like the Egyptian temples—full of spiders, serpents and snakes. It is a treasure house of sin. A gilded palace in a lake of fire.

46 47

4, 5

THE NEW SINS

SENSE OF HUMOR

Humor is the snap, the breaking point, the straw that breaks the camel's back and allows us to turn misery into something else. What is that something else? A cackling, ape-like non-verbal noise. A chuckle, a cackle. A wheezing, sputtering, unmusical disruption. Humor is painful to experience. The expressions of this pain are noises emanating from the sufferer who has reached the saturation point and can only hoot, howl and heave like a being possessed. Laughter, indeed, is a kind of possession—a leaving of one's senses characterized by a series of inarticulate, stuttering moans. One is possessed by something inhuman, cruel and contagious.

Humor allows us to turn others into objects—objects of derision, irony and amusement. To direct our suffering and pain outward, to the nearest helpless person, animal or thing.

Laughter is the sound of animals in distress, helpless and pathetic. Broken at the waist, holding on for dear life.

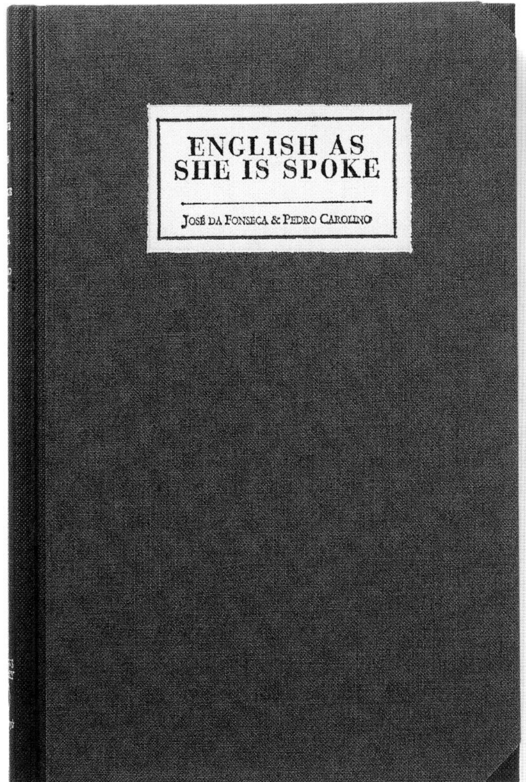


6

## PETER EISENMAN b. 1932

EISENMAN ARCHITECTS

*New York City*

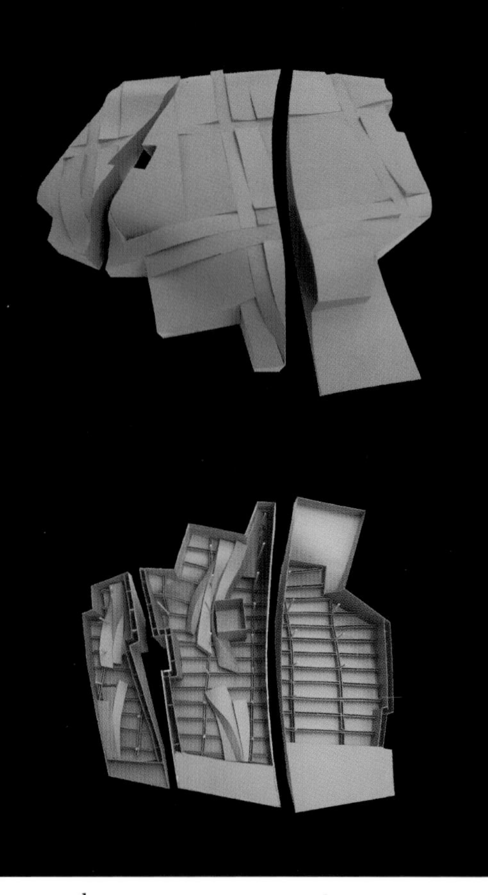

1

Peter Eisenman has devoted his career to making architecture that interrupts our distracted lives. He breaks the horizontal and vertical conventions of Cartesian space to create an architecture that, seemingly frozen at warp speed, rivets our attention the way film does. In his own cinema verité, columns interrupt vistas like unexpected jump cuts; the eye pans across streams of people simultaneously traversing different floors.

If the contemporary frame of reference for Eisenman's work can be found in filmmakers like David Lynch, Michelangelo Antonioni, and Jean-Luc Godard, its historical DNA can be traced to the Italian baroque. Eisenman has internalized the pull and push of forms rhythmically woven by Borromini, and found in Piranesi a powerful antecedent for his own labyrinthine spaces. Synthesizing these ideas with his own, Eisenman generates original forms, using the computer to fuse multiple spatial grids that he teases apart to make space.

In his project for the pilgrimage city of Santiago de Compostela in the northwest Spanish province of Galicia, Eisenman generates an intricate matrix merging three distinct grids: the historical paths of the religious supplicants, the mountainous contours of the site, and the Cartesian grid of traditional architecture. The lines of the historical paths are literally heaved into space by the topographical grid, and the Cartesian grid forms pathways that cut through resulting forms. Conceived to invigorate the region and to serve millions of pilgrims annually, the project covers 750,000 square feet and comprises six buildings sheathed in warmly veined stone, including an opera house, a museum, a center for new technology, and several libraries. Eisenman's aim is to have each building play off the next, not unlike the call and response of a jazz performance, with characteristic stress on movement and improvisation. **SY**

**1**
**CITY OF CULTURE**
Galicia, Spain
Model of roof of opera house and interior ceiling of libraries, 2001
Designer: Peter Eisenman
Client: City of Culture of Galicia Foundation, Santiago de Compostela, Spain
Photography: Eisenman Architects

**2**
**CITY OF CULTURE**
Site map of project and surrounding area, 1999
Designer: Peter Eisenman
Client: City of Culture of Galicia Foundation, Santiago de Compostela, Spain
Rendering: Eisenman Architects

**3, 4**
**CITY OF CULTURE**
**INTERIOR PERSPECTIVES OF BIBLIOTECA**
Digital renderings, 2001
Designer: Peter Eisenman
Client: City of Culture of Galicia Foundation, Santiago de Compostela, Spain
Renderings: Eisenman Architects

2

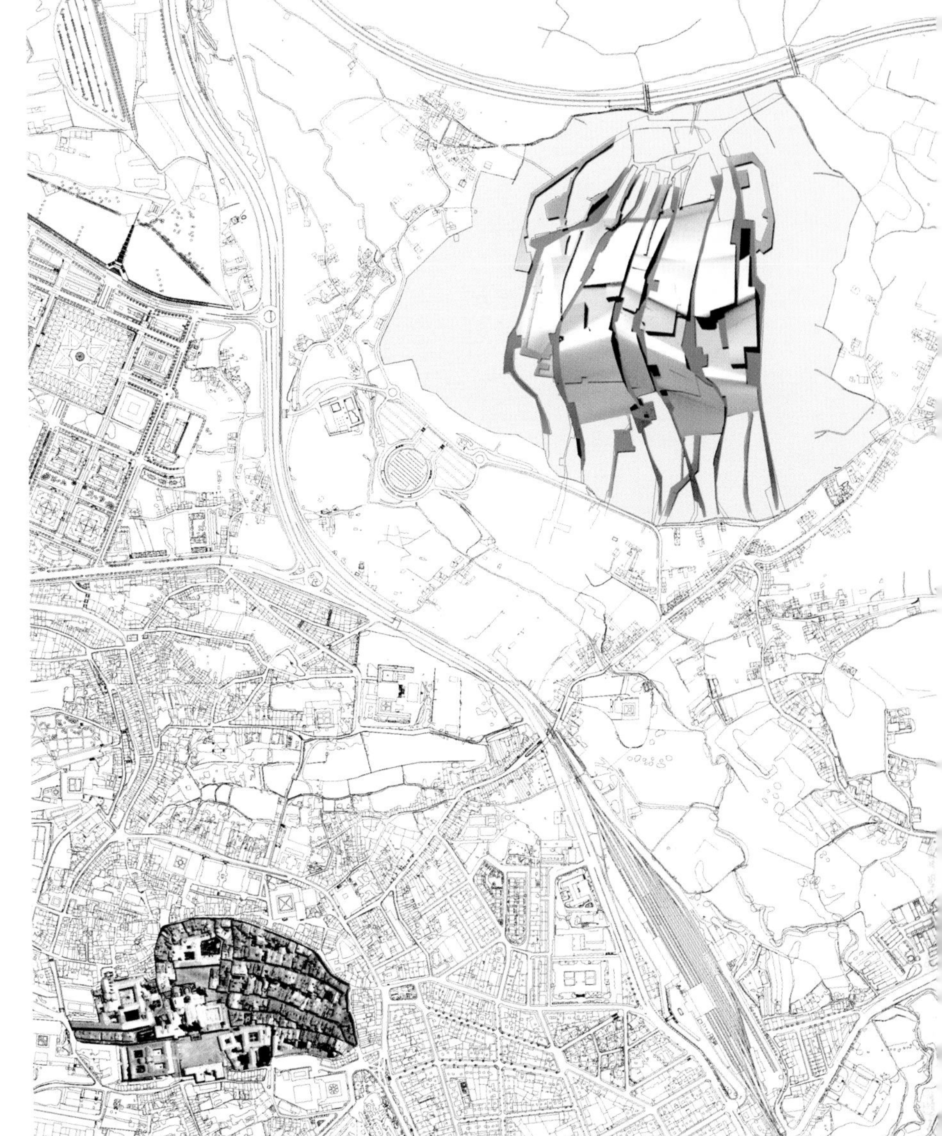

3

4

## PAUL ELLIMAN b. 1961

*New Haven*

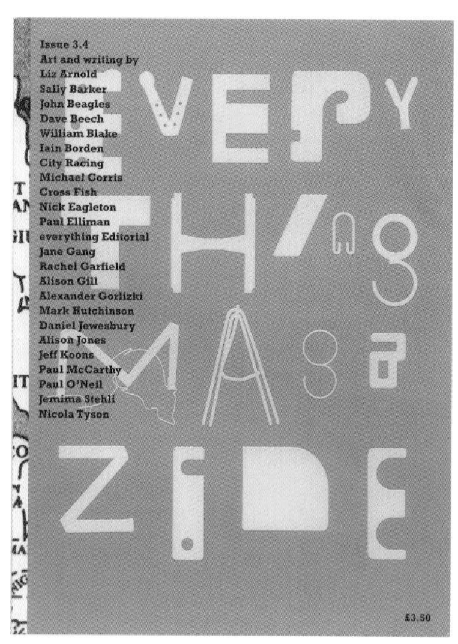


1–3

Typography, which permits the endless repetition of identical characters, is one of the oldest forms of mass production. Through his design as well as his critical writing, Paul Elliman explores the role of typography in a postindustrial, supernetworked world.

His typeface Bits is made from hundreds of pieces of consumer waste—bottle tops, coffee cup lids, computer components, scraps of wire, car-engine parts. Each object's silhouette approximates a specific typographic form. Each is the product of mass manufacture. But each becomes a unique artifact, an archaeological find made precious through the act of preservation.

Whereas letters in a traditional typeface are connected to each other by shared size, weight, proportions, and other features, the characters in Bits are wildly mismatched. Bits is a collection of singular marks that are nonetheless destined to repeat themselves through the typographic system. The cover for *Lost and Found,* an exhibition catalog designed by Anne Odling-Smee and Stephen Coates, plants typographic Bits in a field of grass, where they sit like rusting farm equipment. Covers for *Anything* journal and *Everything* magazine, designed by others in collaboration with Elliman, use letters as *things,* objects of unspecified origin or use.

A poster and identity system for a design conference uses test patterns developed for calibrating digital imaging devices. These tiny marks normally occupy the edge of communication—and are ultimately cut off and discarded. They become the central imagery in Elliman's piece.

Born and educated in Britain, Paul Elliman teaches in the design program at the Yale University School of Art. His work examines the physical intrusion of technology throughout daily life, uncovering the chance beauty and bottomless reach of industrial and digital processes. **EL**

1
**LOST AND FOUND**
Catalog cover, 1999
Offset lithography
Designers: Stephen Coates, Anne Odling-Smee
Publisher: Birkhauser and The British Council

2
**ANYTHING**
Journal, 2001
Offset lithography
Designers: 2x4 with Paul Elliman
Publisher: MIT Press

3
**EVERYTHING**
Magazine, 2001
Offset lithography
Designers: Stuart Bailey and Ruth Blacksell with Paul Elliman
Publisher: Everything Publications

4
**BITS**
Digital typeface, ongoing
Designer: Paul Elliman

4

FRANK ESCHER b. 1960

RAVI GUNEWARDENA b. 1960

## ESCHER + GUNEWARDENA ARCHITECTURE

*Los Angeles*

1, 2

Architects Frank Escher and Ravi GuneWardena, partners since 1995, use direct, inexpensive means to catapult Los Angeles's great modernist tradition into the twenty-first century. They draw inspiration from such twentieth-century masters as Richard Neutra and Pierre Koenig, looking for the poetry of rationalism and making the most of the least.

Combining a straightforward construction system, a no-nonsense plan, and off-the-shelf materials, their Jamie Residence levitates above the hills of Pasadena as both luminous beacon and panoramic observatory. Simple geometries form the basis of their work: the interlocking arrangement of spaces in the Zugsmith House in suburban Los Angeles spring from a single line, while the Sola House is a stack of rectangular tubes, each offering a different perspective of the landscape.

Escher and GuneWardena's three Electric Sun tanning salons push the limits of the firm's pragmatic approach. Not unlike the Berlin installations of Ludwig Mies van der Rohe and Lilly Reich around 1930, where exhibitions *about* silk, velvet, and wood were exhibitions *of* silk, velvet, and wood, the salons' primary architectural medium is the tanning light itself. Rose-colored lights mounted in the walls of the tanning rooms interact with the on-and-off rhythm of the beds' ultraviolet lights to bathe the salon in luminous washes of violet and turquoise. Massive furniture units anchor the ever-evolving space. While the first two salons are purely meditative, the third addresses the visual cacophony of its raucous commercial neighborhood. Radiant translucent-acrylic panels, adorned with giant, colorful images of leaves and flowers by artist Jonathan Williams, are part of the tanning rooms' enclosures, creating privacy and a visual metaphor of the magical "electric sun" within. Rarely has rationalism yielded more poetry. **DA**

1
**SOLA HOUSE**
Los Angeles, California, 2002
Digital rendering of exterior
Designers: Frank Escher and Ravi GuneWardena
Client: Joe and Anne Sola
Rendering: Tom Friedrich

2
**JAMIE RESIDENCE**
Pasadena, California, 2000
Designers: Frank Escher and Ravi GuneWardena
Client: Bryce and Rochelle Jamie
Photography: Gene Ogami

3
**ZUGSMITH HOUSE**
Sherman Oaks, California, 2002
Designers: Frank Escher and Ravi GuneWardena
Client: Mike and Rachel Zugsmith
Digital rendering: Tom Friedrich, Brian Hart, Nils Havermann

4–6
**ELECTRIC SUN I (4, 5) AND ELECTRIC SUN III (6)**
Los Angeles, California, 1997–2001
Designers: Frank Escher and Ravi GuneWardena
Client: Brian Heberling
Photography: Gene Ogami (4, 5) and John Ellis (6)

3

4

5, 6

LAURENS VAN DEN ACKER b. 1965

## FORD MOTOR COMPANY

*Los Angeles*

1, 2

Henry Ford supposedly once quipped that his customers could have any color they wanted, "so long as it's black," bucking an inexorable trend toward greater individualization. Ironically, today Ford Motor Company has proposed the industry's most radical experiment in car customization, the GloCar concept. Launched in the spring of 2002, GloCar was created by a team led by Laurens van den Acker, chief of the company's Advanced Design group. It features a lightweight aluminum frame clad in injection-molded translucent plastic panels that change color, intensity, and frequency by light-emitting diodes (LEDs).

The GloCar anticipates future consumer needs and desires by promising unique design solutions to age-old issues, from safety to sustainability. Its design allows users to easily customize their vehicles. Drivers can express their individuality and mood by varying the color and intensity of LEDs whose mix of red, green, and blue light offers a palette of almost 17 million colors. The panels also increase safety by making the car more visible at night, and when another car comes too close, sensors automat-ically intensify the panels' illumination, warning nearby drivers to move away.

GloCar is unusually eco-friendly. Its soy-based plastic panels eliminate the need for painting. The design also features "smart parts," which perform multiple functions: the rear panel acts as a car-sized brake light, and the side panels double as blinkers, thus reducing the number of parts used.

The GloCar turns Henry Ford's mandate upside down, offering virtually unlimited customization with only one hitch: "You can have any color," a company spokesperson notes, "except for black." **DA**

**1, 2**
**GLOCAR**
**EXTERIOR VIEWS**
Model of concept car, 2002
Designer: Laurens van den Acker
Model: Ford Motor Company

**3**
**GLOCAR**
Digital simulation of GloCar in traffic, 2002
Designer: Laurens van den Acker
Rendering: Laurens van den Acker

**4**
**GLOCAR**
**INTERIOR VIEW**
Model of concept car, 2002
Designer: Laurens van den Acker
Model: Ford Motor Company

3, 4

## BENJAMIN FRY b. 1975

MIT MEDIA LAB

*Cambridge, Massachusetts*

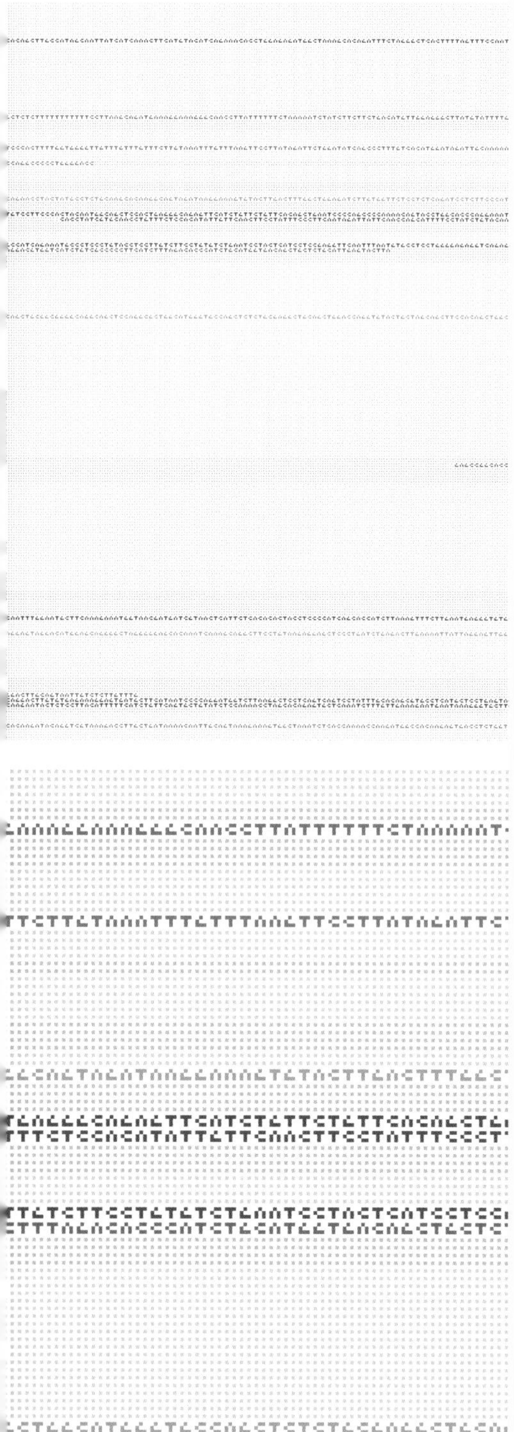

1, 2

Benjamin Fry is creating typographies for the alphabet of life itself: DNA. The design problem Fry confronts is how to make a vast sequence of data intelligible, a challenge that his hybrid education in graphic design and computer science has prepared him for. (Fry is now pursuing his Ph.D. with the MIT Media Lab's Aesthetics and Computation Group.)

One aspect of Fry's chosen task is simply to convey vastness itself in a meaningful way. Only 3 percent of the human genome consists of active information. (The other 97 percent is a byproduct of the evolutionary process.) Geneticists represent the amino acids that make up a genome with sequences of the letters G, A, C, and T. In a series of chromosome maps, Fry has sought to differentiate the unread letters from the live or coded letters. (Chromosomes carry DNA sequences that transmit hereditary traits.) To represent Chromosome 20, Fry replaced the non-coding data with single-pixel dots, while the genetically significant letters appear in a nine-pixel typeface, tiny yet intelligible. The viewer can thus perceive the coded data against the larger field of inactive dots.

Fry took a different approach to representing Chromosome 14 (which is about 107 million letters long and, when Fry mapped it, contained 347 known genes). Here, yellow wireframe boxes depict the uncoded data, whereas blue wireframes indicate a gene.Within a blue gene box, the solid plane represents the coded portion of the gene. The coded data is thus accurately scaled in relation to the uncoded part, but the significance of the live material is vividly emphasized.

Typography articulates the flow of letters into navigable passages. Benjamin Fry's work makes the astonishing seas of data found within the human genome more understandable but no less sublime. **EL**

**1, 2**
**CHROMOSOME 20**
Gene map (details), 2002
Designer: Benjamin Fry,
MIT Media Lab

**3**
**CHROMOSOME 14**
Gene map (detail), 2002
Designer: Benjamin Fry,
MIT Media Lab

3

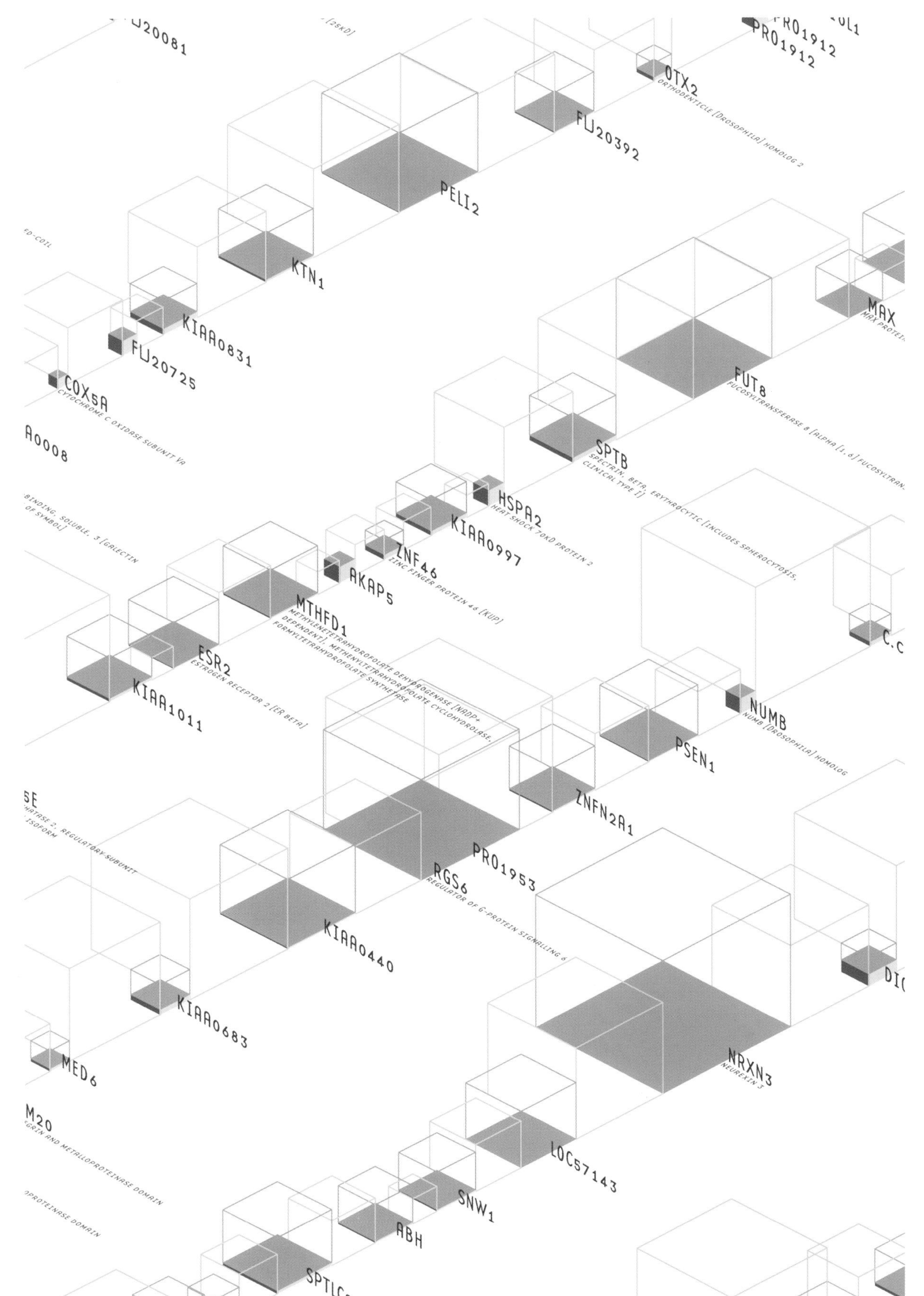

FLJ20081
PRO1912
PRO1912
OTX2
ORTHODENTICLE [DROSOPHILA] HOMOLOG 2
FLJ20392
PELI2
KTN1
KIAA0831
FLJ20725
COX5A
CYTOCHROME C OXIDASE SUBUNIT VA
MAX
FUT8
SPTB
HSPA2
HEAT SHOCK 70KD PROTEIN 2
KIAA0997
ZNF46
ZINC FINGER PROTEIN 46 (KUP)
AKAP5
MTHFD1
ESR2
ESTROGEN RECEPTOR 2 (ER BETA)
KIAA1011
NUMB
PSEN1
ZNFN2A1
PRO1953
RGS6
REGULATOR OF G-PROTEIN SIGNALLING 6
KIAA0440
KIAA0683
MED6
NRXN3
NEUREXIN 3
LOC57143
SNW1
ABH

YVES BEHAR b. 1967

## FUSEPROJECT

*San Francisco*

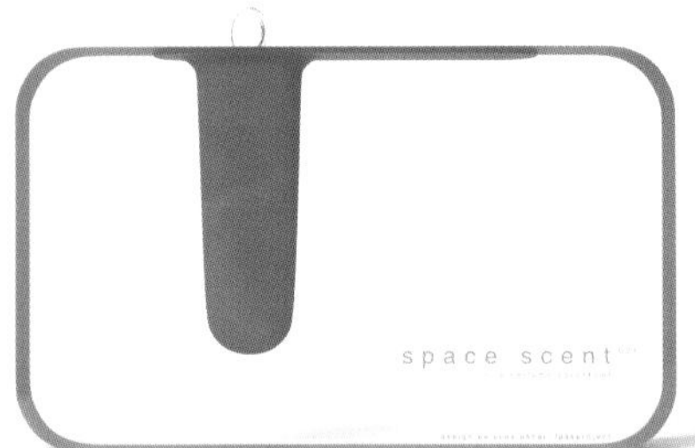


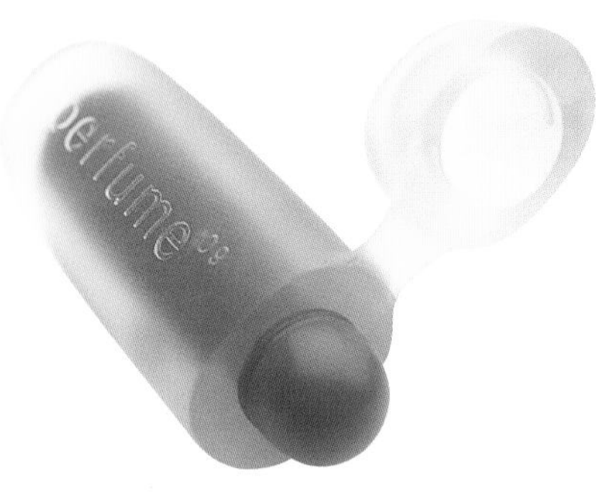


1, 2

As their double-barreled name suggests, fuseproject blends design and brand development. They invent (and sometimes reinvent) products for young consumers using a bold and sensuous aesthetic that appeals to both the eye and the hand. Founded by Yves Béhar just a few years ago, fuseproject has already revolutionized the highly competitive field of body-care products. While their shampoo bottles for Philou reinterpret in candy-colored plastic the biomorphic shapes of such modern designers as Russel Wright and Eva Zeisel, fuseproject discards the traditional bottle altogether in their design for Space Scent in favor of a red capsule suspended in a clear resin block. For the same company, Haasprojekt, fuseproject created packaging for Perfume 09. By encasing the traditional glass perfume vial (again colored red) in rubber, they have protected the new scent from spills and made it travel ready.

Mobility also informs fuseproject's new shoe designs, which enhance comfort for driving and walking. The MINI Motoring Gear shoe is the first specially designed for both functions. Most iconoclastic of all fuseproject's efforts, however, is their redesign of that symbol of hippie culture 255 years in the making—the Birkenstock shoe. While retaining its ergonomic, repairable construction, fuseproject added nineteen new models, sophisticated shapes, and brighter colors (think Jaguar racing green). They made Birkenstock's cork-and-rubber sole more comfortable by introducing a soft inner pad and even created an entirely new line, footprints, complete with a sexy silver box and sleek "fp" logo. What better way to inaugurate the new century than by reinventing an icon of the last? **DA**

**1, 2**
**SPACE SCENT + PERFUME 09**
Perfume bottles, 2000, 2001
Polyurethane resin, elastomeric rubber, ink
Designers: Yves Behar, Johan Liden
Manufacturer: haasprojekt
Photography: Marcus Hansche

**3, 4**
**FOOTPRINTS BY BIRKENSTOCK**
Shoes, 2002
Cork, natural rubber, leather
Design team: Yves Béhar/Fuseproject, Johan Liden, Geoffrey Petrizzi
Client: Birkenstock
Photography: Fuseproject

**5**
**PHILOU**
Product, 2001
Low-density soft-touch polyurethane, ABS
Designer: Yves Béhar
Manufacturer: Philou Inc.
Photography: Marcus Hanschen

**6, 7**
**MINI MOTORING GEAR**
Two-part driving shoe, 2003
Breathable thermal-fit sock
Designer: Yves Béhar (lead), Shawn Sinyork
Client and manufacturer: MINI USA
Photography: Alias Image/Eskil Tomozy

3, 4

5

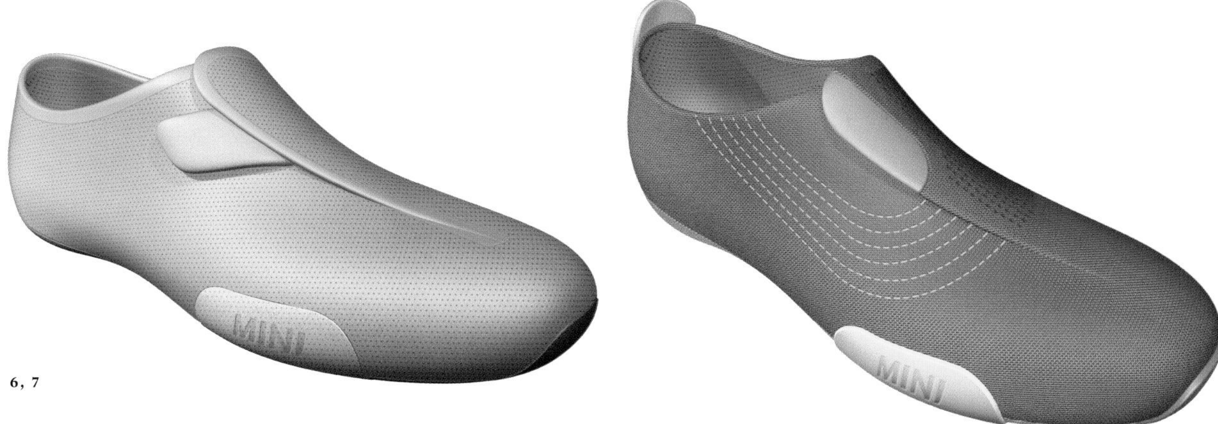


6, 7

AMY FRANCESCHINI b. 1970

FUTUREFARMERS

*San Francisco*

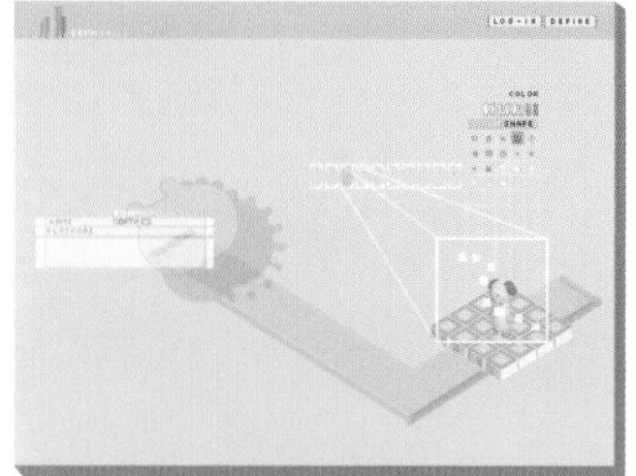

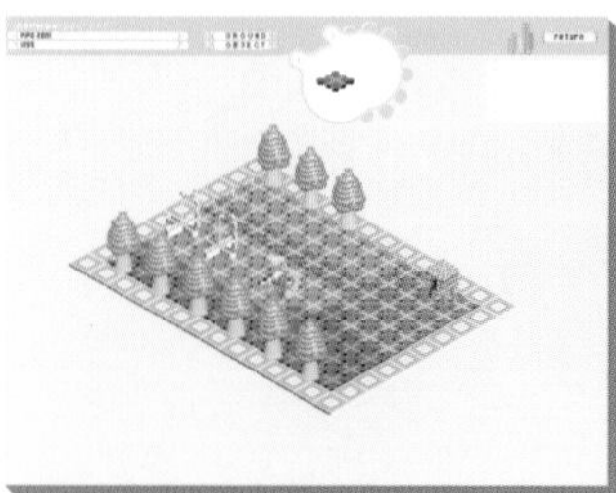

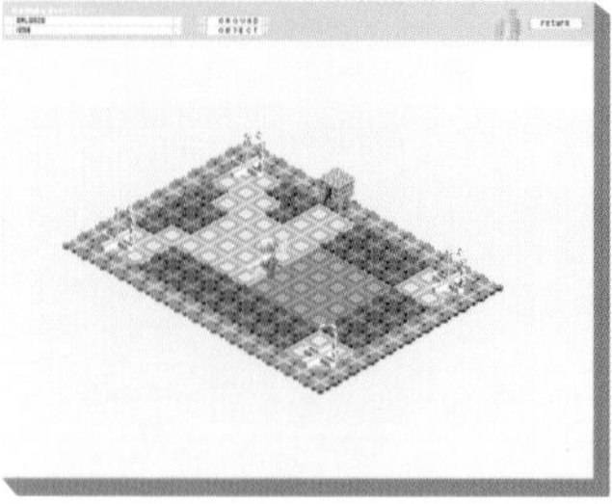

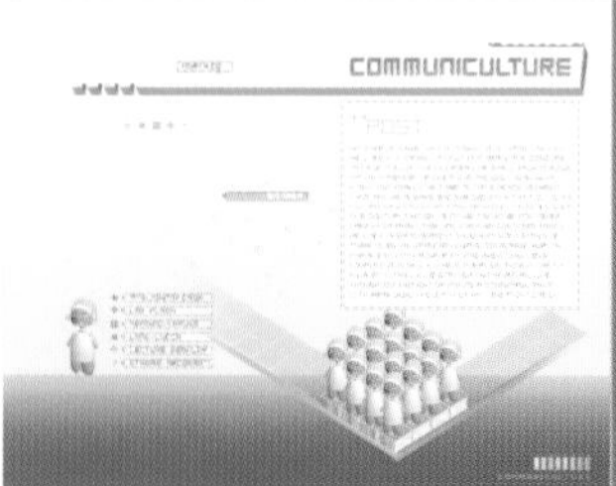


1–4

Amy Franceschini grew up on a farm. A recent graduate of Stanford University's MFA program, she is the founder of Futurefarmers, a multimedia art and design practice. As reflected in the motto "cultivating your consciousness," her agrarian roots are crucial to her digital work.

Franceschini and her collaborators strive to sow the Web with ecosensitive games and communitarian experiences. The visual environments they create are not, however, plain granola. The shimmering three-dimensional characters that bounce and float through Futurefarmers' luminous landscapes have a toylike simplicity that helps them conserve digital resources in the networked worlds they inhabit.

Communiculture is a virtual forest grown by visitors to the site. Each tree in the forest is built from six modules, and each module is claimed by one visitor. The forest grows as the community grows. The site provides each user with an animated avatar, or on-line persona, generated in response to his or her selections from a library of personality traits. A plot of "land" allows users to share resources, such as music or image files.

The computer game Tak Tak 7 stars an elf who must rescue seven gypsies trapped in a series of mazes. Working against him are the Block Kids, little monsters who wear blinding ice blocks over their eyes. Tak Tak defeats them not with weapons but with his mind: he must learn to camouflage the color of his "consciousness"—represented by a dot over his head—to match theirs.

Many of Futurefarmers' projects move off the screen into the physical environment. The Back Pack Theater is a prototype for a portable projection system that would allow hikers to enjoy films in the wilderness. For Amy Franceschini, there is no necessary conflict between natural and virtual worlds; each can be used to better understand the other. **EL**

**1–4**
**COMMUNICULTURE**
Website, 1999
Designers: Amy Franceschini, Keetra Dixon, and Joshua Walton
Programmers: Justin Bakse and Sascha Merg, Futurefarmers

**5**
**TAK TAK 7: BLOCK KID**
Computer game, 1998
Designers: Amy Franceschini and Sascha Merg

**6**
**BACKPACK THEATER**
Digital rendering of prototype, 2002
Designers: Amy Franceschini and Michael Swaine
Commissioned by Cooper-Hewitt, National Design Museum

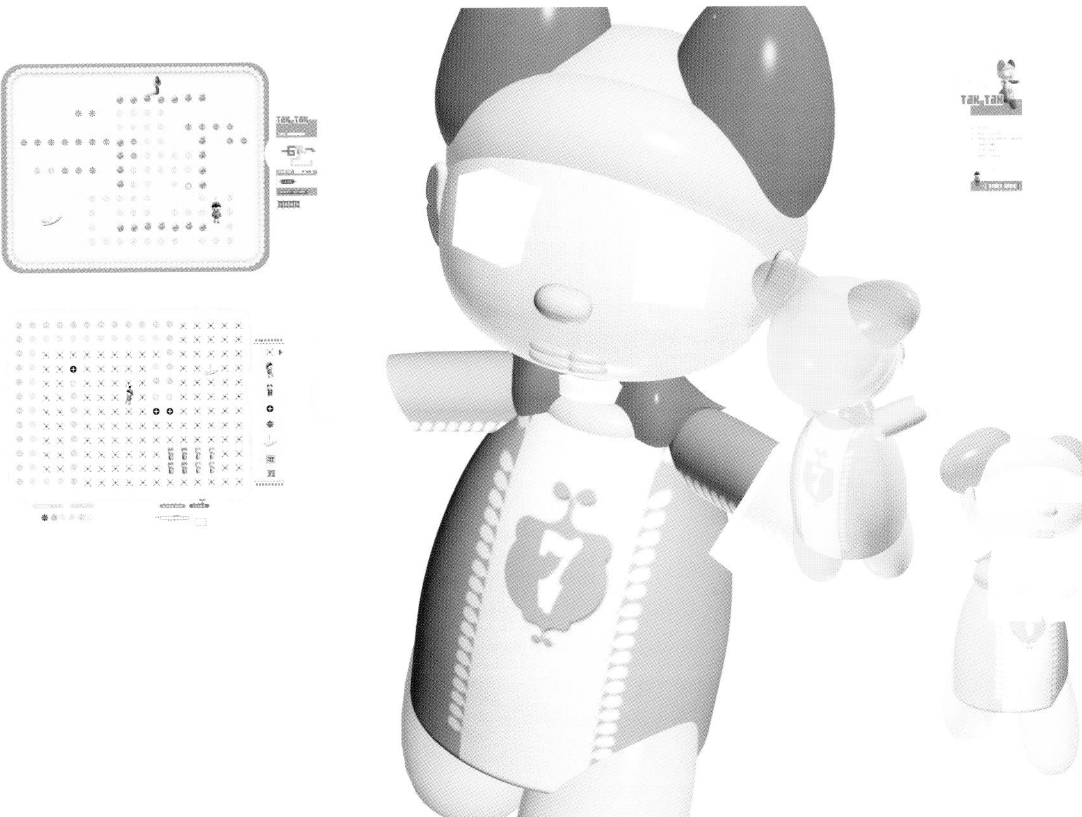

5

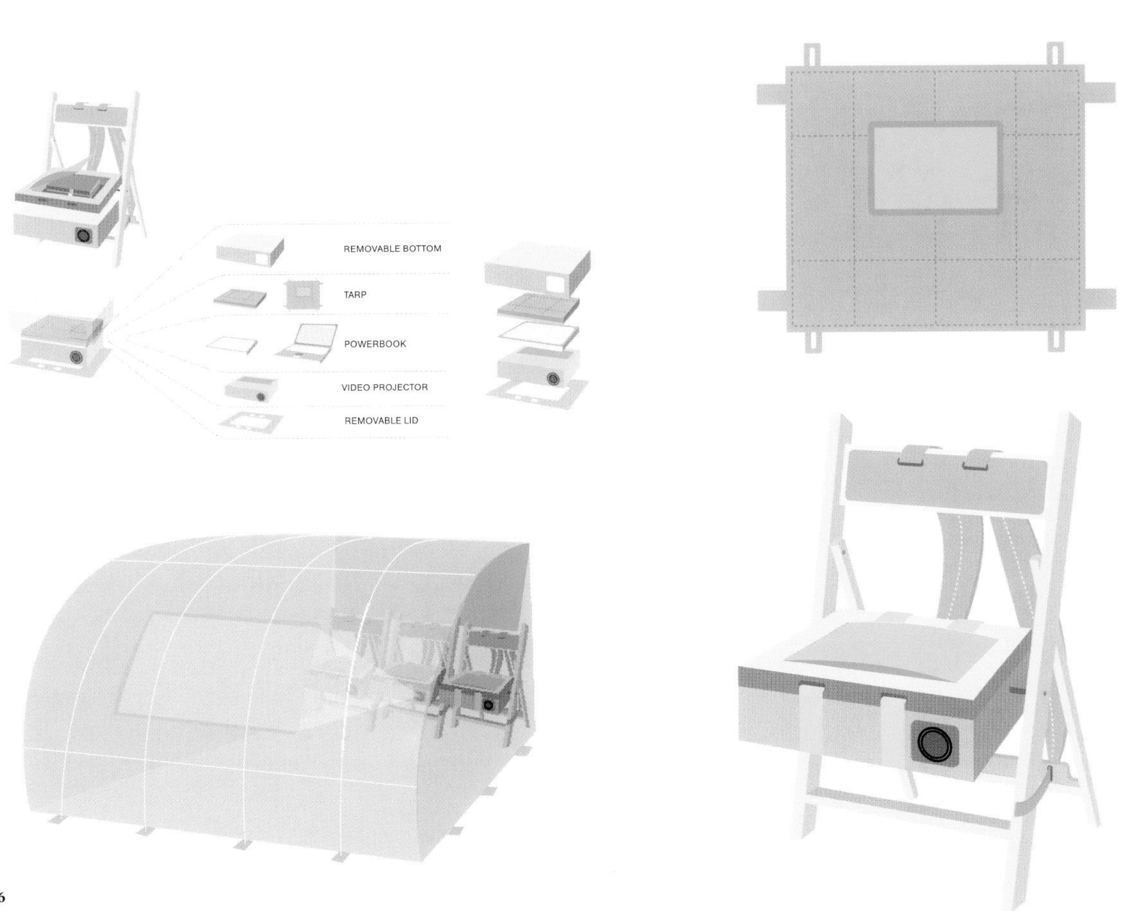
REMOVABLE BOTTOM
TARP
POWERBOOK
VIDEO PROJECTOR
REMOVABLE LID

6

## TESS GIBERSON b. 1971

*New York City*

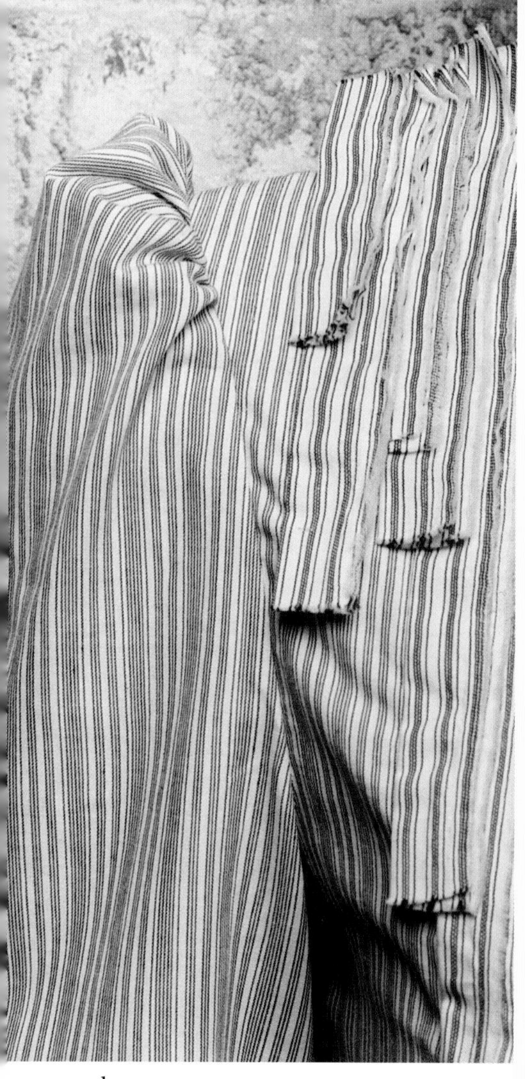

1

There is prim hedonism in Tess Giberson's clothing design. Like the fabled secretary whose good looks hide behind her eyeglasses, a garment by Giberson operates on a system of mixed signals. She understands the power of beauty and unleashes it guardedly, in increments. And while there is a bit of "come hither" to her work—diminutive Liberty floral prints used as peekaboo linings for slouchy blouses—it is not salacious and it does not tease. Instead, the clothes caution against a vapid prettiness and argue for a way of dressing that gains its potency from a subtle combination of references to both genders.

Men's shirting is overtly feminized with ruching and stitching. Tattered, fringed skirts maintain their shape (and dignity) by virtue of their stolid gray wool. Subdued palettes and classic fabrics provide a conservative foil for Giberson's obsessive stitching, off-kilter appliqués, and frayed edges. Garments are only partly preconceived; they are, in fact, made. For instance, Giberson will stitch fragments of lace to the inside of a blouse—its private side—yielding crude line drawings of flowers on the right side, offering a new take on the Surrealist game of automatic writing.

Giberson is constitutionally unable to produce work that she hasn't sewn herself. Brought up by bona fide back-to-the land idealists in the 1970s, Tess Giberson comes by her commitment to hand work honestly. With her fall 2002 collection, she found herself drawing even more deeply on her family's ethos of making. Involving her sister, husband, friends, and mother in a latter-day sewing bee, Giberson found herself working in the communal, utopian tradition that has always been a strong streak in American culture. She understands clothing as both the most public and private of design acts and that understanding is poignantly mirrored in her process. **SY**

1
**STRIPED SHIRT WITH FRAGMENTED CHEST**
Cotton shirting, shell buttons, 2001
Designer: Tess Giberson
Photography: Greg Sorenson

2
**FLARED SKIRT WITH MULTI-PIECED HEM**
Wool, thread, 2002
Designer: Tess Giberson
Photography: Matt Flynn

3
**BLOUSE WITH FLOWER COLLAGE**
Cotton, cotton lace, shell buttons, 2002
Designer: Tess Giberson
Photography: Matt Flynn

2

3

TODD ST. JOHN b. 1969

GARY BENZEL b. 1970

## GREEN LADY + HUNTERGATHERER

*New York City and San Diego*

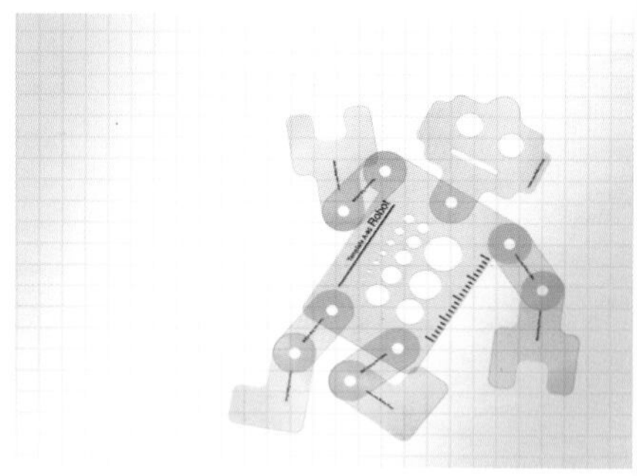

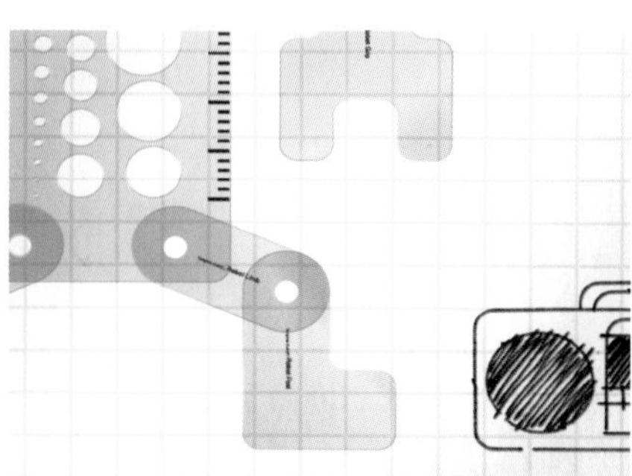

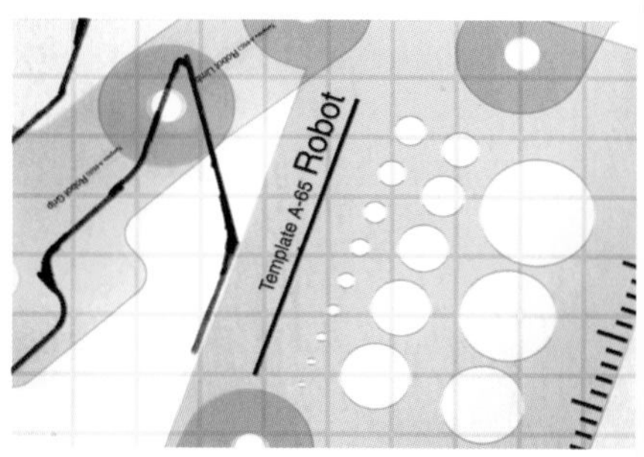

1–4

The t-shirt has replaced the poster as graphic design's ideal medium of public expression. Inexpensive, uncensored, and mobile, t-shirts carry countless graphic messages through the streets of the world.

Designers Todd St. John and Gary Benzel have used the humble and ubiquitous t-shirt as the seed for a much broader practice that now includes furniture, objects, housewares, and films. Their fashion company Green Lady, founded in San Diego in 1995, quickly attracted an international following. HunterGatherer (HuGa) is a separate firm, established in Brooklyn in 2000, that collaborates with outside companies and manufactures its own product line.

Green Lady and HunterGatherer create garments and objects that are powered by graphic messages. Many pieces express a primitivist compulsion within a technology-obsessed culture. On a sweatshirt, simulated masking tape spells the name "GRN LDY." A t-shirt depicts the evolution of the human species with flat silhouettes based on textbook illustrations—but the evolution moves in reverse, from man to ape.

Domestic objects convey a similar spirit. A foldable magazine rack is covered with an enlarged woodgrain pattern, poking fun at the paneled basements and faux finishes of previous generations. The piece also refers to portable camping gear—the factory-made equipment of the modern hunter/gatherer. A star map printed on a throw pillow traces icons of contemporary life, including an old-school Macintosh computer, a strip of DNA, an electric guitar, and a Playboy bunny.

Setting this wacky primitivism to motion, a video by Todd St. John features a break-dancing robot made of plastic stencils. One of St. John's and Benzel's mottos is "Building tomorrow's yesterdays today." That would make a great t-shirt. **EL**

**1–4**
**ROBOT DANCE**
Film stills, 2001
Director/illustrator: Todd St. John, HunterGatherer
Additional design help: Gary Benzel
Animation: Todd St. John, Stuart Weiner
Client: Gasbook 11 (Shift, Japan)

**5, 6**
**GREEN LADY**
Silkscreened sweatshirt, 2000
Designers: Todd St. John and Gary Benzel, Green Lady

**7**
**WOODGRAIN MAGAZINE RACK**
MDF, silkscreen, 2001
Designer: Todd St. John, HunterGatherer

**8**
**MODERN CONSTELLATIONS**
Silkscreened pillow, 2001
Designers: Todd St. John and Gary Benzel, HunterGatherer

**9**
**DE-EVOLUTION**
Silkscreened shirt, 1998
Designers: Todd St. John and Gary Benzel, Green Lady

5, 6

7

8

9

TOBIAS FRERE-JONES b. 1970

JONATHAN HOEFLER b. 1970

## THE HOEFLER TYPE FOUNDRY

*New York City*

Some typefaces rush to the foreground of communication, while others excel in supporting roles. The Hoefler Type Foundry has produced typefaces that are willing and able to do both. Founded by Jonathan Hoefler in 1989, The Hoefler Type Foundry has created custom fonts for magazines and institutions—from *Sports Illustrated* to the Guggenheim Museum—as well as typefaces for general sale. In 2000, Hoefler was joined by Tobias Frere-Jones, who created Interstate, based on U.S. highway signs, one of the most prominent typefaces of the 1990s.

Recent projects of The Hoefler Type Foundry include Gotham, derived from letters used at the Port Authority Bus Terminal. Gotham aspires to become North America's Gill Sans (a font widely used in Britain, also derived from transit lettering). At the very least, Gotham, with its clunky geometry and working-class curves, could be the next Interstate.

The typeface Retina was created for the financial pages of the *Wall Street Journal*. Legible at tiny sizes, Retina is available in ten weights, each of which—unlike standard font variants—occupies an identical slot of space. Notches in Retina's interior spaces keep the letters sharp, defending against cheap paper and high-speed presses.

You are reading a font called Mercury, a neutral, classical typeface designed to meet the rigors of contemporary publishing. The font's four main variants, No. 1—No. 4, are rendered with progressively more heft, yet characters from each series occupy the same slice of space, enabling designers to substitute fonts without altering line lengths.

The Web address for The Hoefler Type Foundry is, quite simply, typography.com. This wonderfully universal tag is well-deserved for a design team whose reliable, carefully wrought letterforms both satisfy and transcend need. **EL**

1

1
**ASSORTED TYPEFACES**
Designer: The Hoefler Type Foundry

2
**GOTHAM**
Digital typeface, 2000
Designer: Tobias Frere-Jones

3
**RETINA**
Digital typeface, 2000
Designer: Tobias Frere-Jones

4
**MERCURY**
Digital typeface, 1997–2000
Designer: Jonathan Hoefler

DETERMINE
GOTHAM LIGHT

*SIGNATURE*
GOTHAM LIGHT ITALIC

REVERSION
GOTHAM BOOK

*CONDITION*
GOTHAM BOOK ITALIC

GOTHAM

**BILLBOARD**
GOTHAM MEDIUM

***DEFENSIVE***
GOTHAM MEDIUM ITALIC

**DESERTION**
GOTHAM BOLD

***CHAMBERS***
GOTHAM BOLD ITALIC

**DORIC**
GOTHAM BOLD CONDENSED

**ORDER**
GOTHAM MEDIUM CONDENSED

COURSE
GOTHAM BOOK CONDENSED

MODERN
GOTHAM LIGHT CONDENSED

| YTD %CHG | 52 WEEKS HI | LO | STOCK (SYM) | DIV | YLD % | PE | VOL 100S | LAST | NET CHG |
|---|---|---|---|---|---|---|---|---|---|
| +19.6 | 83.4 | 46 | **AKZ** AkzidenzGrot | | ... | dd | 10033 | 20.8 | +0.94 |
| - 5.3 | 83.8 | 55.6 | **AltG** AltrntGothic | | ... | dd | 10996 | 74.9 | -1.78 |
| -18.5 | 16.9 | 5.6 | **ANTQ** AntiqOlive | | ... | dd | 9690 | 42.8 | -1.20 |
| +26.4 | 82.7 | 25.5 | **AvtG** AvantGarde | | ... | 7 | 6213 | 78.1 | +1.64 |
| +28.5 | 99 | 28.8 | **BANK** BankGothic | | ... | dd | 8911 | 28.4 | +1.54 |
| + 5.1 | 63.2 | 21.7 | **BASE** BaseNine | | ... | dd | 1862 | 47.5 | +0.39 |
| - 3.1 | 83.6 | 37.5 | **BASK** Baskerville | | ... | dd | 938 | 14.5 | -0.45 |
| -10.1 | 94.1 | 54.9 | **BDNI** BauerBodoni | | ... | cc | 2206 | 47.3 | -1.46 |
| -13.1 | 106.3 | 90.1 | **BELL** BellGothic | | ... | dd | 10453 | 36.6 | -0.19 |
| -17.8 | 65.2 | 7.4 | **BKMN** Bookman | | ... | ... | 5626 | 9.1 | -1.05 |
| -12.2 | 93.4 | 32.1 | **BMBO** Bembo | | ... | dd | 5156 | 40.9 | -1.14 |
| -10.0 | 31.2 | 11.7 | **BRSH** BrushScript | | ... | 6 | 9881 | 62.2 | -1.07 |
| -15.1 | 52.3 | 6 | **CASL** Caslon540 | | ... | dd | 9029 | 64.9 | -1.82 |
| -13.2 | 105.9 | 14.7 | **CNTR** Centaur | | ... | dd | 9587 | 91.2 | -0.41 |
| **+26.4** | **95.1** | **19.5** | **CHMP** ChmpnGthc | **.64** | **1.8** | **dd** | **1509** | **40.2** | **+1.17** |
| + 2.5 | 109.2 | 5 | **CLRN** Clarendon | | ... | dd | 2587 | 77.1 | +1.81 |
| + 8.3 | 98.2 | 26.1 | **COOP** CooperBlack | | ... | dd | 5612 | 54.3 | +0.56 |
| + 8.6 | 46.6 | 11.2 | **COUR** Courier | | ... | dd | 8931 | 41.8 | +1.20 |
| **+ 6.1** | **89.4** | **23.3** | **DIDO** DidotHTF | **.80** | **1.6** | **cc** | **6467** | **4.2** | **+1.03** |
| -29.1 | 89.6 | 83.7 | **DIN** DINGrotesk | | ... | dd | 1558 | 6.0 | -0.48 |
| - 4.0 | 99.8 | 32.3 | **DOM** DomCasual | | ... | 26 | 7451 | 57.0 | -1.88 |
| +18.0 | 73.8 | 16.1 | **EGIZ** Egiziano | | ... | dd | 2789 | 61.6 | +1.53 |
| - 9.7 | 32.7 | 18.5 | **EURO** Eurostile | | ... | 9 | 1449 | 99.5 | -1.15 |
| + 9.4 | 69.6 | 59.4 | **FKTR** FetteFraktur | | ... | dd | 3944 | 87.0 | +1.01 |
| + 7.5 | 66.8 | 2.8 | **FRNK** FrnklinGthc | | ... | dd | 11712 | 48.8 | +0.55 |
| - 4.3 | 17 | 7 | **FRUT** Frutiger55 | | ... | ... | 1814 | 34.5 | -1.31 |
| +14.8 | 35.8 | 15 | **FUTU** FuturaBook | | ... | 18 | 11325 | 20.5 | +0.42 |
| -19.1 | 52.3 | 10.1 | **GDY** GoudyOldStyl | | ... | dd | 2685 | 46.5 | -1.77 |
| + 4.6 | 95.3 | 26.8 | **GILL** GillSans | | ... | dd | 10748 | 72.3 | +0.39 |
| -18.7 | 96.2 | 35.4 | **GLRD** Galliard | | ... | 26 | 1566 | 1.1 | -0.46 |
| -16.4 | 72.7 | 9.6 | **GMND** Garamond | | ... | 27 | 2376 | 62.3 | -0.71 |
| -18.3 | 102.3 | 20.7 | **GROT** Grotesque9 | | ... | 47 | 6147 | 8.0 | -1.66 |
| + 4.0 | 87.8 | 19.1 | **HLV** Helvetica | | ... | dd | 3009 | 63.3 | +0.35 |
| +28.0 | 79.3 | 35.6 | **HOBO** Hobo | | ... | dd | 5981 | 25.2 | +0.79 |
| **+19.4** | **97.3** | **56.9** | **HTXT** HoeflerText | **.5e** | **1.3** | **dd** | **4548** | **93.7** | **+0.99** |
| **+29.3** | **85.1** | **11.4** | **INTR** Interstate | **.32** | **2.1** | **dd** | **10127** | **19.3** | **+1.86** |
| +10.2 | 72.7 | 59.1 | **JNSN** Janson | | ... | 17 | 8065 | 63.2 | +1.11 |
| - 5.3 | 84.8 | 68.7 | **KIS** KisJanson | | ... | dd | 4641 | 80.9 | -0.29 |
| + 8.5 | 65 | 7.9 | **KSMK** FFKosmik | | ... | 20 | 510 | 26.3 | +0.92 |
| +22.8 | 35.9 | 8.9 | **LTHS** LithosBlack | | ... | dd | 1669 | 39.8 | +0.19 |
| +16.5 | 104.7 | 1.5 | **LtrG** LetterGothic | | ... | dd | 8091 | 20.6 | +0.06 |
| +10.7 | 96.9 | 30.8 | **MEMP** Memphis | | ... | ... | 11742 | 64.0 | +1.16 |
| -21.5 | 78.4 | 61.6 | **META** FFMeta | | ... | 9 | 5229 | 69.6 | -0.41 |
| -23.3 | 54.1 | 31.1 | **MTRO** Metroblack | | ... | 10 | 4162 | 97.5 | -1.44 |
| + 3.1 | 85.9 | 27.7 | **MrsE** MrsEaves | | ... | dd | 8850 | 21.3 | +0.72 |
| -19.7 | 93.7 | 71.3 | **NEWS** NewsGothc | | ... | ... | 6615 | 72.5 | -1.68 |
| + 8.9 | 27 | 1 | **OCR** OCR-A | | ... | dd | 10166 | 93.4 | +1.87 |
| -22.7 | 110 | 72 | **OPTM** Optima | | ... | dd | 4906 | 63.6 | -0.18 |
| + 8.8 | 54.1 | 16.4 | **PALA** Palatino | | ... | 34 | 10695 | 10.4 | +0.93 |
| +29.2 | 91.2 | 23.5 | **PKAV** ParkAvenue | | ... | ... | 4006 | 95.6 | +0.67 |
| **+22.7** | **62.2** | **48.7** | **REQ** RequiemHTF | **.02** | **.44** | **dd** | **3691** | **74.8** | **+0.78** |
| - 9.2 | 61.1 | 37.2 | **RTIS** Rotis | | ... | dd | 9562 | 0.0 | -1.33 |
| -21.1 | 97.7 | 56 | **SCLA** FFScala | | ... | cc | 2176 | 35.5 | -1.23 |
| -26.7 | 60.6 | 51.3 | **SNEL** SnellRndhnd | | ... | dd | 502 | 60.1 | -1.45 |
| + 6.1 | 99.2 | 1 | **THES** FFThesis | | ... | 6 | 8966 | 23.9 | +1.70 |
| + 1.5 | 60.5 | 43.6 | **TMS** TimesRoman | | ... | dd | 9682 | 1.2 | +1.98 |
| - 0.8 | 107.5 | 74.2 | **TJN** Trajan | | ... | ... | 674 | 6.6 | -0.65 |
| - 6.1 | 70.3 | 7.1 | **TRXE** FFTrixie | | ... | dd | 2343 | 77.8 | -0.96 |
| + 9.3 | 93.7 | 31.5 | **UNIV** Univers55 | | ... | 10 | 7603 | 3.8 | +1.29 |
| -17.4 | 85.3 | 2.4 | **WLBM** Walbaum | | ... | dd | 746 | 52.4 | -1.24 |
| **+ 8.6** | **45.9** | **45.8** | **WTNY** Whitney | **.44** | **.1** | **dd** | **3856** | **4.3** | **+1.10** |
| -20.0 | 94.9 | 45.5 | **ZAPF** ZapfChancry | | ... | ... | 1757 | 72.6 | -1.32 |

RETINA AGATE

**Newspaper type** faces a unique set of challenges, and requires the *most specialized* design. This type family is Mercury News 1.
MERCURY NEWS 1

**Newspaper type** faces a unique set of challenges, and requires the *most specialized* design. This type family is Mercury News 2.
MERCURY NEWS 2

**Newspaper type** faces a unique set of challenges, and requires the *most specialized* design. This type family is Mercury News 3.
MERCURY NEWS 3

**Newspaper type** faces a unique set of challenges, and requires the *most specialized* design. This type family is Mercury News 4.
MERCURY NEWS 4

MERCURY

Aa
MERCURY DISPLAY ROMAN

Aa
MERCURY DISPLAY SEMI

**Aa**
MERCURY DISPLAY BOLD

**Aa**
MERCURY DISPLAY BLACK

2–4

## DAVID HOEY b. 1957

BERGDORF GOODMAN

*New York City*

1

Every other week, in closet-sized spaces, store window designers fashion whole universes of drama, fantasy, and desire. David Hoey, window director for Bergdorf Goodman, works with Linda Fargo, Vice President of Visual Merchandising, to respond to this unique challenge. Bold visual concepts delight the speeding pedestrian or driver, while people with more time are treated to the finer points of Hoey's comic sensibility and knowledge of art, design, and popular culture. Hoey's irony is evident in his juxtaposition of Bergdorf's couture fashion and everyday objects, such as a grid of toasted Wonder Bread (a baker's homage to artist Sol LeWitt) and dribbled house paint (an irreverent nod to Jackson Pollock).

Hoey adores extreme design: his windows are either minimally simple or maximally obsessive. He answered the question, "How much can you stuff in there without the window exploding," with his all-white displays for Christmas 2001, which took a year to plan and were executed in paper by in-house artisans. Described by Hoey as "1940s commercial Surrealism combined with neo-Victorian 1960s ice cream parlor chic," this hallucinatory quartet of psychodramas featured handwritten notes with dreamlike quotes, disembodied hands and arms, and a menagerie of exotic animals. Keys dangling from mannequins' mouths alluded to Surrealism's goal of unlocking the unconscious. In place of the typical strategy of making merchandise stand out from the background, Hoey hid mink bathrobes and other outlandish paraphernalia within the thickets of his mythological forest.

Like the great display designers before him, from Salvador Dalí to Andy Warhol, David Hoey plays with the store window's capacity to present goods seductively while keeping them out of touch behind glass in complete worlds unto themselves. **DA**

1
**LETTERS AND SHADOWS**
Window display, 2002
Designer: David Hoey
Additional support: Linda Fargo, Visual Merchandising

2
**CHRISTMAS**
Window display, 2001
Designer: David Hoey
Additional support: Bergdorf Goodman Visual Department and Linda Fargo, Visual Merchandising

3
**WIGS**
Window display, 2001
Designer: David Hoey
Additional support: Linda Fargo, Visual Merchandising

4
**TOAST**
Window display, 2001
Designer: David Hoey
Additional support: Linda Fargo, Visual Merchandising

Photography: Zehavi + Cordes

2

3

4

## JOSEPH HOLTZMAN b. 1957

*New York City*

1–3

In the pages of *nest*, Joseph Holtzman, as publisher, has become a collector of other people's rooms. A quarterly of interiors, *nest* is a lavishly decorated object in and of itself. Its pages are pierced, scalloped, notched, beribboned, and otherwise altered, issue to issue. *Nest* has given a whole new meaning to the term "shelter magazine," taking its readers inside submarines, palaces, ice huts, crematoria, and country houses. *Nest* is nothing if not eclectic.

In the *Triennial*, Joseph Holtzman, as interior decorator, creates his own room in someone else's house. Wholly conceived and strictly proportioned, Holtzman's room is the antithesis of eclectic, though it may be the definition of eccentric. In what was once Andrew and Louise Carnegie's dressing room, he has rescued the parlor—the non-utilitarian room—from anachronism, reinventing it for the twenty-first century through a calculated strategy of decoration.

Holtzman has designed every aspect of the room's decor himself: its furnishings and fabrics, even its floor and ceiling. Striped jacquard wallcoverings hang from a molding of "buttons" that double as a hanging system for contemporary art. Chairs are upholstered in his marijuana-leaf chintz. Below a low railing, spiral vines are reverse-painted on glass. Ceiling beams grow stalactites that hold hanging lanterns. Tinted window blinds admit natural light while suggesting the greenery outside. Every surface, from the vinyl sunflower centers to the soft damask they sprout from, was designed to react with the room's natural and artificial light.

The room's intelligence goes beyond the carefully calibrated relationships of color and form, material and light. It is redolent with historical references, yet it is consummately personal. No one will mistake this "period room" as dating from any but our own. **SY**

**1–3**
**NEST**
Magazine covers, 1999–2002
Photography: Courtesy *nest*

**4**
**INSTALLATION IN COOPER-HEWITT, NATIONAL DESIGN MUSEUM**
Rendering of interior, preliminary study, 2002
Designer: Joseph Holtzman
Rendering: Joseph Holtzman

**5**
**MARIJUANA LEAF CHINTZ FABRIC**
2001
Designers: Joseph Holtzman, Kazumi Yoshida
Photography: Courtesy *nest*

ANDY CRUZ b. 1972

RICH ROAT b. 1965

KEN BARBER b. 1972

ADAM CRUZ b. 1976

CHRIS GARDNER b. 1972

TAL LEMING b. 1975

CHRISTIAN SCHWARTZ b. 1977

## HOUSE INDUSTRIES

*Yorklyn, Delaware*

House Industries was founded in Wilmington, Delaware, in 1993 by Andy Cruz and Rich Roat, who burst on to the burgeoning scene of digital font production with typefaces such as Badhouse, Poorhouse, and Openhouse. The fonts they made were raw and ephemeral; some, such as Crackhouse and House Gothic, became instant icons of pop culture.

Ten years after its inception, House Industries has grown and matured. The company has left the realm of the one-liner to draw on rigorous research and sustained development.

Neutraface is based on letters used by architect Richard Neutra in the 1940s and 1950s. Dropped crossbars and a small body-height give a stylized, decorative quality to these sans-serif letterforms. Working from samples of Neutra's original lettering, House designer Christian Schwartz created digital typefaces for use as text, headlines, and on architectural signs. The loopy, lyrical forms of Delvue, designed by Ken Barber, are both decorative and functional, inspired by local Delaware signage. Tal Leming's type family United captures the tough, amateur quality of military lettering, which is typically applied by hand to vehicles and equipment.

Product development is an increasing preoccupation at House. Promotional wallets, t-shirts, and packages are now joined by typographic textiles and a new line of clothing using the United fonts. House is putting Neutra's one-off Boomerang chair into production, and is planning the manufacture of aluminum architectural letters.

Cruz, the son of an automotive pinstriper, studied graphic arts in the 1980s at a trade school, where hand-lettering was still a valued skill. Other House artists are dexterous painters and illustrators. By merging traditional media with contemporary technologies, they aim to invigorate today's digitally processed culture. **EL**

1–3

**1–3**
**BOOMERANG, DELVUE, AND UNITED**
Drawings, source images for digital typefaces, 2002

**4**
**NEUTRAFACE**
Digital typeface, 2002
Designers: Christian Schwartz
Type directors: Andy Cruz, Ken Barber, Dion Neutra
Publisher: House Industries

**5**
**DELVUE**
Digital typeface, 2002
Designer: Ken Barber
Publisher: House Industries

**6**
**UNITED**
Digital typeface, 2002
Designer: Tal Leming,
Type directors: Andy Cruz, Ken Barber
Publisher: House Industries

Neutra Boomerang Chair

SILVERLAKE

CASE STUDY HOUSE

4

Dolly's salt water taffy

Charcoal Pit

Rehoboth Beach Patrol

5

Camouflage

BELL AH-1 GUNSHIP

COBRA COMMANDER

6

## VIKTOR JONDAL b. 1976

*New York City*

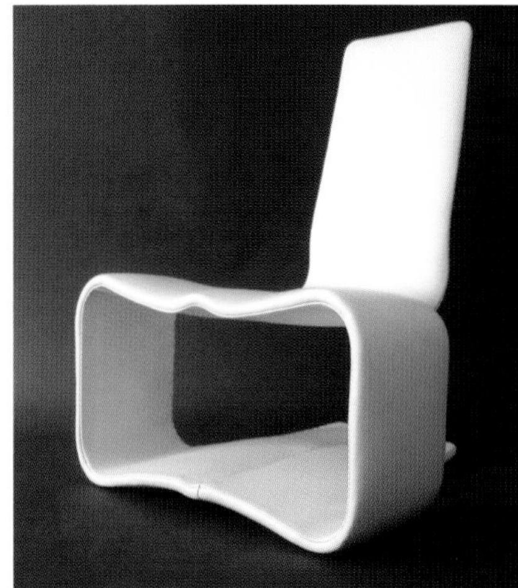

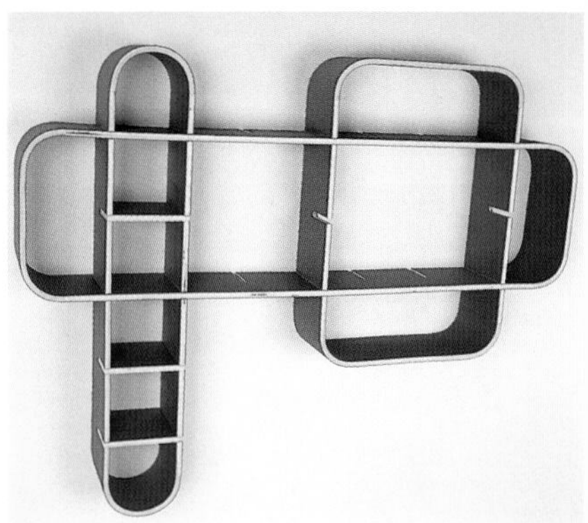

1, 2

Viktor Jondal's design approach puts the cart before the horse. Often the Swedish-born designer identifies what a material can do, and then designs an object that exploits those properties. "I don't usually start with finding a solution to a particular problem," says Jondal. "But sometimes it ends up that way."

Classic molded plywood is one of Jondal's favorite materials. In his Mr. Tall, Big & Slim wall-mounted shelving, interlocking molded-plywood and rubber-laminate components allow users to customize individual configurations that are as graphic as they are practical. Plywood is also the inspiration for the designer's Fly! chair, which softens the material with foam-padded, vinyl-clad curves that seem less molded than casually draped over thin air.

Sometimes Jondal's material musings lead him to pose—and then solve—wholly original problems. After contemplating aluminum, Japanese micro architecture, and the work of modernists like Joe Colombo, Jondal developed HUS, modular rooms that give a whole new meaning to the term "self-storage" (the initials stand for Hotel Unit System and slyly echo the Swedish word for house). Conceived for individuals Jondal calls "involuntary tourists"—i.e., any air traveler forced into an unexpected layover—each HUS is a freestanding 4 x 8 x 8-foot box made of powder-coated stamped aluminum, paper pulp, or polypropylene, and equipped with storage, a stool, waste disposal, outlets, and a cushioned daybed. Basically lockers for humans, HUS capsules can be set up in a terminal or alongside airport hotels for low-cost, high-volume usage. In answer to a thoroughly unpleasant byproduct of today's overburdened travel environment, Jondal has created a sanctuary that combines pragmatism and whimsy in one tidy universal package. **MO**

1
**FLY!**
Chair prototype, 2001
Molded plywood, foam, vinyl
Designer: Viktor Jondal
Photography: Viktor Jondal

2
**MR. TALL, BIG & SLIM**
Prototype for modular shelf system, 2001
Molded plywood, rubber laminate
Designer: Viktor Jondal
Photography: Viktor Jondal

3–9
**HUS (HOTEL UNIT SYSTEM)**
Concept renderings, 2002
Designer: Viktor Jondal

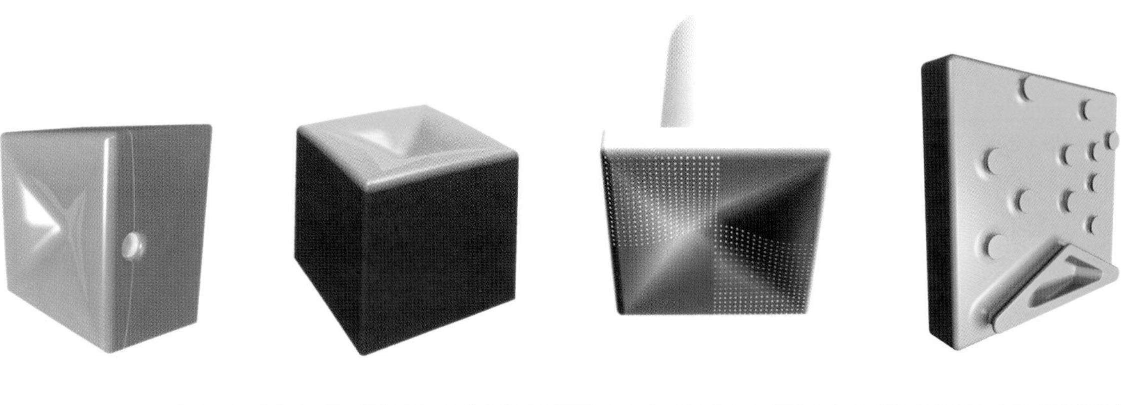

3-9

## MAIRA KALMAN b. 1949

*New York City*

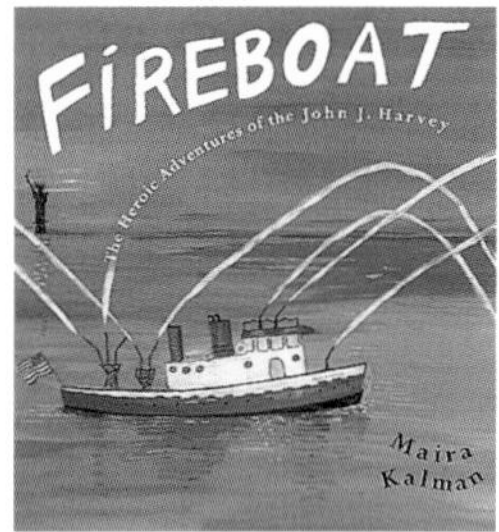


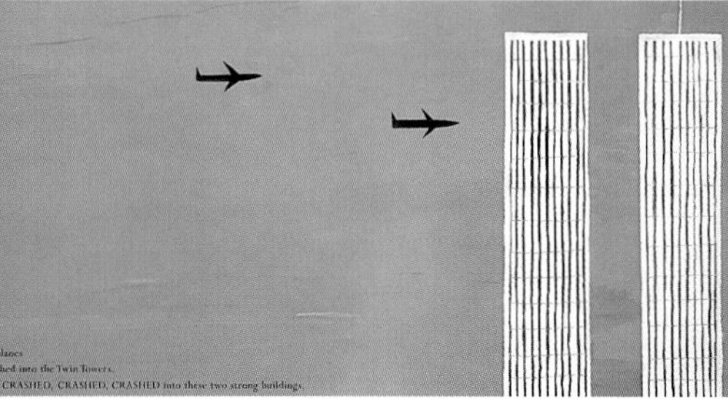

1–4

Quirky. Fearless. Whimsical. Provocative. Naive. Inscrutable. Divine. The giddy, optimistic artistry of Maira Kalman, in which childlike wonder meets manic urban energy, has inspired adjectives as varied as the idiosyncratic works she produces each year.

Born in Tel Aviv, raised in New York, and one of the founders of M&Co—an influential graphic design firm run by her late husband, Tibor Kalman—Maira Kalman is a phenomenon with a frolicsome command of mediums. She has designed fabrics, mannequins, and theatrical sets, collaborating with such eminences as Isaac Mizrahi, Mark Morris, and David Bryne. The sketchy, scratchy, jewelly images of her sassy children's books wed Ludwig Bemelmans to Florine Stettheimer; one of her latest is entitled *What Pete Ate from A–Z: Where We Explore the English Alphabet (In Its Entirety) in Which a Certain Dog Devours a Myriad of Items Which He Should Not*. And to captivate commuters discomfited by the renovation of New York City's Grand Central Terminal, Kalman produced temporary murals aswarm with oddly dressed world citizens, from sour-faced matrons to ecstatic dancers to historical figures.

Recently, amid the despair and paranoia that followed the terrorist attacks of 2001, Kalman injected a welcome note of good cheer with a satirical cover illustration for *The New Yorker*. She and Rick Meyerowitz reimagined New York City as a map of special-interest mini-states, among them Kvetchnya, Botoxia, and Hiphopabad. Just as mirthful but infinitely more soothing is Kalman's children's book about a brave little fireboat plying the city's harbor after 9/11, with efficiency, purpose, and most of all, sympathy. One thing shines through the artist's intellectual hijinks and good-natured mockery, one thing shines through: generosity of spirit. **MO**

1–4
**FIREBOAT: THE HEROIC ADVENTURES OF JOHN J. HARVEY**
Illustrated book, 2002
Offset lithograph
Artist: Maira Kalman
Publisher: Penguin Putnam, New York

5–7
**COUTURE VOYEUR**
Magazine illustrations, 2000
Offset lithograph
Artist: Maira Kalman
Publisher: *The New York Times Magazine*

8
**FOUR SAINTS, THREE ACTS**
Set decoration, 1999
Brooklyn Academy of Music
Designer: Maira Kalman
Choreographer: Mark Morris

9
**MAX MAKES A MILLION**
Illustrated book
Offset lithograph
Artist: Maira Kalman
Publisher: Viking, New York, 1990

10
**WHAT PETE ATE FROM A–Z**
Illustrated book
Offset lithograph
Artist: Maira Kalman
Publisher: Putnam, New York, 2001

11
**NEW YORKISTAN**
Cover illustration, 2001
Designers: Maira Kalman, Rick Meyerowitz
Publisher: *The New Yorker*

Photography: Courtesy Maira Kalman

11.5.00
Style
Couture Voyeur
By Maira Kalman

JEAN-PAUL GAULTIER
Paris

VERSACE
JEAN CHARLES DE CASTELBAJAC
OSCAR de la Renta
FOR BALMAIN

5–7

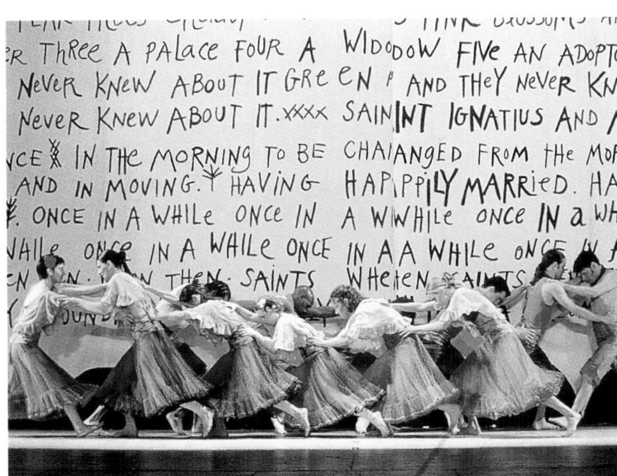
THREE A PALACE FOUR A WIDODOW FIVE AN ADOPT
NEVER KNEW ABOUT IT GREEN AND THEY NEVER KN
NEVER KNEW ABOUT IT. XXXX SAININT IGNATIUS AND
IN THE MORNING TO BE CHAIANGED FROM THE MO
AND IN MOVING. HAVING HAPPPILY MARRIED. HA
ONCE IN A WHILE ONCE IN A WHILE ONCE IN A WH
WHILE ONCE IN A WHILE ONCE IN A A WHILE ONCE
THEN. SAINTS WHEHEN SAINTS

8

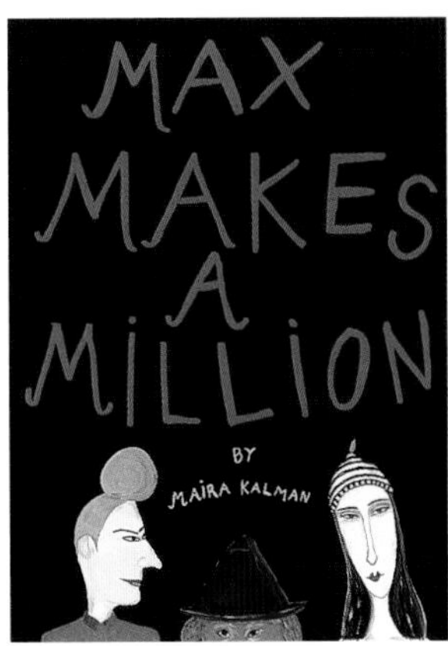
MAX MAKES A MILLION
BY MAIRA KALMAN

9

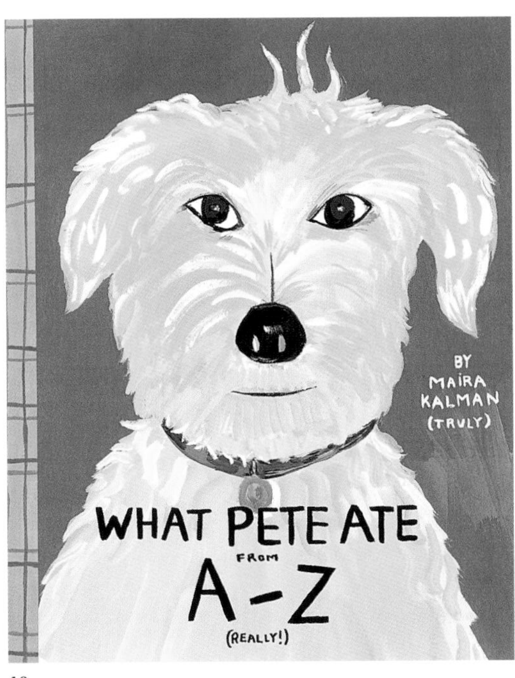
BY MAIRA KALMAN (TRULY)
WHAT PETE ATE FROM A-Z
(REALLY!)

10

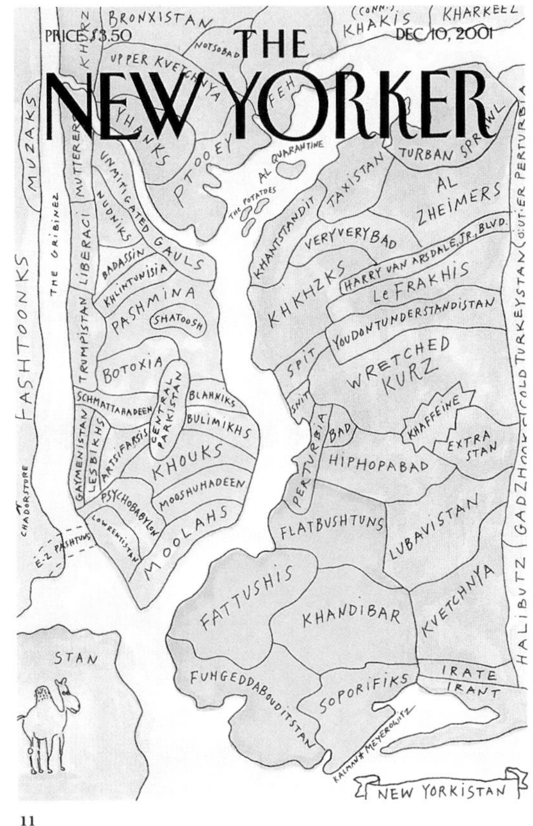
PRICE $3.50
THE NEW YORKER
DEC 10, 2001
BRONXISTAN
KHAKIS
KHARKEEL
UPPER KVETCHNYA
MUZAKS
PTOOEY
AL QUARANTINE
TURBAN SPRAWL
TAXISTAN
AL ZHEIMERS
VERYVERYBAD
HARRY VAN ARSDALE JR. BLVD.
LE FRAKHIS
YOUDONTUNDERSTANDISTAN
KHKHZKS
WRETCHED KURZ
FASHTOONKS
LIBERACI
TRUMPISTAN
GAULS
PASHMINA
SHATOOSH
BOTOXIA
SCHMATTAHADEEN
BLAHNIKS
BULIMIKHS
KHOUKS
MOOSHUHADEEN
MOOLAHS
PERTURBIA
HIPHOPABAD
KHAFFEINE
EXTRA STAN
FLATBUSHTUNS
LUBAVISTAN
KVETCHNYA
FATTUSHIS
KHANDIBAR
FUHGEDDABOUDITSTAN
SOPORIFIKS
IRATE
IRANT
STAN
HALIBUTZ
NEW YORKISTAN

11

PAUL KARIOUK b. 1963

MABEL O. WILSON b. 1963

## KW:A

*Oakland*

1

Home may be where the heart is, but for the migrant it is equally true that "anywhere I hang my hat is home." This conflict, the impact of migration on domesticity, is an important theme in KW:a, the practice of architects Paul Kariouk and Mabel O. Wilson, whose traveling installation *(a)way station* gives shape to their belief that migration is a metaphor for the human search for domestic stability in a turbulent world.

In conceiving *(a)way station*, the architects began with the recognition that domestic space for most of the world's forty million migrants is not divided into separate rooms but is layered into "a dense amalgam of belongings and overlapping daily activities." For Kariouk and Wilson these residences are "way stations where the migrant assembles a temporary home out of material possessions—transplanted objects of sentimental value and newly acquired objects of consumer culture."

The exhibition is designed as a room—simultaneously a bedroom, living room, bathroom, and kitchen—that may have been inhabited by migrants. Kariouk and Wilson then divided the "room" into fifteen equal-sized units, slicing through domestic objects and furnishings. Like migrants' belongings, the units are rearranged for each exhibition site. Visitors walk among these units, temporarily occupying the transitional domestic space of itinerants.

Many of the objects from the original room—plates, chairs, and clothing—are encased like natural history specimens in amber-colored cast resin and backlit to impart the importance migrants give to such everyday things. Taped interviews with local residents provide the soundtrack. Synthesizing objects, images, texts, and sounds, *(a)way station* forces us to consider how frequent uprooting disrupts domestic life and to rethink the notion of home as a symbol of stability, memory, and promise. **DA**

**1–5**
**(A)WAY STATION**
Exhibition design, 2000
Designers: Paul Kariouk and Mabel Wilson with Yusuke Obuchi, Bob Carbon, Sarah Heller, Jason Scroggins
Project funding: NYSCA, LEF Foundation, Graham Foundation
Photography: Peter Tolkin (1, 2, 4); Kelli Yon (3, 5)

2

3

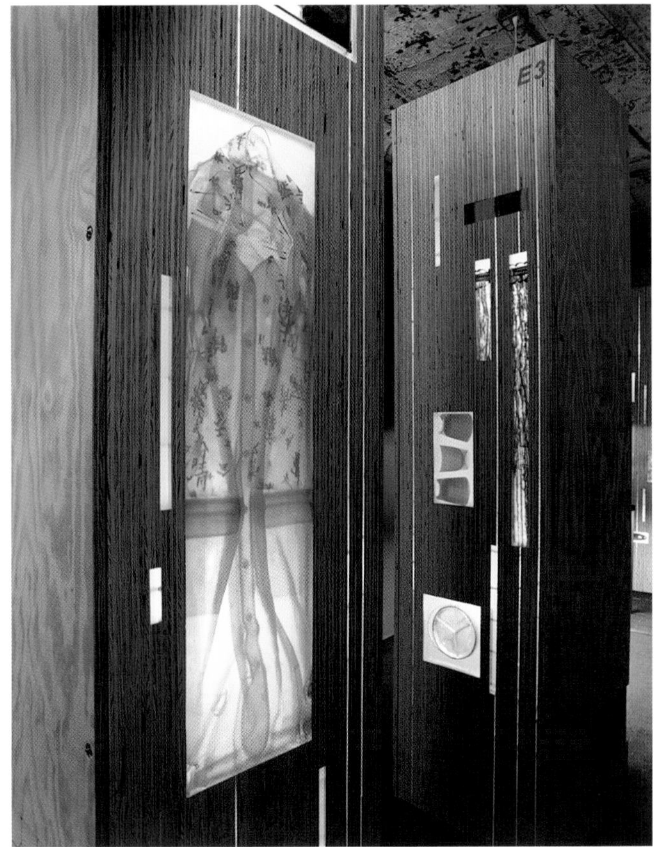


4

5

STEFAN LOY b. 1965

FRANK FORD b. 1966

## LOYANDFORD

*Los Angeles*

1

Shards of men's gray flannel suiting meet flowered silk and pleated chiffon. Old jackets are turned inside out, transforming once-hidden seams into decorative details. Take the power suits and glamorous evening gowns from the 1980s television series *Dynasty*, cut and reassemble them into inventive fashion collages, and an image of LoyandFord's fall 2001 couture collection emerges. Fashion references are genetically recombined: Yves Saint Laurent's masculine glamour fuses with Gianni Versace's hypersexuality, Vivienne Westwood's punk with Martin Margiela's deconstructionism. Surprisingly, all this ripping and reassembling yields clothing that is expertly constructed into strong, asymmetrical silhouettes. The mood is conceptual and sensual, streetwise and salon-suave.

Launching LoyandFord in 2000, the German-born designers Stefan Loy and Frank Ford, in the words of *Wallpaper* magazine, "unleashed a joyous fashion anarchy upon L.A." LoyandFord design one-of-a-kind couture as well as ready-to-wear shirts, pants, sweaters, and accessories. Making their reputation in Europe's underground fashion-cum-art club scene, they have reached a much broader audience in America, where their ready-to-wear collection is available in more than forty stores and earned over $1 million in its second year.

"Mostly," Loy says, "it starts with the fabric. We are trying to find new ways of defining a new shape or a new color.... We'll like pieces that are wrong in a way. The concept is to rework how clothes were made in the past. It's about craftsmanship." In addition to buying fabric, they purchase ready-made clothes. Loy and Ford then deconstruct the clothes, and before reassembling them, dye, print, and sometimes embroider the fabrics by hand. While Loy and Ford say fashion is not an art, the process they follow is as inspired and thoughtful as a painter's or sculptor's. **DA**

1
**SUNBURN AND INSIDE**
Garments, 2001
Taffeta, mohair, silkscreen image
Designers: Stefan Loy and Frank Ford
Manufacturer: LoyandFord

2
**LINING TOO LONG**
Garments, 2001
Wool, silk lining
Designers: Stefan Loy and Frank Ford
Manufacturer: LoyandFord

3
**FRONT ON BACK JACKET**
Garments, 2001
Wool, mohair
Designers: Stefan Loy and Frank Ford
Manufacturer: LoyandFord

4
**HALF JACKET + MADE OUT OF TWO SKIRT**
Garments, 2001
Gabardine, wool
Designers: Stefan Loy and Frank Ford
Manufacturer: LoyandFord

5
**TITANIC COCAINE DRESS**
Garments, 2001
Hand-dyed chiffon
Designers: Stefan Loy and Frank Ford
Manufacturer: LoyandFord

Photography: Marc Lecureuil

2

3

4

5

TINA LUTZ b. 1966

MARCIA PATMOS b. 1969

## LUTZ + PATMOS

*New York City*

1

Concept fashion can be a loaded gun. Too precious, and nobody will get the point. Too broad and the fashionistas whose fickle passions spark trends will take a wide berth. But Tina Lutz and Marcia Patmos have won respect by developing concept-rich garments that recognize the body underneath, respect the brain on top, and tap into an honest female ideal.

Designing together since 2000, the duo creates products based on a provocative character study of the modern woman, independent of mind and strong in outlook, who is aware of the world's temptations but understands that not all vices are corrosive. Taking inspiration from wildly disparate sources—actress Charlotte Rampling's nonchalant wrinkles, France's TGV high-speed passenger train—Lutz & Patmos's high-ply cashmeres adhere to personal style not popular fashion. Ergonomic seams acknowledge physical curves without denigrating them. The turtleneck of a sweater cannily incorporates a coil that can be unwound when the weather (or the room) gets a bit warm. And the pair's quirky decision to invite an artist to create one item each season speaks of a creative inclusiveness rare in the fashion world.

For Lutz & Patmos's spring 2002 collection, for example, Yves Béhar of fuseproject, an industrial design firm, devised a Teflon-infused, water-resistant cashmere windbreaker. American painter and filmmaker Sarah Morris's contribution to the fall 2002 collection was a limited-edition 4-ply cashmere sweater whose intarsia pattern reworks a motif from Morris's 2001 subway-system painting *Metro Center (Capital)*.

Even the presentation of the goods—Lutz & Patmos's tailored plastic pouches are travel-ready and conservation-conscious—advances an aesthetic philosophy that clothing is merely one of the ingredients of a lifestyle that's already well under way. **MO**

1
**MARLY FUNNEL NECK SWEATER**
Cashmere, 2002
Designers: Lutz + Patmos

2
**METRO CENTER SWEATER**
Based on painting *Metro Center (Capital)* by Sarah Morris
Cashmere, 2002
Designers: Lutz + Patmos with Sarah Morris

3
**MARTINEZ REVERSIBLE SCOOP SWEATER**
Cashmere, 2002
Designers: Lutz + Patmos

4
**FENICIA REVERSIBLE WRAP TOP**
Cashmere, 2002
Designers: Lutz + Patmos

5
**INFINITY SCARF**
Cashmere, 2002
Designers: Lutz + Patmos

Photography: Matt Flynn

2, 3

4, 5

## TOD MACHOVER b. 1953

MIT MEDIA LAB

*Cambridge, Massachusetts*

1, 2

Tod Machover designs music. In addition to having composed five operas, commissioned and performed by renowned theaters the world over, he even designs the instruments that make his music. But what truly makes him a designer—in the fullest sense of the word—is the radical way he has found to make music tangible. Machover uses highly sophisticated computers in tandem with intriguing objects to translate familiar physical gestures—squeezing, tapping, pulling, pushing—into the shapes, colors, and patterns of music.

While his work has captured the imagination and professional interest of his musical peers, Machover's newest project, the Toy Symphony, is designed especially for children and the rest of us who don't read music. Indeed, he completely sidesteps the obstacles of scores and notes.

His instruments don't even look like instruments—or at least not ordinary ones. Machover's Beatbugs glow like high-tech fireflies when you tap them in a pattern. One tap more lets you send the pattern to another Bug, and another, superimposing beats and sounds. In contrast to the Bugs, which look like kissing cousins of computer mice, the embroidered Music Shapers hark back to the era before recorded music, except that they are stuffed with twenty-first-century sensate technology. A simple squeeze of the hand controls the timbre and density of the sound. The wireless Hyperviolin—a bow and mysteriously disembodied neck—allows virtuoso violinists, like frequent collaborator Joshua Bell, to exchange and modify music with children when the Toy Symphony is performed in concert halls from Dublin to Tokyo.

With Tod Machover, you don't read music. You feel it and you see it. **SY**

1
**TOY SYMPHONY: MUSIC SHAPER**
Digital musical instrument, 2001
Design team: Tod Machover, Maggie Orth, Roberto Aimi
Client: International Fashion Machines and MIT Media Lab
Photography: Paul McCarthy

2
**TOY SYMPHONY: BEATBUG**
Digital musical instrument, 2002
Design team: Tod Machover, Roberto Aimi, Peter Colao, Gil Weinberg, MIT Media Lab
Photography: Paul McCarthy

3
**TOY SYMPHONY: MUSIC SHAPERS IN USE**
Photograph, 2002
Photography: Paul McCarthy

4
**HYPERVIOLIN AND HYPERBOW**
Photograph, 2001
Design team: Tod Machover, Diana Young, Tristan Jehan
Client: Jensen Muscial Instruments and MIT Media Lab
Photography: Webb Chapel

3

4

## MAHARAM

*New York City*

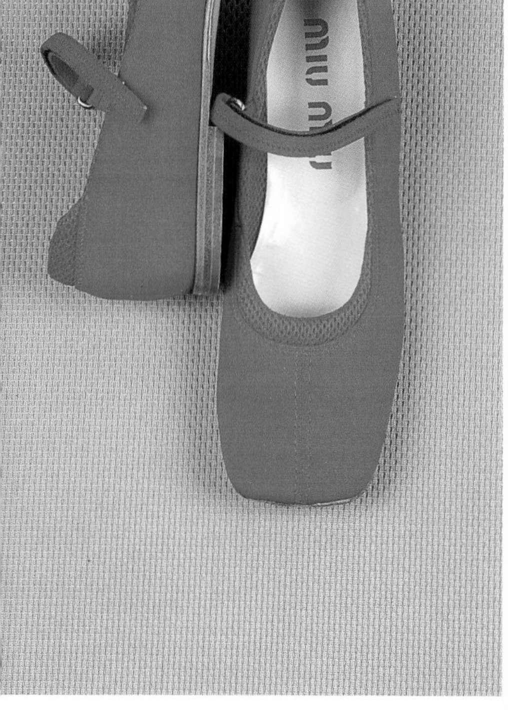


1

Something's up when your furniture starts dressing better than you do. Your desk chair may not be wearing Prada, but if it's clad in a Maharam textile, it may have been made in the same mill that your tote was. A design-forward resource for architects, interior designers, and furniture manufacturers, Maharam has turned the category of contract textiles inside out. The newest (and fourth) generation of the Maharam family did it by looking beyond the bounds of their business to fashion, art, and design—while meeting and surpassing industry standards.

Their Content Series uses a dedicated wool source, metal-free dyes, and chemical-free finishing, reducing resource consumption in the manufacturing process. These handsome wovens both transform the pinstripe sensibility and bring an environmental ethos to the office.

Work or workouts, suits or sneakers—they're all the same to Maharam. Their vivid, two-toned bonded Action Fabric knits marry runway chic and athletic endurance. Demonstrating that performance is as much about resilience as strength, Maharam has taken knits to the third dimension with a new line of stretch upholstery fabrics that are easy to wrap around a cushion. The rippled surface of this new breed of Action Fabrics is inviting to touch and has the same sense of freedom associated with synthetics since the invention of "wash and wear."

Pose reprises Op Art in microcosm. Composites, a line of woven plastic wallcoverings based on a collaboration with Andrée Putman, has an industrial elegance that stems from the luggage that inspired it. More recently, Maharam sponsored Hella Jongerius's first foray into textile design. The Dutch designer's Repeat is an eccentric concatenation of stripes, florals, polka dots, and factory markings. It is also an apt metaphor for the permeable boundaries of design at Maharam. **SY**

1, 3
**ACTION FABRICS™**
Polyester, 2001
Design team: Maharam Design Studio
Manufacturer: Maharam
Photography: John Gettings (1), Phillipe Regard (3)

2
**COMPOSITES™**
Wallcovering, 2002
Polyethylene, polyester
Design team: Maharam Design Studio
Manufacturer: Maharam
Photography: John Gettings

4
**POSE**
**READY-TO-WEAR™**
Vinyl, polyurethane, 2002
Design team: Maharam Design Studio
Manufacturer: Maharam
Photography: Davies + Starr

5
**REPEAT™**
Fabric (detail), 2002
Cotton, polyester, rayon
Designer: Hella Jongerius in collaboration with the Maharam Design Studio
Manufacturer: Maharam
Photography: Phillipe Regard

2

3

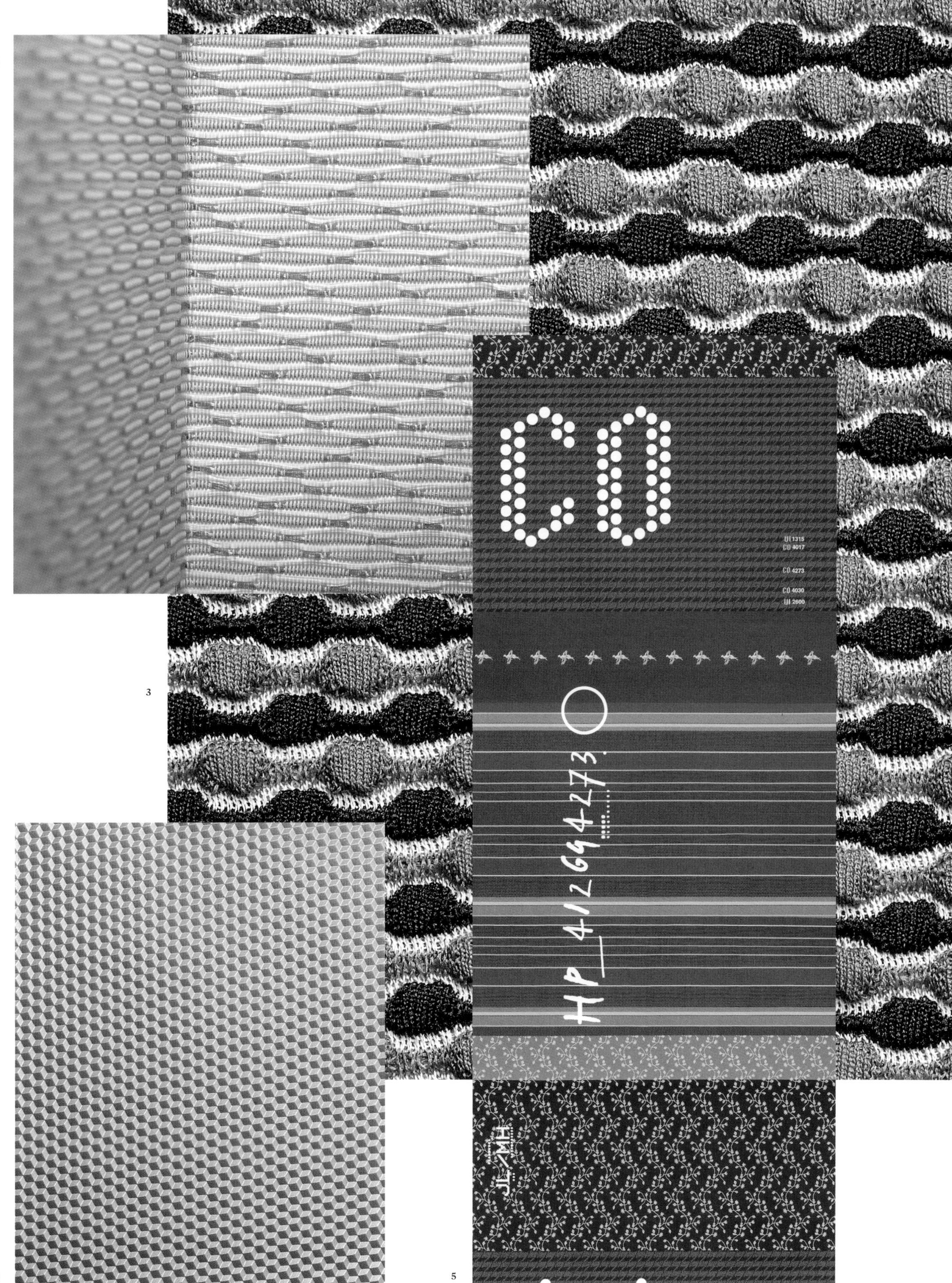


4

5

GEOFF MCFETRIDGE b. 1971

CHAMPION GRAPHICS

*Los Angeles*

1, 2

Geoff McFetridge was drawn to graphic design as a teenager living in Calgary, Alberta, where he produced t-shirts, flyers, and zines for garage bands and fellow skateboarders. Today, from his firm Champion Graphics in Los Angeles, he designs the same kinds of ephemera he produced as a teenager, but for an international audience.

McFetridge creates psychologically charged ornament that combines aspects of cartooning, graffiti, and adolescent doodling with crisp, formal modernism. His camouflage patterns invite close reading, each one a text packed with symbols both arbitrary and loaded. Nature and culture collide, as cityscapes become wilderness and forests are populated with lumbering "stoners" and snow monsters. A swarm of sharks decorates a fabric called Fearless, suggesting a tightly packed society of lone predators. Rush, a series of snowboards for Burton, depicts urban vistas, from New York to Tokyo. One board shows a dense tourist village wedged between a forest and a mountain—the view from the snowboard is a road heading directly into town.

McFetridge's urban view of nature takes on another dimension in a set of animated commercials for the Winter XGames, a televised competition of "extreme" sports. McFetridge developed each spot with the same primitive yet formalized flatness seen in his pattern designs. Taking the motto "Safety First" to promote the willfully dangerous XGames, the ads depict cuddly creatures performing absurd acts of recklessness that result in death or dismemberment. The bear in "Don't Ski with Scissors" cuts off his own head; the squirrel in "Don't Drink Gas" poisons himself by drinking from his own fuel tank.

Geoff McFetridge uses the dangers of daily existence—real or imaginary—to unsettle his gorgeously designed surfaces. **EL**

**1, 2**
**RUSH**
Snowboards, 2001
Silkscreen on P Tex1000
Designer: Geoff McFetridge
Manufacturer:
Burton Snowboards, Vermont

**3**
**SAFETY FIRST/XGAMES**
Posters for television commercials, 2001
Designer: Geoff McFetridge
Agency: Wieden and Kennedy
Client: ESPN/Winter XGames

**4**
**ALL TOGETHER NOW**
Pattern design, 2001
Lithograph on canvas
Designer: Geoff McFetridge

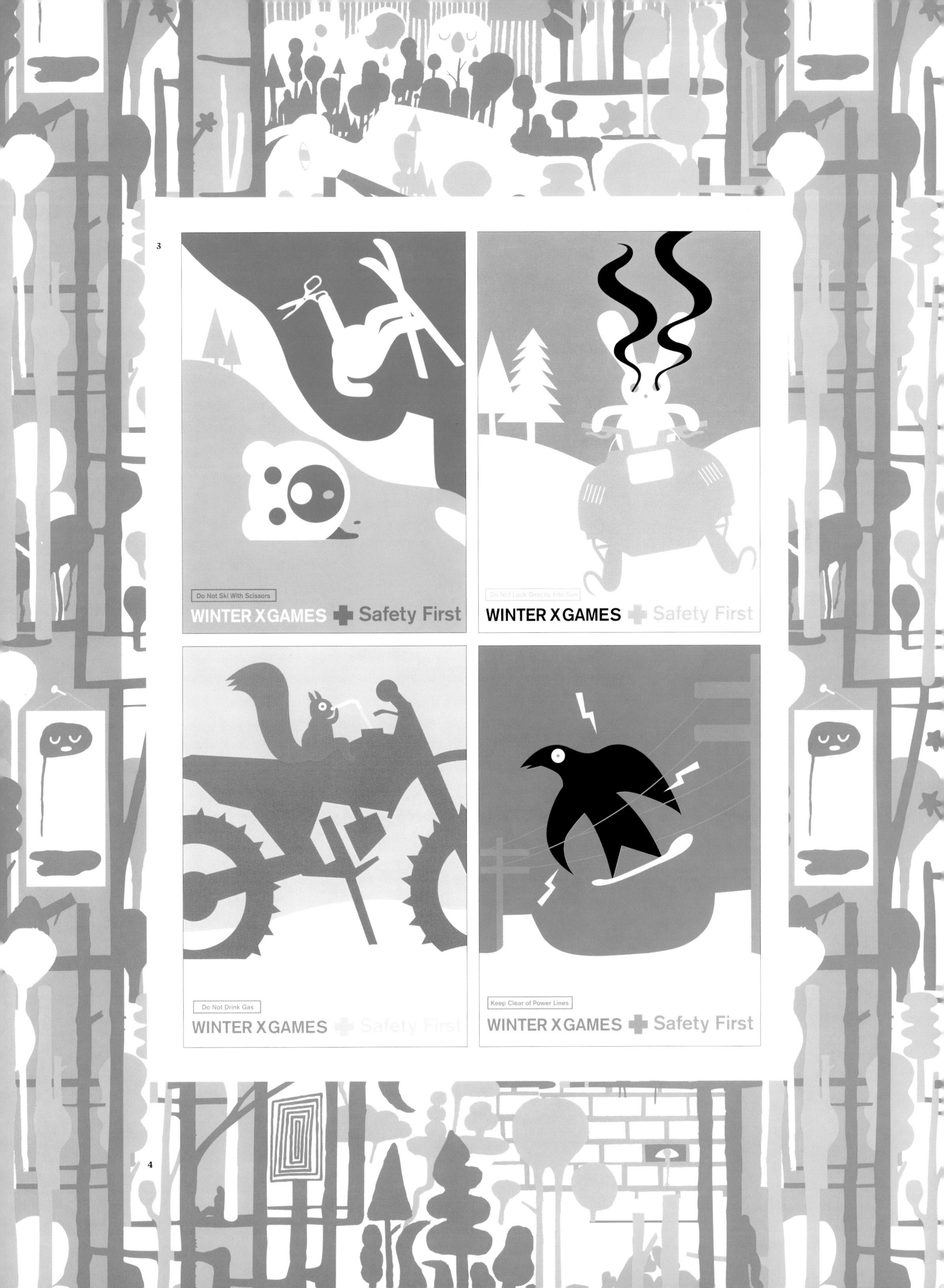
3
Do Not Ski With Scissors
WINTER X GAMES Safety First
Do Not Look Directly Into Sun
WINTER X GAMES Safety First
Do Not Drink Gas
WINTER X GAMES Safety First
Keep Clear of Power Lines
WINTER X GAMES Safety First
4

## STEPHEN MCKAY b. 1951

*New York City*

1

2

Stephen McKay's Modern Pioneer series, launched in the late 1990s and today including tables, chairs, and light fixtures, updates the minimalist vocabulary of the great modern architects. McKay's sensibility stems from a background in architectural studies and interior design acquired before the founding of his lighting and furniture workshop in 1997. Although he now designs and manufactures almost two hundred light fixtures, ranging from contemporary to traditional styles, the Modern Pioneer collection is his most visually sophisticated work, merging a deeply personal interpretation of design history with a keen sense of form and proportion.

McKay views the Modern Pioneer pieces less as furniture design than as distillations of buildings by Ludwig Mies van der Rohe, Le Corbusier, and Rudolph Schindler. Each piece in the series, he says, attempts to "strip down and lay bare" the formal devices of these modern architects—hovering cantilevers, simple forms, and facades of abstract grids that "reverberate for me," McKay says, "in completely new ways." The Shadow Box Pendant Fixture converts the traditional lampshade into a crisply tailored, translucent volume floating within a rectangle of thin metal rods. The Lafayette Pendant espouses a Shaker simplicity in its orchestration of horizontal and vertical lines, complemented by the march of four subtly angled cylindrical shades. Thin planes of solid walnut serve as arms, shelves, or tabletops in the Book Table and Book Chair.

Stephen McKay aspires to create work like that of Florence Knoll, the legendary mid-twentieth century American designer. Just as Knoll worked with such celebrated architects as Eero Saarinen, McKay collaborates with contemporary leaders in the field to custom design elegant furnishings that seamlessly blend with their environments. "Nothing works," McKay humbly notes, "unless it's a disappearing act." **DA**

1
**SHADOW BOX PENDANT FIXTURE**
Lighting, 2002
Bronze frame, parchment box shade
Designer: Stephen McKay

2
**BOOK CHAIR**
Walnut, 2001
Designer: Stephen McKay

3
**LAFAYETTE PENDANT**
Lighting, 2001
Bronze body, parchment shades
Designer: Stephen McKay

4
**BOOK TABLE**
Walnut, 2001
Designer: Stephen McKay

Photography: Matt Flynn

3

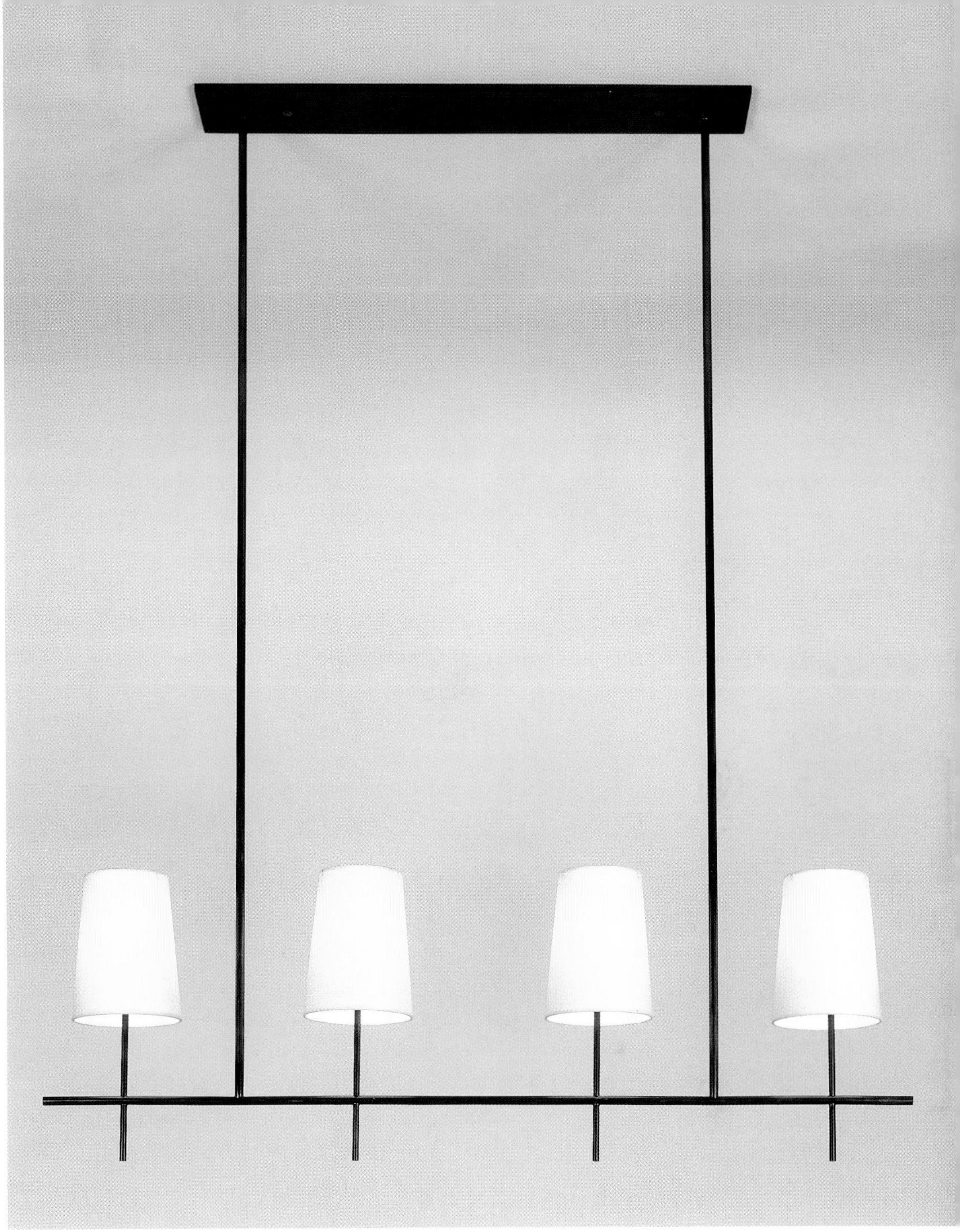

4

## GENE MEYER b. 1954

*New York City*

1

Born in Louisville, Kentucky, and educated at the Parsons School of Design in New York, Gene Meyer began his fashion-design career in the atelier of iconoclast Geoffrey Beene. It's an influence readily apparent in his own artistic resumé. But that is where all comparison ends.

Mathematical calculations wrapped in dazzling color combinations, Meyer's chromatically saturated runway creations—from accessories like scarves, ties, and boxer shorts to the body-conscious menswear he has been creating since 1995—are a continuing exploration of the indefinable wonders inherent in basic geometry, executed in eye-popping colors that recall Miami Beach swimming pools, Carmen Miranda's fruit-laden toques, and Fourth of July fireworks. They are also tributes to the award-winning designer's curious creative process.

The classic image of a fashion designer is a man or woman who creates directly on a human body—pinning, tucking, and draping—or who begins with a sketch or a doodle. Gene Meyer, on the other hand, follows the cut-and-paste technique of Henri Matisse. Like the famed French artist, he prefers the medium of collage. Meyer laboriously cuts colored paper into circles, squares, wavy oceanic lines, and other totemic geometric shapes and then combines them into mosaics that become the templates for his sprightly garments, as well as his newly introduced collection of wool floorcoverings. What's behind his inspiration? The designer cites Ivy League chic of the 1960s and Elvis Presley movies, not to mention his own father's kaleidoscopic weekend golf wardrobe, which made the Duke of Windsor's clashing plaids, stripes, and polka-dots seem positively subdued in comparison. Gene Meyer's vision is a joyful jaunt over the rainbow to an all-man's land where the dandy meets the surfer dude in Technicolor splendor. **MO**

**1, 5**
**MUFFLERS**
Cotton, wool, mohair, 2001
Designer: Gene Meyer
Photography: Dan Lecca

**2–4**
**RUGS FROM GENE MEYER COLLECTION**
Handspun Himalayan wool, 2001
Designer: Gene Meyer
Manufacturer: M & M Design International, New York
Photography: Courtesy Gene Meyer

**6**
**MENSWEAR FROM GENE MEYER**
Cotton/poplin shirt, wool/cashmere suit, 2001
Designer: Gene Meyer
Photography: Dan Lecca

**7**
**SCARF**
Cotton/wool, 2000
Designer: Gene Meyer
Photography: Corina Lecca

2–4

5–7

## J. ABBOTT MILLER b. 1963

PENTAGRAM

*New York City and Baltimore*

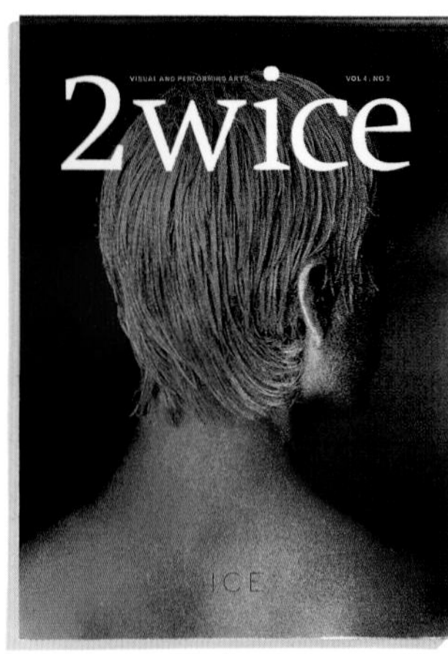


1–3

To J. Abbott Miller the space of design is limitlessly fungible. He views books as platforms for performances and exhibitions, and he stages exhibitions and performances in the language of books. He seeks out projects that allow him to work not only as designer but also as curator, author, or—in the case of *2wice* magazine—editor.

With *2wice*'s editor-in-chief, Patsy Tarr, Miller chooses the subject (and commissions the articles) for each issue with the vision of a curator creating a collection. As designer of *2wice*, he plays with words as pictures and pictures as words. In the "Picnic" issue, for example, he places a photograph of choreographer Mark Morris in a gingham suit (read: human picnic table) opposite an article written in a gingham typeface.

The catalog for the Guggenheim Museum's planned retrospective of Matthew Barney, creator of the *CREMASTER* cycle, needed no such excess. Barney's surreal bio-fictions about a third sex found a classical foil in Miller's choice of two highly rational typefaces, Didot and Univers, and a system of elongated dictionary "thumb indexes."

Though he is a gifted formalist, Miller eschews one-size-fits-all projects for a custom fit between medium and message, particularly in exhibition design. Having honed his storytelling skills on the small stage of the museum, he moved into the big top in 2002, designing three 20,000-square-foot pavilions to celebrate Harley-Davidson's 100th anniversary. Enormous letters make up words in four languages that surround each tent; a 45-foot tower of typography lists all the Harley-Davidson engines. A paean to the street theater of the Russian avant-garde becomes a spirited tribute to a populist American icon.

Whether dealing with the monumental or the modest, with biker culture or dance culture, Miller articulates what's being said by sight. **SY**

**1–3**
**2WICE**
Biannual publication, *Camera*: Spring 2001; *Picnic*: Spring 2002; *Ice*: Fall 2001
Offset lithography
Designer: J. Abbott Miller
Cover photographs: Martin Schoeller, Andrew Eccles, Christian Witkin, Martin Parr
Publisher: 2wice Arts Foundation, New York
Photography: Joseph Mulligan

**4**
**HARLEY-DAVIDSON OPEN ROAD TOUR**
Touring exhibition, July 2002–August 2003
Designer: J. Abbott Miller, Pentagram
Team: James Hicks, Jeremy Hoffman
Consulting architects: Ziger/Snead
Tent design: FTL Happold
Lighting: Katz/Mather
Sites: Atlanta, Baltimore, Los Angeles, Toronto, Mexico City, Sydney, Tokyo, Barcelona, Hamburg, Milwaukee
Photography: Timothy Hursley

**5, 6**
**MATTHEW BARNEY: THE CREMASTER CYCLE**
Exhibition publication, 2002
Offset lithography, vinyl, silkscreen
Designer: J. Abbott Miller and Roy Brooks
Publisher: Guggenheim Museum, New York
Photography: Joseph Mulligan

4

5, 6

## MIKE MILLS b. 1966

THE DIRECTORS BUREAU

*Los Angeles and New York City*

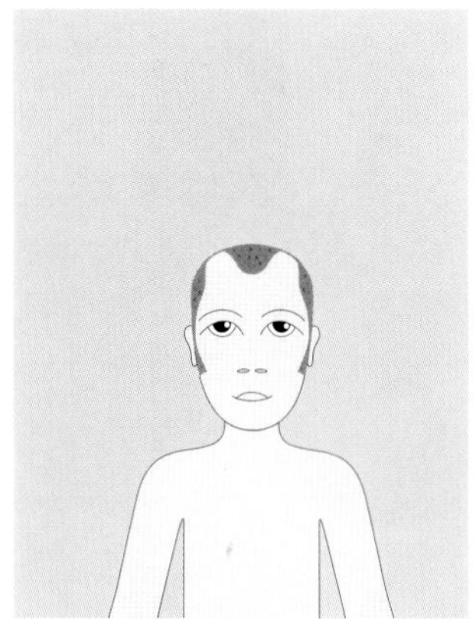

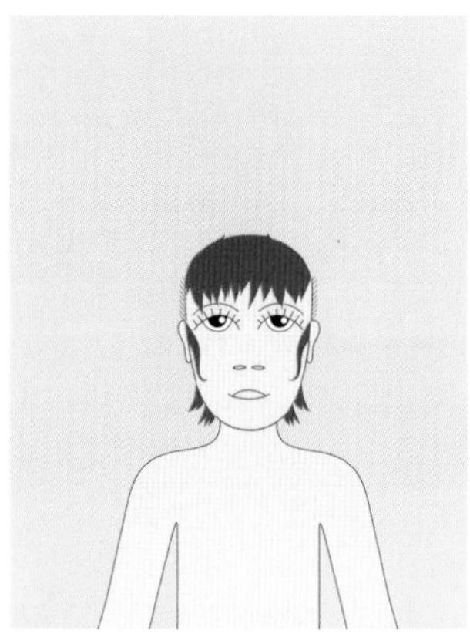

1–3

The films and graphics of Mike Mills are populated with strange heroes, from suburban kids to erstwhile celebrities.

His acclaimed documentary film *Paperboys* examines the lives of teenagers in a Minnesota suburb. Like an anthropologist, Mills carefully observes the boys' homes, hobbies, and family lives, allowing each subject to appear both as an individual and as a representative of his group. The portraits in a group of digital prints called *Every Face Is Exactly the Same* have matching features; only their hairstyles and eyelashes change.

Although the prints were presented in an art gallery, Mills calls them graphic design, asserting his roots in a discipline he has been able to both master and more or less walk away from. After studying art and design at the Cooper Union in New York City in the mid-1980s, Mills created album covers, posters, logos, and t-shirts for bands, skateboard companies, and streetwear labels. In 1998 he cofounded The Directors Bureau (TDB) with filmmaker Roman Coppola in Los Angeles. At TDB, a company whose low-key, low-gloss persona has made it fashionably at odds with Hollywood's dominant slickness, Mills has directed music videos for Air, Moby, and other bands, and commercials for Adidas, Nike, The Gap, and Volkswagen, while also directing his own independent films.

Along the way, Mills has continued to create graphic design. A set of postcards for the Paris boutique Colette assembles an odd crew of twentieth-century personalities, from Jane Goodall and Yves Saint Laurent to Princess Leah. A skateboard deck sports the face of political outsider Ralph Nader, a surprising yet fitting icon for young skaters searching for independence.

Mike Mills, something of an outsider himself, has fueled his own ride to independence with the energy of pop culture. **EL**

**1–3**
**EVERY FACE IS EXACTLY THE SAME**
Iris prints, 1999
Designer: Mike Mills

**4**
**RALPH NADER/PUBLIC CITIZEN**
Skateboard deck, 1998
Silkscreen on composite material
Designer: Mike Mills
Client: Subliminal

**5**
**PAPERBOYS**
Film, 2001
Director: Mike Mills
Producers: Ned Brown, Katherine Kennedy, Julia Leach
Client: Jack Spade

**6–8**
**COLETTE**
Postcards, 1999
Offset lithography
Designer: Mike Mills
Publisher: Colette, Paris

4

5

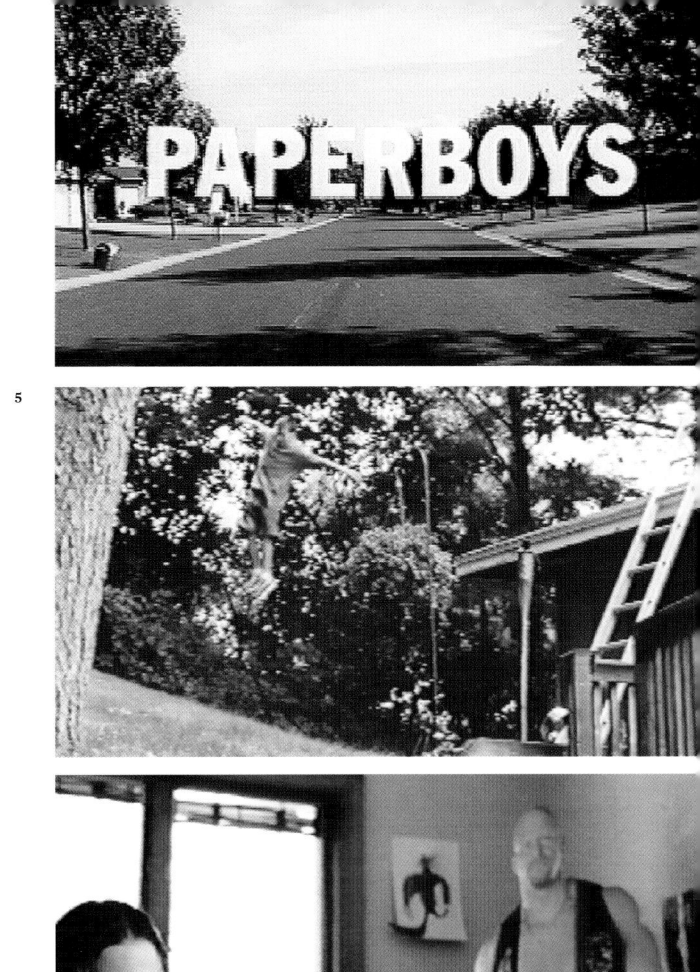

6–8

YVES SAINT LAURENT FASHION DESIGNER

## ISAAC MIZRAHI b. 1961

*New York City*

1

In the 1995 film *Unzipped*, Isaac Mizrahi declares he would like to create a fur outfit inspired by the old *Banana Splits* television series that could be worn to walk the dog. That remark is the key to why Mizrahi, among the most influential fashion designers of the 1990s, is today one of the most important designers for the stage. A glamorous, expensive monkey suit for a common chore is both exotic and absurd, a refusal to take fashion seriously and a knowing use of clothing as theater.

A performer himself, with his own cable TV show, Mizrahi has created costumes for Twyla Tharp, Bill T. Jones, Mikhail Baryshnikov, and Mark Morris. Two projects for Morris—an opera and a ballet—neatly illustrate the breadth of Mizrahi's range.

*Platée* is the story of a vain and silly frog duped into believing Jupiter loves her in a cruel cosmic prank. Mizrahi complemented Morris's wildly eclectic interpretation of this eighteenth-century *ballet bouffon* by drawing on references from Weegee photographs to Marx Brothers movies to French couture. The collaboration yielded a cast of dowager socialites, Bowery bums, and sailors transformed into spoiled goddesses, satyrs, and nymphs. The surreal snakes, birds, and newts in *Platée*'s amphibious world are both literal and larger than life, familiar yet wholly new.

With the Indonesian-inspired ballet *Gong*, Mizrahi rejected the idea of any literal adaptation of Balinese clothing as the equivalent of a duty-free shopping mentality. Instead, he used color to create a climate for movement and an extension of the score.

Mizrahi is the design equivalent of a good listener. At this stage of history, he feels we are far too exposed to adhere to a single philosophy, unless it's that of a chameleon, who, after all, may be nature's most sophisticated colorist. **SY**

1
**GONG**
Costumes, 2001
Silk shantung, lycra knit, tulle
Designer: Isaac Mizrahi
Client: American Ballet Theater Company
New York City
Photography: Paul Kolnik

2–5
**PLATÉE**
Costumes, 1998
Designer: Isaac Mizrahi
Client: Mark Morris Dance Company
New York City
Photography: Ken Friedman (1);
Robbie Jack (2), Bill Cooper (3, 4)

2–5

## TED MUEHLING b. 1953

*New York City*

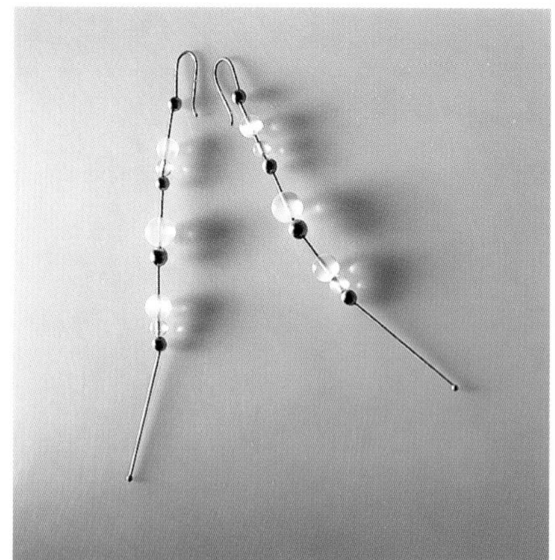

1–3

Ted Muehling is a romantic modernist. His jewelry, porcelain, glass, and metalwork dance on the edge of abstraction, but never stray far from the natural forms that inspire them. Birds' eggs, twigs, moth wings, and seashells become vases, cutlery, earrings, and tableware. It is a testament to the strength of his eye and the discipline of his aesthetic that his work—which is unafraid of the sweet and the pretty—escapes sentimentality and never suffers from banality. Instead, the beauty Muehling creates triggers deep-seated emotional responses, reverberations that remind us of the secret pleasures of nature, the intimate details of which many of us haven't bothered to notice since childhood.

Muehling has managed to build an entire career on childhood pastimes of solitary walks and endless scavenging. But it was at Pratt Institute in New York that his passion became a professional pursuit. A student of industrial design, he chose to create jewelry—instead of appliances or cars—because it offered a degree of control and intimacy that working with large companies would never permit. Designing in a personal cabinet of curiosities, Muehling faces only his own limitations.

During twenty-seven years of successful practice, Muehling has expanded his repertoire and his client base, most notably with his work at the Nymphenburg Porcelain factory in Munich, Germany. Plates decorated with *trompe l'oeil* insects and butterflies, pitchers that look to be made of the milk they carry, and seashells that serve as salt cellars all gently evoke the Romantic era of the eighteenth century when Nymphenburg was founded. In much the same spirit, Muehling interprets nature with a classical vocabulary to elicit a sense of the sublime—what Wordsworth called "emotion recollected in tranquility." Art is a meditation and design is a negotiation. Muehling deftly situates his practice between them. **SY**

1
**BEAD CHAIN EARRINGS**
Moonstones, 14-karat gold, 2000
Designer: Ted Muehling

2
**HAND-CUT AQUAMARINE EARRINGS**
Aquamarine, 14-karat gold, 2002
Designer: Ted Muehling

3
**HAND-CUT AMBER EARRINGS**
Amber, 14-karat gold, 2002
Designer: Ted Muehling

4
**CORAL LANTERN**
Porcelain, 1999
Designer: Ted Muehling
Manufacturer: Nymphenburg, Germany

5, 6
**INSECT PLATE AND BONBONIERE**
Porcelain, 1999
Designer: Ted Muehling
Manufacturer: Nymphenburg, Germany

Photography: Dan Howell

4

5, 6

## CHRISTOPH NIEMANN b. 1970

*New York City*

1

The editorial illustrations of Christoph Niemann use images as a poetic language packed with double meaning. Each drawing—like a cartoon without copy or a joke without a punch line—is a compressed hieroglyph whose richly funny content unfolds in the mind.

A cover design for *The New Yorker*'s 2002 fashion issue presents a serene Japanese courtesan clothed in Asian exports: a cell-phone fan, an earphone hair ornament, and a Pokémon kimono with a circuit-board sash. Another *New Yorker* cover shows a darkened war room, where a team of trigger-happy hawks leap to action as Fourth of July fireworks flash on a screen. Niemann infuses the image with emotional intensity as the warriors dwarf the innocuous celebration at the vortex of the scene.

Niemann, a German-born illustrator and designer, pursued summer internships with Paul Davis and Paula Scher while he was a student in Stuttgart. He returned to New York after graduating in 1997 and quickly found a place working with the city's most important venues for editorial illustration, from *The New York Times* and *The New Yorker* to *Rolling Stone* and other publications, including the underground zine *Nozone*, edited and published by Niemann's friend Nicholas Blechman.

In many of Niemann's illustrations, ordinary objects perform multiple functions. He created an x-ray view of a skeleton hand holding a skeleton gun to represent gun culture in America. For an article about innovation, Niemann used the familiar image of the matchstick to construct the hand that holds it. The match ignites an idea, providing the small but dangerous spark that sets in motion a larger process.

All of Christoph Niemann's work is fueled by ideas. Like a poet, he uses symbols both literally and figuratively; like a prankster, he raises our expectations and then turns them upside down. **EL**

1
**PRET-A-PORTER**
Cover illustraton (detail), 2002
Illustrator: Christoph Niemann
Art director: Françoise Mouly
Publisher: *The New Yorker*

2
**JULY 4: STAR-WARS AND STRIPES FOREVER**
Cover illustraton, 2001
Illustrator: Christoph Niemann
Art director: Françoise Mouly
Publisher: *The New Yorker*

3
**INNOVATION (HAND WITH MATCHES)**
Editorial illustraton, 2001
Illustrator: Christoph Niemann
Art director: Scott Davis
Publisher: *Fortune Small Business*

4
**GUN CULTURE IN AMERICA**
Editorial illustraton, 2000
Illustrator: Christoph Niemann
Art director: Steven Heller
Publisher: *The New York Times Book Review*

2

3

4

## FRANK NOUVO b. 1961

*Los Angeles*

1, 2

Ease of use, instant access, 24/7 communication: ah, the wonders of modern life. The trouble, however, is that great leaps in technology often can have nothing to do with advancing the state of design or its appreciation by the public at large. And what, asks Frank Nuovo, Vice President of Global Design for Nokia Corporation, is the point of that?

Nuovo and his team at Nokia Design have altered the face of telecommunications in barely seven years, working out of a top-secret office. What they produce is definitely a result of form following consumer demand—color screens, improved dial pads, elaborate innards to transmit streaming video—but Nokia Design's array of mobile phones also subtly incorporates cause-and-effect design solutions that have radically and permanently altered the way human beings communicate.

The discovery that some users were painting their phones with bright auto paint so they could find them more easily inspired Nuovo et alia to invent removable faceplates that could be changed at whim, sparking an international craze for do-it-yourself personalized communication devices. Curving contours are constantly devised and refined to mold phones more comfortably to the user's palm. And because mobile-phone owners typically dial on the run, using an agile thumb, along came artfully angled numerical keys, like those on the Nokia model 3585.

Outside his work for Nokia, Frank Nuovo has recently taken communications back to the future for Vertu, a British-based independent subsidiary of Nokia that he conceived. The centerpiece product of the Vertu Studio, led by Nuovo, is a limited series of bench-made communication instruments (née mobile phones) made of materials that would have passed muster with that Italian master of precious *objets d'art*, Benevenuto Cellini—gold, platinum, leather, stainless steel. **MO**

**1**
**NOKIA 8890**
Mobile phone, 2000
Brushed aluminum finish
Design team: Frank Nuovo and Nokia Design
Manufacturer: Nokia, Finland
Photography: Courtesy Nokia

**2**
**NOKIA 7290**
Mobile phone, 2001
Plastic
Design team: Frank Nuovo and Nokia Design
Manufacturer: Nokia, Finland
Photography: Courtesy Nokia

**3–5**
**VERTU SIGNATURE SERIES**
**SIDE, BACK, AND FRONT VIEWS**
Mobile phone, 2002
Platinum, sapphire crystal display, leather frame, ceramic back cover
Designer: Frank Nuovo
Manufacturer: Vertu, United Kingdom
Photography: Courtesty Vertu

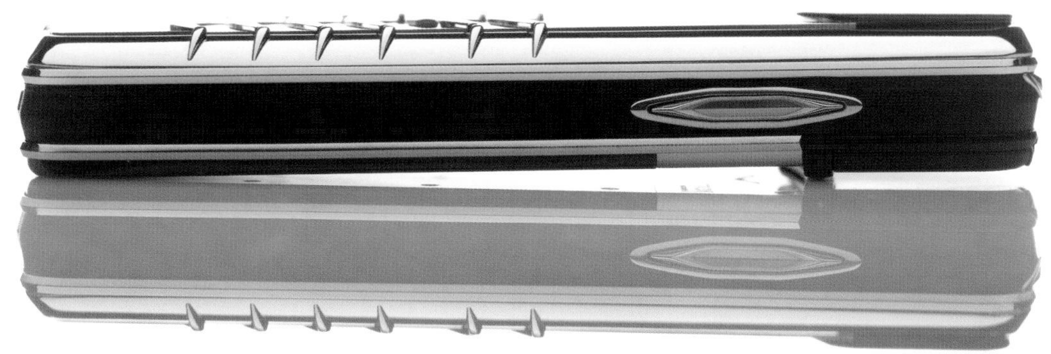

3–5

## YUSUKE OBUCHI b. 1969

*New York City*

1, 2

Yusuke Obuchi's proposed Wave Garden represents a new synthesis of architecture, science, and social needs. Initiated as Obuchi's master's thesis project at Princeton University's School of Architecture, the Wave Garden will probably never be built, but it is a provocative prototype for a renewable power plant. Located just off Southern California, it is a floating artificial landscape of 480 acres, approximately half the area of New York's Central Park. Monday through Friday, the Wave Garden is a power plant to replace the nearby Diablo Canyon nuclear facility. On the weekend, however, it becomes a buoyant public park accessible by boat. This remarkable transformation is achieved by the connection Obuchi forges between natural and man-made forces, linking the ebb and flow of the ocean's waves to the societal wave of fluctuating energy consumption.

A three-dimensional representation of this relationship, the Wave Garden consists of 1,734 three-inch-thick ceramic tiles linked together and supported on the water's surface by tubular buoys. During the week, the motion of the ocean's waves causes the flexible tiles to bend, generating energy through piezoelectricity. (Discovered by Pierre and Jacques Curie in the 1880s, piezoelectricity is the electric charge produced by mechanical stress on crystals; it commonly powers quartz wristwatches.)

Demand for the energy the Wave Garden produces from Monday through Friday determines its shape and function on the weekend, when energy consumption decreases. If Californians consume little energy during the week, they are rewarded: the tiles rise to the surface to create stable recreational platforms and swimming ponds. But if weekday demand is too high, the Wave Garden remains strictly a power plant. The Wave Garden acts as a barometer of energy use and makes invisible power visible. **DA**

1
**WAVE GARDEN**
Installation at Storefront for Art and Architecture, New York City, 2002
Designer: Yusuke Obuchi
Installation assistance: Storefront staff and volunteers
Photography: Anthony Hamboussi

2
**WAVE GARDEN: SITE MAP**
Digital rendering, 2002
Designer: Yusuke Obuchi
Rendering: Yusuke Obuchi

3
**WAVE GARDEN**
Installation (detail) at Princeton University, Princeton, New Jersey, 2002
Designer: Yusuke Obuchi
Installation assistance: Jason Scroggin, Martina Schaefer, Jonathon Winton, and student volunteers
Photography: Yusuke Obuchi

4
**WAVE GARDEN: STUDY MODEL**
Digital rendering, 2002
Designer: Yusuke Obuchi
Rendering: Yusuke Obuchi

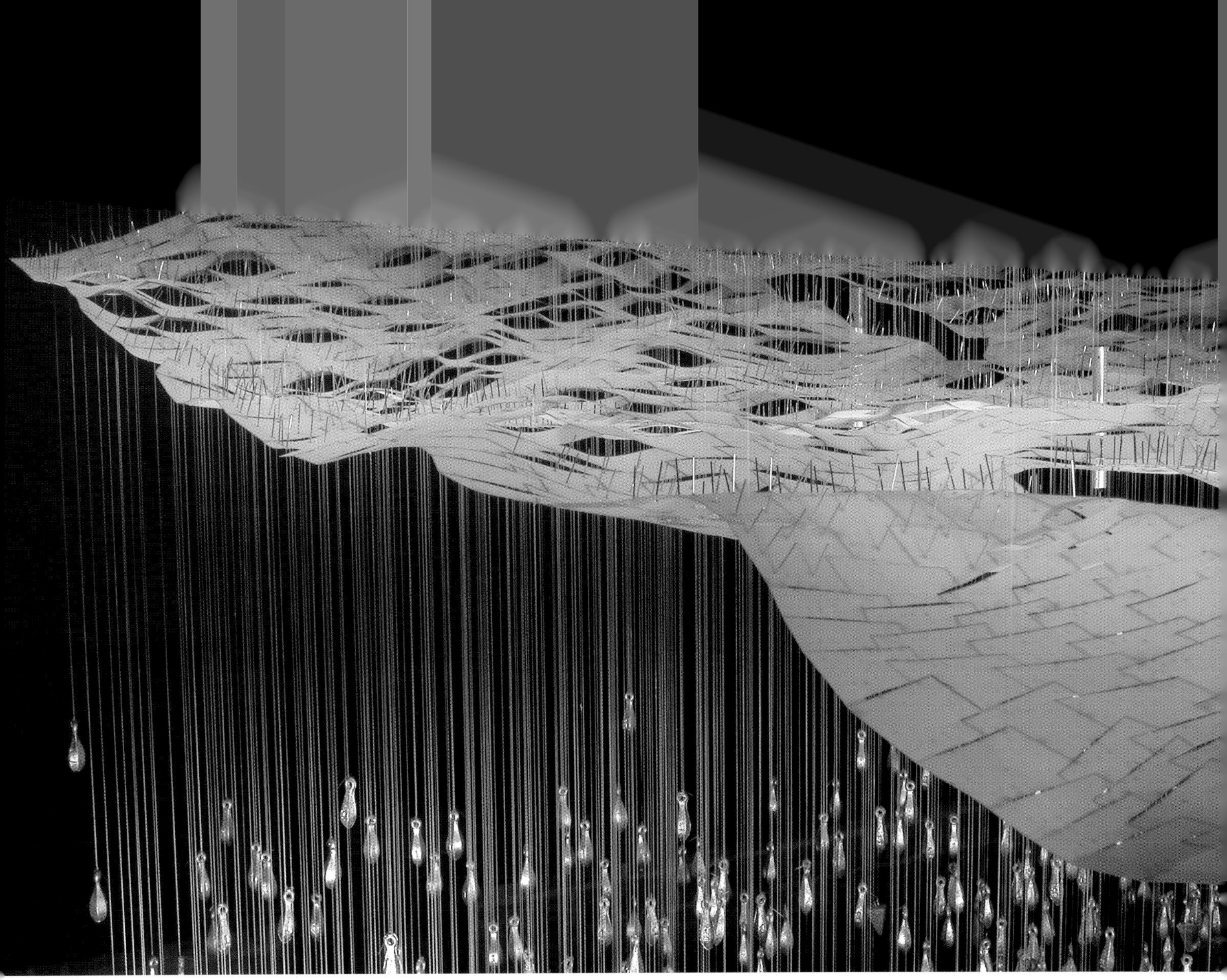

3

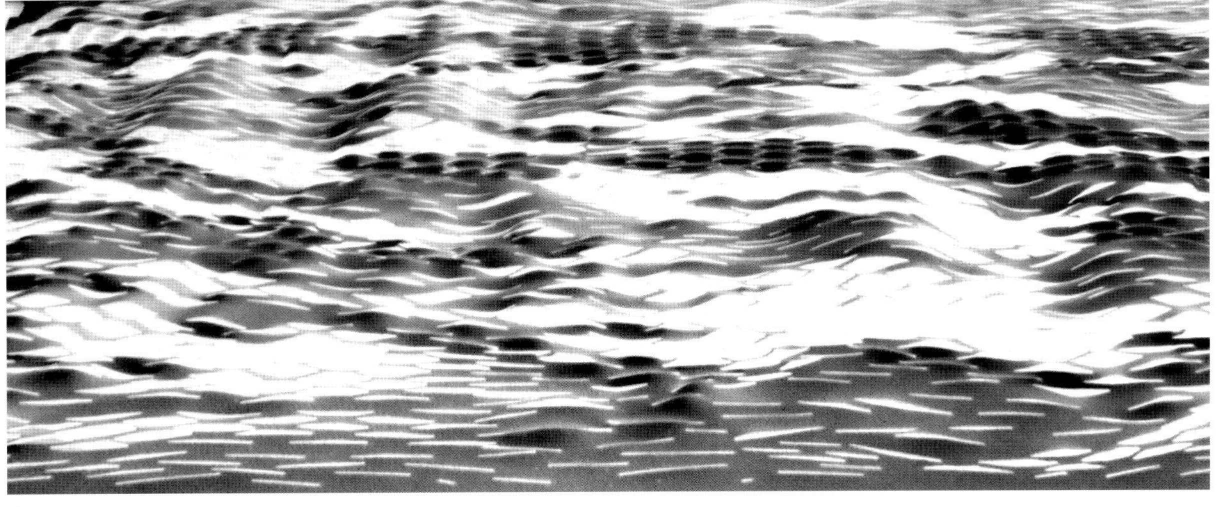

4

## MICHELE OKA DONER b. 1945

*New York City*

1

An orb of diamond-splashed bronze that must be threaded onto a band of ribbon before it is strapped onto a wrist or tied around the neck. Quivering gold tentacles that creep insinuatingly over a bare shoulder or tantalizingly around a clothed breast. A bracelet of bronze grape twigs dappled with discreet diamond buds.

Michele Oka Doner's renowned oeuvre is crowned by *A Walk on the Beach*, a site-specific work created in 1995 for Concourse A of Miami International Airport, in which thousands of cast-bronze starfish, sea worms, and jellyfish are embedded in a stretch of coal-dark terrazzo more than half a mile long. But less known are the Miami Beach–born sculptor's more intimate works of art. She creates gold brooches, bracelets, and necklaces via the lost-wax process, in which wax maquettes are melted away to create highly detailed molds for molten metal. The resulting jewelry rejects the form's traditional passive role as applied ornament and instead embraces its promise as an interpersonal work of art. In short, Oka Doner's jewels carry on intimate dialogues with the woman who wears them, whether they caress the skin like a secret lover or delight the eye with diamonds deeply embedded in a matrix of precious metal.

While their small size and superficially decorative purpose may place them outside Oka Doner's monumental works, her jewels are logical extensions of the artist's fascination with the natural world. Throughout her career, she has removed the earth's detritus—fallen leaves, exotic seeds, strange fruits—from its usual context and arrested its ephemeral qualities in eternal metal. Michele Oka Doner's jewels refine that exploration into a personal message that cannot be misunderstood. When worn, they tap into Everywoman's inner Eve, the Ur-mother, present at the moment of the world's creation. **MO**

1
**BARK SERVER**
Cast silver, 1998
Designer: Michele Oka Doner
In the collection of Dennis Gallion and Daniel Morris

2
**BURNING BUSH**
Candelabrum, 1995
Cast bronze
Designer: Michele Oka Doner

3
**FROND NECKLACE**
18-karat gold, 2000
Designer: Michele Oka Doner
In the collection of Barbara Fleishman

4
**CORAL REEF BRACELETS**
2001
Bronze, pearls (left)
Bronze, diamonds (right)
Designer: Michele Oka Doner for ELP Studio, Rome
In the collection of Vera Graff

5
**BROOCH WITH SEEDS**
18-karat gold, canary diamonds, 1999
Designer: Michele Oka Doner
In the collection of Barbara Tober

Photography: Nick Merrick/Hedrich Blessing

2

4

5

3

## GAETANO PESCE b. 1939

*New York City*

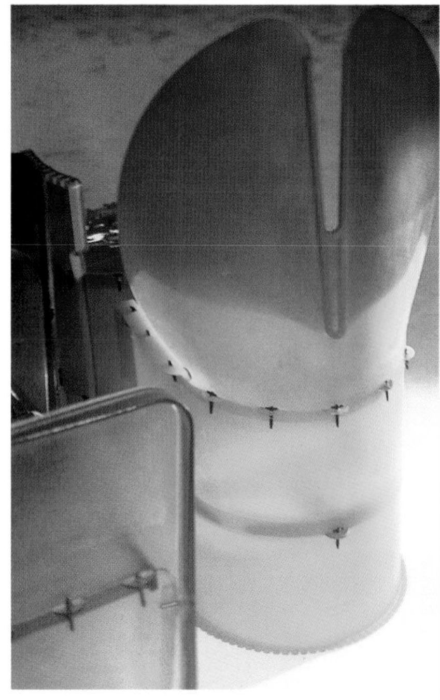

1, 2

In today's design culture, the idiosyncratic and the personal—values that define the seminal work of Gaetano Pesce—have become highly prized. As early as 1971, he pioneered the concept of nonhomogeneous furniture production to encourage variation in the manufacture of each piece.

Thirty years later the influence of Pesce's cult of the imperfect, which finds pleasure and beauty in the flaw, is evident in design practices as diverse as architecture, fashion, and typography. However, his is not a purely aesthetic preference, but a deeply held political position. When mistakes are valued, there is no waste and no worker too unskilled. Environmental impact is lessened and social capital increased.

*13 Goccie Separabili* (13 Separable Drops) is his latest advancement in participatory design. In a new level of collaboration, each worker modifies the proportions and color composition of the pieces they make and, ultimately, sign. The title of the series refers to the large "drops" of liquid resin that harden into furniture components that are assembled with pegs.

In his unbuilt project for the French city of Avignon, Pesce brings his process of modular, crude fabrication to the realm of architecture. Intended as a shop featuring products typical of Provence, Pecse's translucent box requires no separate structural elements, apart from frames for doors and windows. Silicon is poured, like concrete, between planks of plywood, and the boards are removed after the silicon has cured. The result is a proposition for an architecture of the future that is elastic, translucent, and self-supporting, created with the most rudimentary building skills. In this and all his work, Pesce has created a design process and aesthetic that incorporates the random, yet preserves the integrity of his ideas, forging an unlikely alliance of hedonism and humility. **SY**

**1–4**
**I SEPARABILI**
Chairs, 2001
Resin
Designer: Gaetano Pesce
Manufacturer: Zero Disegno
Alessandria, Italy
Photography: Germana Soldano

**5**
**PAVILION FOR THE SOUVENIRS OF PROVENCE**
Architectural model, 1999
Translucent silicon on plywood mold
Designer: Gaetano Pesce
Photography: Courtesy Gaetano Pesce

3, 4

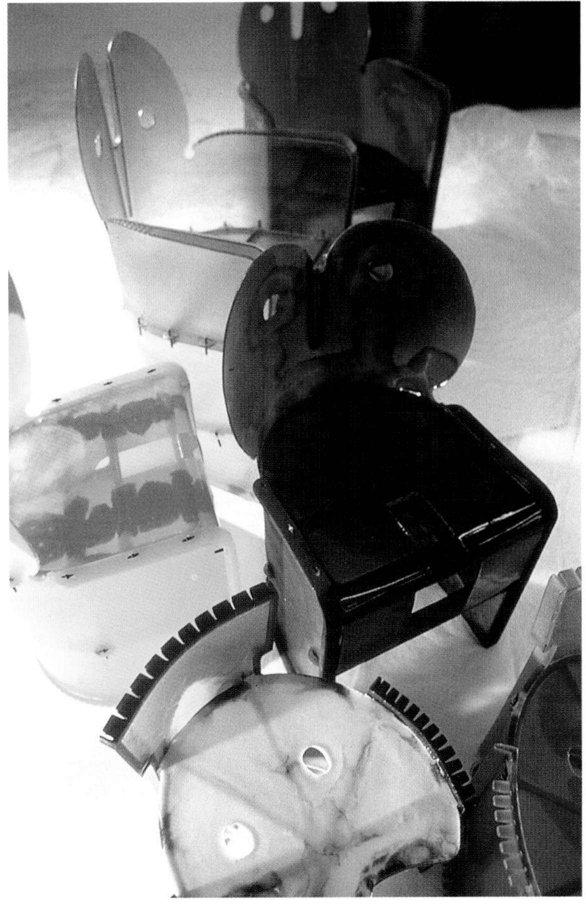

5

ALISON CORNYN b. 1965

SUE JOHNSON b. 1969

## PICTURE PROJECTS

*New York City*

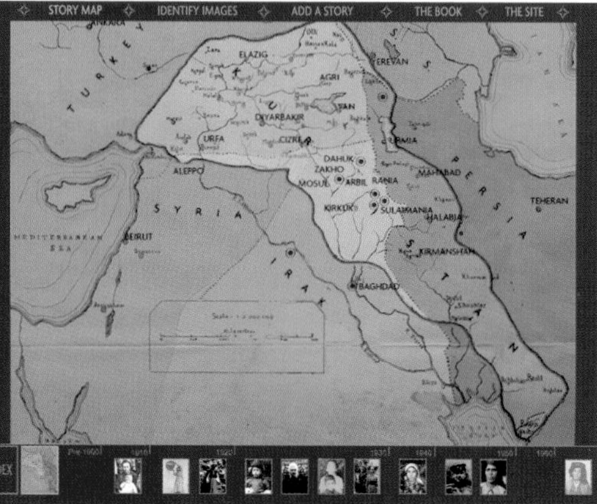


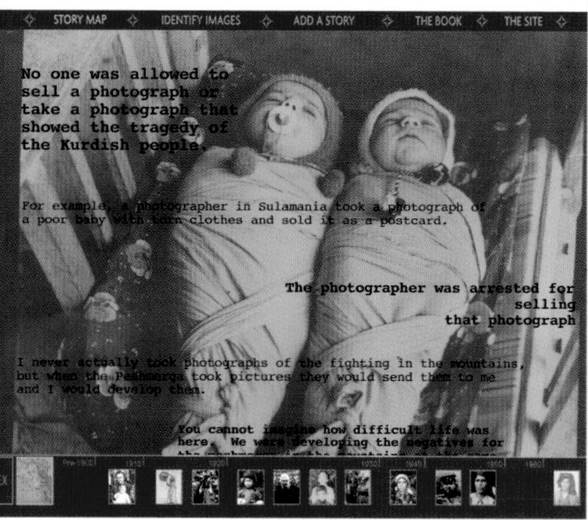


**1–3**

Picture Projects, cofounded by multimedia artists and photographers Alison Cornyn and Sue Johnson in 1995, uses the Web as a documentary medium. Working with other photographers, journalists, and activists, the team explores social issues of national and international significance.

360Degrees.org is an ongoing study of the United States prison system. The site's central component records the "stories" of people whose lives have been defined by jail—prisoners, their families, their victims, and prison workers. The phrase "360 degrees" reflects the site's panoramic photographs of prison cells, courtrooms, intake halls, and other spaces. The photographs indicate the panoptic experiences of total enclosure and surveillance that are fundamental to the prison concept.

The elemental sweep of the circle structures the site's interface, framing the faces of participants as well as marking levels of content. As the site loads, animated rings of white ripple over the deep gray screen, accompanied by the clank of prison doors. Throughout the site, concentric circles suggest confinement as well as the possibility of release. Cornyn comments, "Each choice made by a visitor to the site has a ripple effect. Visitors are asked to place themselves in the 'system.' "

Other sites by Picture Projects include akaKurdistan.com, chronicling the history of the Kurdish people of the Middle East, who have no sovereign territory. Building on Susan Meiselas's book *Kurdistan: In the Shadow of History*, the Website presents photographs of Kurds and their region, annotated with observations by travelers, British officers, Kurds, and others, from the late nineteenth century to the present. Visitors to the site are invited to add their own photographs and help identify pictures.

The astonishing work of Picture Projects exploits the Web's capacity as a responsive, content-rich publishing medium. **EL**

**1–3**
**AKAKURDISTAN**
Website, 1998
Designers: Alison Cornyn and Sue Johnson
Photography: Picture Projects and Susan Meiselas

**4–10**
**360DEGREES.ORG**
Website, 2001
Designers: Alison Cornyn and Sue Johnson
Photography: Picture Projects

**11, 12**
**360DEGREES.ORG**
Panoramic photographs from Website, 2001
Photography: Picture Projects

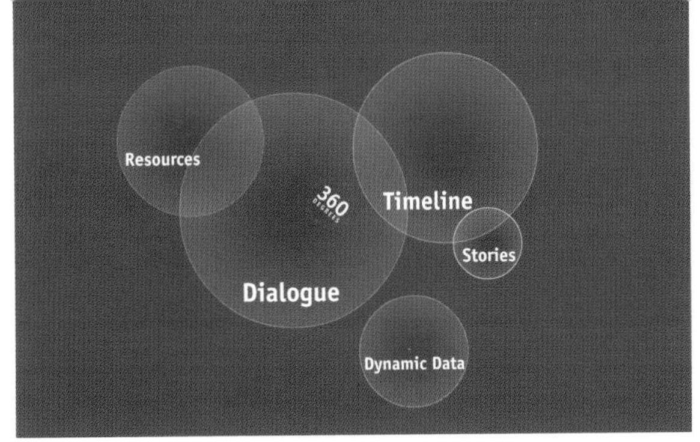
Resources
360 DEGREES
Timeline
Stories
Dialogue
Dynamic Data

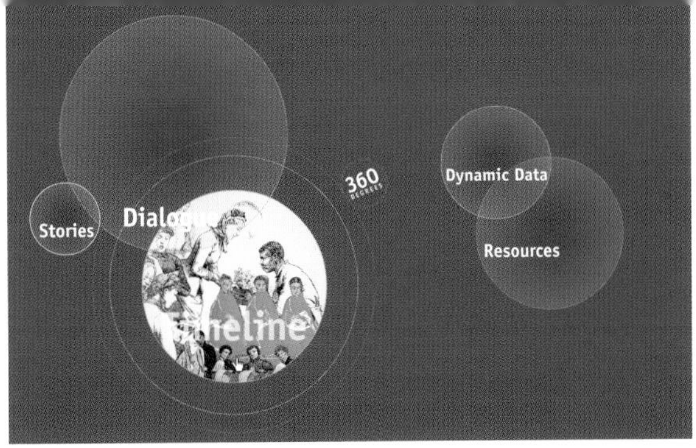
Stories
Dialogue
Timeline
360 DEGREES
Dynamic Data
Resources

4–10

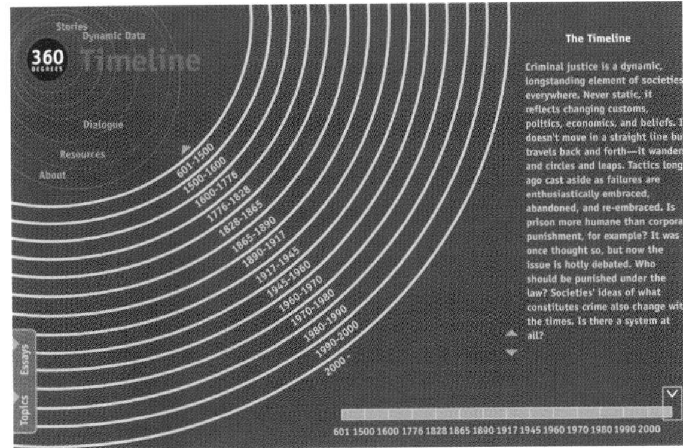
Stories
Dynamic Data
360 DEGREES
Timeline
Dialogue
Resources
About
601-1500
1500-1600
1600-1776
1776-1828
1828-1865
1865-1890
1890-1917
1917-1945
1945-1960
1960-1970
1970-1980
1980-1990
1990-2000
2000 -
The Timeline
Criminal justice is a dynamic,
longstanding element of societies
everywhere. Never static, it
reflects changing customs,
politics, economics, and beliefs. I
doesn't move in a straight line bu
travels back and forth—it wander
and circles and leaps. Tactics long
ago cast aside as failures are
enthusiastically embraced,
abandoned, and re-embraced. Is
prison more humane than corpora
punishment, for example? It was
once thought so, but now the
issue is hotly debated. Who
should be punished under the
law? Societies' ideas of what
constitutes crime also change wit
the times. Is there a system at
all?
Essays
Topics
601 1500 1600 1776 1828 1865 1890 1917 1945 1960 1970 1980 1990 2000

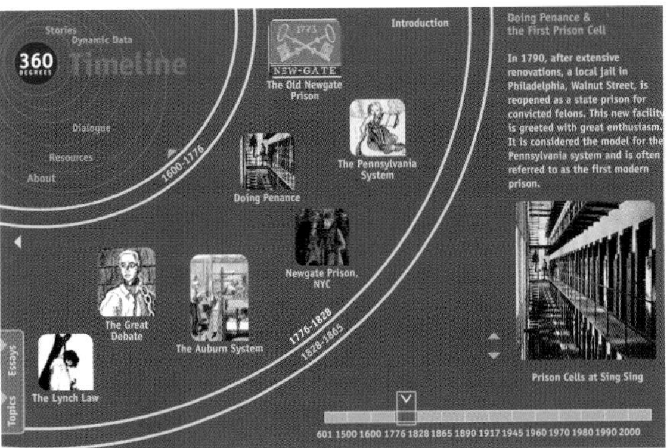
Stories
Dynamic Data
360 DEGREES
Timeline
Dialogue
Resources
About
The Old Newgate Prison
Introduction
The Pennsylvania System
Doing Penance
Newgate Prison, NYC
The Great Debate
The Auburn System
The Lynch Law
1600-1776
1776-1828
1828-1865
Doing Penance &
the First Prison Cell
In 1790, after extensive
renovations, a local jail in
Philadelphia, Walnut Street, is
reopened as a state prison for
convicted felons. This new facility
is greeted with great enthusiasm.
It is considered the model for the
Pennsylvania system and is often
referred to as the first modern
prison.
Prison Cells at Sing Sing
Essays
Topics
601 1500 1600 1776 1828 1865 1890 1917 1945 1960 1970 1980 1990 2000

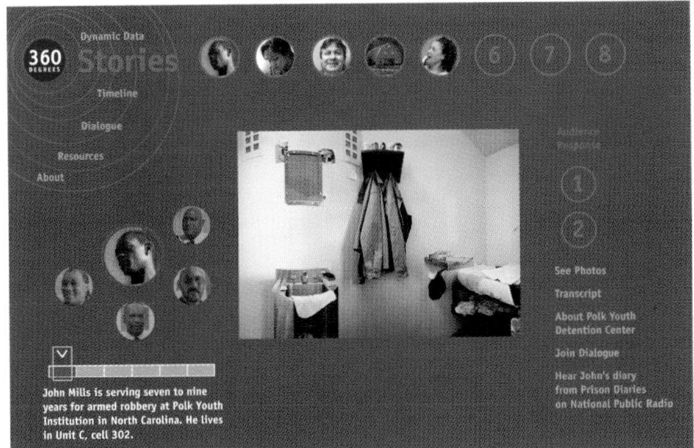
Dynamic Data
360 DEGREES
Stories
Timeline
Dialogue
Resources
About
6
7
8
1
2
See Photos
Transcript
About Polk Youth
Detention Center
Join Dialogue
Hear John's diary
from Prison Diaries
on National Public Radio
John Mills is serving seven to nine
years for armed robbery at Polk Youth
Institution in North Carolina. He lives
in Unit C, cell 302.

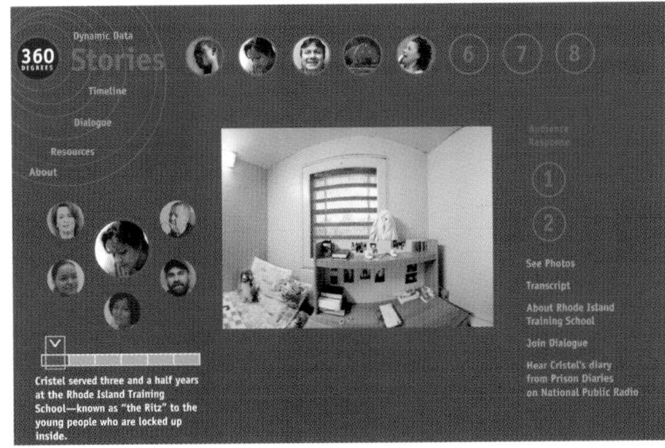
Dynamic Data
360 DEGREES
Stories
Timeline
Dialogue
Resources
About
6
7
8
1
2
See Photos
Transcript
About Rhode Island
Training School
Join Dialogue
Hear Cristel's diary
from Prison Diaries
on National Public Radio
Cristel served three and a half years
at the Rhode Island Training
School—known as "the Ritz" to the
young people who are locked up
inside.

5, 6

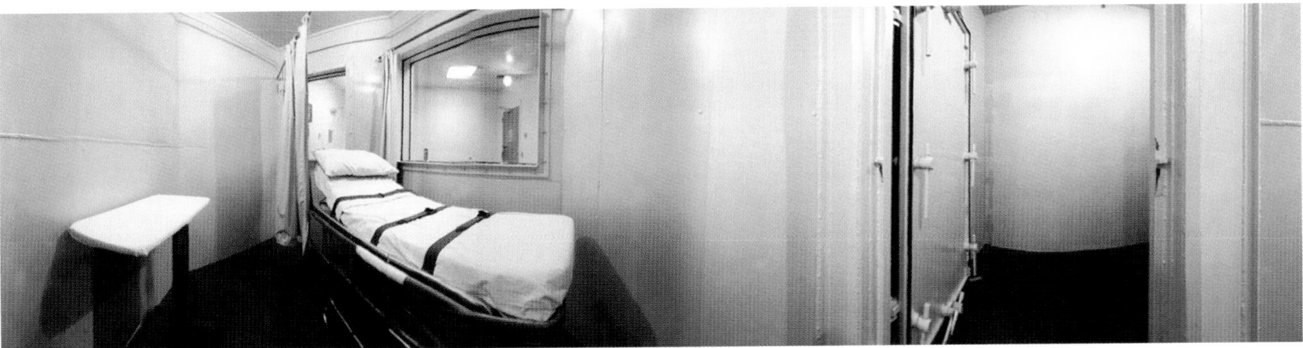
11, 12

## MARK POLLACK b. 1954

POLLACK

*New York City*

1

Mark Pollack combines a genius for technique and an unerring eye with a deep understanding of the richness inherent in woven cloth. An artist who studied weaving at the Rhode Island School of Design (RISD) in the 1970s, Pollack is now the design director of his eponymous fabric company, founded fifteen years ago. Pollack produces what might be best described as crossover textiles. What began as a contract furnishings business has grown to include an elegant line of residential fabrics.

Truly designed, not styled, this fabric is the product of integrated material engineering and a highly developed aesthetic. With Flapper, Pollack breaks the dimensional barrier of textiles flatland. Extra wide looms are repurposed to produce a diaphanous, three-dimensional textile that appears to have extensions sewn to it, but, in fact, is a single fabric with no less than seventeen edges, or selvages.

In the end, however, tour-de-force technique is the silent partner in a material marriage. For in truth, we respond to what we can see. And with Pollack's fabrics for windows the visual rewards are especially rich. Light filters through the floating lines of Strand, creating shadows with its sinuous pattern. Ravenna's tiled surface glows like the ancient mosaics of its namesake. Woven with reflective threads, Pollack's window fabrics are a light source onto themselves. An entire line of textiles—including Flapper and Strand—was inspired by the RISD Museum's historic fashion collection in a generous homage to Pollack's alma mater.

Mark Pollack's commitment to experimentation in a field known for its pragmatism is quite extraordinary. A full 20 percent of his designs are never realized—a design investment repaid in full by the stunning beauty of those that are. **SY**

1
**RAVENNA**
Silk, polyester, 2002
Design team: The Pollack Studio
Manufacturer: Pollack

2
**DOUBLE TAKE**
Polyester, cotton, 2002
Design team: The Pollack Studio
Manufacturer: Pollack

3
**PEEKABOO**
Linen, viscose, slk, polyester, Lurex polyester, 2002
Design team: Mark Pollack and The Pollack Studio
Manufacturer: Pollack

4
**FLAPPER**
Polyester, cotton, 2002
Design team: Mark Pollack and The Pollack Studio
Manufacturer: Pollack

5
**STRAND**
Polyester, polyamide nylon, 2002
Design team: Mark Pollack and The Pollack Studio
Manufacturer: Pollack

Photography: Maryanne Solensky

2, 3

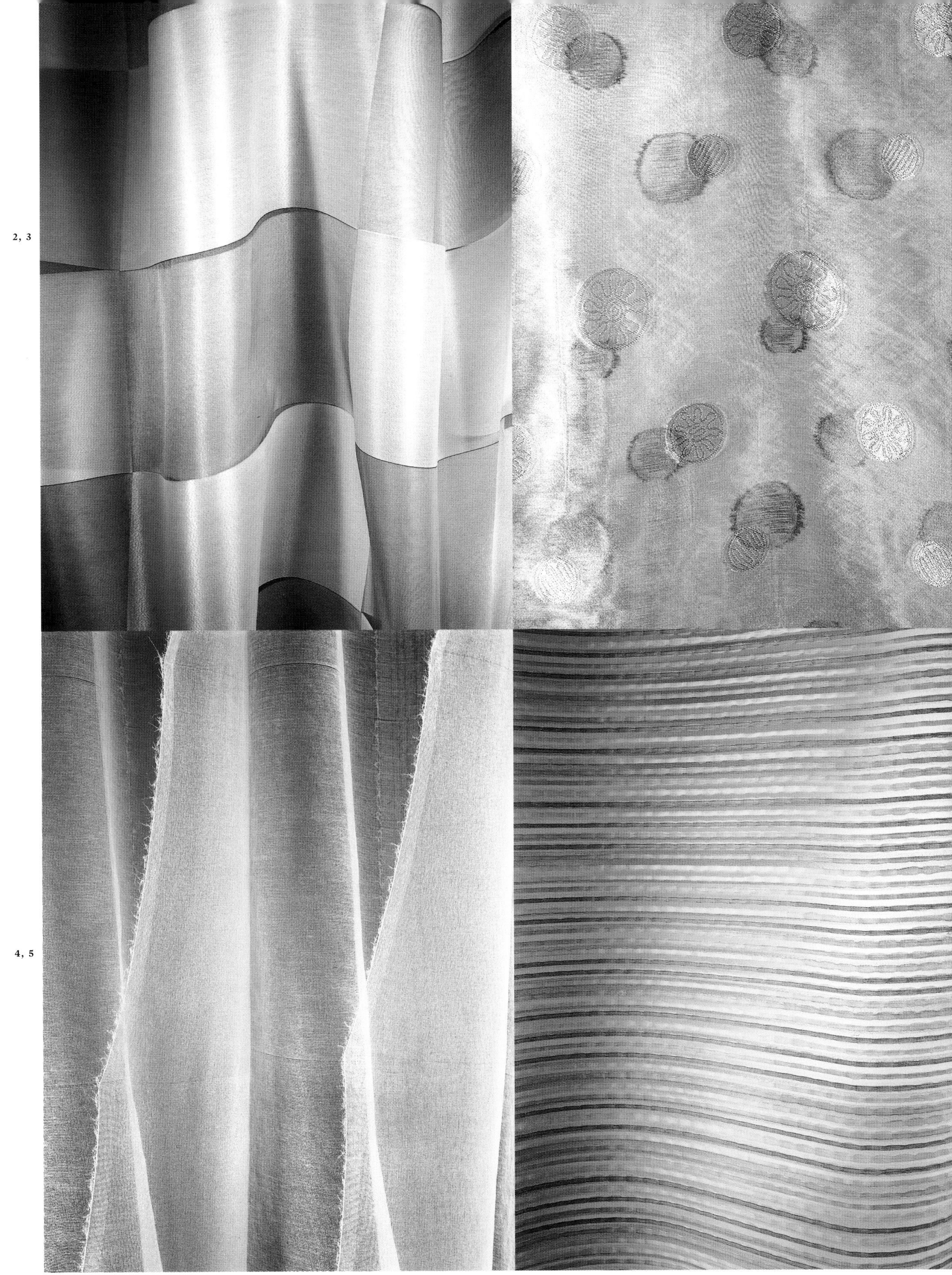

4, 5

## MICHAEL RAKOWITZ b. 1973

*Baltimore*

1

Air is the medium chosen by sculptor Michael Rakowitz for three recent projects he describes as both "radical design research" and "a subtle form of cultural agitation." For paraSITE, an ongoing effort he launched in 1997 to provide individual homeless shelters in Boston and New York, Rakowitz works with homeless people to design tent structures that he makes and gives away. Costing $5 each, ParaSITEs are made of a double membrane of garbage bags, inflated and heated via an inner network of tubes connected to the air ducts and steam vents of nearby buildings. A social critique of—and, Rakowitz admits, a Band-Aid solution to—a national problem, paraSITE led to the lighthearted Climate Control. This contraption of fans and sheet-metal ducts at the PS1 art center in Queens, New York, was, the artist says, "an absurd, autonomous, self-perpetuating machine" that maintained ideal climactic conditions for its own preservation.

Neighborhood preservation was the goal of Rise, created by Rakowitz for a show in a Manhattan Chinatown building whose owners wanted to replace community centers with high-rent art galleries. Rakowitz helped subvert their efforts with an exterior duct that brought the smells of food preparation from a ground-floor bakery into the rarified art world above.

Rakowitz's sculptures are an intervention in existing, overlooked spaces that offer metaphors for power and cultural politics. Rise achieved what he calls "a critique of gentrification through the innocence of smell." The paraSITE shelters attracted controversy because, when former Mayor Rudolph Giuliani was seeking to eliminate homelessness from New York's streets, they provided warmth and shelter and were powered by air that Rakowitz terms "an extension of private property." (Many police let the homeless stay.) Not unlike air, Michael Rakowitz's works at first seem invisible but gain potency as we recognize their social acuity. **DA**

**1**
**RISE**
Installation in New York City, 2001
Flexible aluminum duct, fan
Designer: Michael Rakowitz

**2, 3**
**PARASITE**
Inflatable shelter, 2000
Polyethylene tubing
Designer: Michael Rakowitz

**4, 5**
**CLIMATE CONTROL**
**INTERIOR AND EXTERIOR VIEWS**
Installation at P.S. 1 Contemporary Art Center, New York City, 2001
Galvanized steel duct, fans
Designer: Michael Rakowitz

Photography: Michael Rakowitz

**2, 3**

**4, 5**

## BOB SABISTON b. 1967

FLAT BLACK FILMS

*Austin*

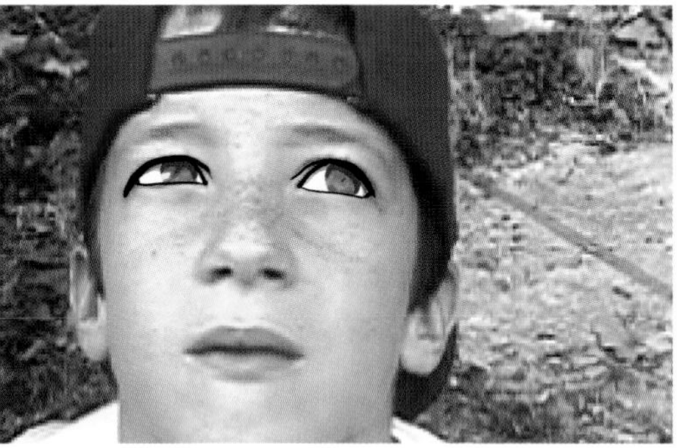

1–3

Most animators make drawings come alive. In a kind of digital second coming, Bob Sabiston flips that equation, bringing real people to life through drawing. With proprietary software, he has reinvented the century-old technique of rotoscoping—the process of tracing over film images of live actors. The movement is unmistakably human, the surface blatantly artificial, the effect uncanny.

The in-between state conjured by Sabiston's animation proved the perfect vehicle for Richard Linklater's 2001 feature film *Waking Life*. Protagonist Wiley Wiggins slips in and out of sleep, caught up in a mesmerizing series of philosophical conversations, rants, and raves. The script's metaphysics and the floating sensation of dreaming are mirrored in the imagery of the film. Characters—drawn in flat, camouflagelike patterns of color—move like real people inhabiting unstable skins.

Like *Waking Life, Snack and Drink,* Sabiston's short about an autistic child, has an intentionally jittery quality that both complements his subject matter and reflects his process. Advancing frame by frame, the animator chooses which sections of live-action footage to trace. Using an interpolation feature, the computer fills in the in-between frames. The more drawing or tracing of the original footage, the more accurate the movement feels. Reduce the number of frames traced and you increase the feeling of flow, or what Sabiston calls "computer smoothness."

Backed by acres of algorithms, Sabiston has realigned the tension between the visual and the narrative in animated film. He embeds the motion of his hand into the movement of his characters and spawns a new species of motion pictures. **SY**

**1–3**
**STEP BY STEP**
**TREVOR SEQUENCE**
Film stills showing process of animation, 2000
Designer: Bob Sabiston
Photography: Richard Linklater

**4**
**WAKING LIFE**
Animation still, 2000
Designer: Bob Sabiston
Photography: Richard Linklater

**5, 6**
**SNACK AND DRINK**
Animation stills, 1999
Designer: Bob Sabiston
Photography: Tommy Pallotta

4

5

6

## STANLEY SAITOWITZ b. 1949

*San Francisco*

1

After more than twenty-five years in practice, Stanley Saitowitz stills hews to a singular architectural vision. Whether designing a series of luxurious houses, urban lofts, or a campus laboratory—three recent projects that represent his diverse range—Saitowitz's work remains rooted in its formal properties, and he approaches each new commission with a straightforward look. "The essential medium of architecture," Saitowitz has said, "is space: a void to be filled with life."

Rather than seek singular and unusual shapes, Saitowitz designs buildings by adopting an aesthetic of simple, repetitive forms, like minimalist sculpture. His serial technique is evident in the row of six glass towers he designed for the Holocaust Memorial in Boston and in the gridded facade and finned brise soleil at his Energy Efficiency and Electricity Reliability building at the University of California, Berkeley. For the Yerba Buena Lofts Saitowitz conceived a dynamic honeycomb of concrete and glass modules that evokes both the vernacular buildings in the surrounding industrial neighborhood as well as the visual density and verticality of the city's famous Victorian "painted ladies."

Saitowitz's "bar" houses apply his approach to a group of projects. Confronted with a profusion of residential commissions at the peak of the Bay Area's dot-com economy in the 1990s, Saitowitz created a single spatial module (one-story tall and about 20-feet wide) that stacks, curves, and interlocks. Facades alternate between closed and open, translucent and transparent. Interior spaces, loggias, and walled courtyards frame views of the spectacular Napa Valley landscape. Stanley Saitowitz's work demonstrates the rewards of both an architecture based on form and purpose and a professional commitment to staying the course. **DA**

**1**
**YERBA BUENA LOFTS**
San Francisco, 2001
Designer: Stanley Saitowitz
Client: YBL LLC, Ed Transev
Photography: Tim Griffith

**2–4**
**BAR HOUSES:**
**DAVIS, VITERBI, AND**
**SLEEPY HOLLOW RESIDENCES**
Digital renderings, 2001
Designer: Stanley Saitowitz
Renderings: Stanley Saitowitz

**5, 6**
**ENERGY EFFICIENCY AND**
**ELECTRICITY RELIABILITY BUILDING**
Berkeley, CA, 2001
Digital renderings
Designer: Stanley Saitowitz
Client: Lawrence Berkeley Labs
Renderings: Stanley Saitowitz

2

3

4

5, 6

## PAULA SCHER b. 1948

PENTAGRAM

*New York City*

1

For over three decades, Paula Scher has designed posters, packages, publications, and identities that use typography in a richly popular way—her work can be at once witty and decorative, contemporary and Victorian. One of her obsessions is to cover a surface with letterforms, as seen in recent projects that apply text to buildings.

Lucent Technologies Center for Arts Education is a school of the arts in Newark, New Jersey. Scher chose to paint the building white and cover it with words, declaring to the public the activities studied inside: dance, music, theater, drama. Scher decreed every surface worthy of inscription, even the duct work. Her exterior signage for the Peter Norton Symphony Space in New York uses more elaborate materials to emblazon a building with its purpose. Here, letters cut out of the stainless steel awning (designed by architect James Polshek) are illuminated via fiber optics.

In her designs for hallways and public areas in the New 42nd Street Studios and Duke Theater, also in New York, Scher overstates the obvious—for dramatic effect. Huge letters, wrapping from the floor onto the walls, announce elevators, stairs, and restrooms. Modestly produced with paint and laser-cut linoleum, the graphics take their cue from stage directions chalked on the floor for actors. Scher has also created large-scale exterior signage for the building.

Over the past several years, Scher has produced a series of map-based paintings that are densely covered with lettering. In these works, text becomes intimate and handmade, and landscapes become tapestries of text. One imagines the scale of Scher's alphabetic compulsion expanding to cover the entire globe. **EL**

**1, 2**
**LUCENT TECHNOLOGIES CENTER FOR ARTS EDUCATION**
Newark, New Jersey, 2001
Architectural graphics
Designer: Paula Scher
Client: New Jersey Performing Arts Center

**3**
**PETER NORTON SYMPHONY SPACE**
New York City, 2002
Architectural graphics
Designer: Paula Scher
Client: Symphony Space

**4, 5**
**THE NEW 42ND STREET STUDIOS AND DUKE THEATER**
New York City, 2002
Architectural graphics
Designer: Paula Scher
Client: The New 42nd Street

Photography: © Peter Mauss/ESTO

2

MUSIC
THEATER
DANCE
POETRY
DRAMA
WRITING
CATHEDRAL HOUSE

3

PETER NORTON
symphonyspace
BROADWAY
W 95ST
ONE WAY
7AM-7PM
FAMILY
WALL TO WALL
MUSIC
FILM
THEATRE
SELECTED SHORTS
EDUCATION
LITERATURE
DANCE

ELEVATOR
FLOOR
3

4, 5

## JENNIFER SIEGAL b. 1965

OFFICE OF MOBILE DESIGN

*Los Angeles*

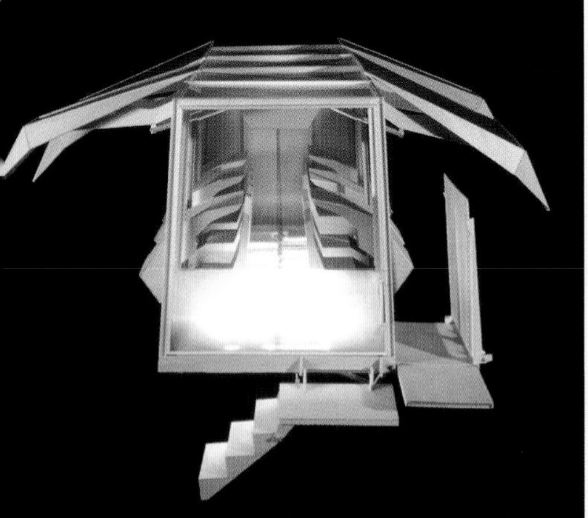

1–3

Owning your own home is the American dream, but for many it's compromised when the only affordable choice is a trailer. Rethinking the mobile home is Jennifer Siegal's dream.

Designing compact, flexible environments comes naturally to Siegal. It's part of her family tradition. Her grandfather had a hot-dog cart, and two generations later she did too. So for Siegal, her deployable ZEVO Kiosk was more a logical step than a leap. Originally designed as a bicycle-driven locksmith shop, Siegal has turned it into a bookmobile for the *National Design Triennial*. Reconfigured and renamed as Storehouse, the winged vehicle serves as a display for Siegal's models and a bookstall dedicated to publications on mobile design.

Like the portable library, much of the work of Siegal's Office of Mobile Design, has an educational objective. The Mobile EcoLab is a community-based project that is an important, fully realized precedent for Siegal's ambitions to redefine prefabricated housing, one of the fastest growing industries in the U.S.

Siegal's prototype Portable House offers a critical alternative to the stereotypes associated with mobile housing and the poverty of form that afflicts it. Siegal's proposed iMobile proves that sometimes a room is more useful than a house. A roving computer lab designed to bring cyberspace to the neighborhood the old-fashioned way—on wheels—the iMobile is a direct response to the ever-widening technology gulf between the haves and have-nots.

Direct is the operative word. A proponent of design-build architecture, Siegal is in sync with a burgeoning grassroots, do-it-yourself movement among designers across the country who are looking for ways to inject the personal into the social. **SY**

1
**IMOBILE**
Model, 2000
Design team: Jennifer Siegal,
Elmer Barco, Arona Witte, Ashley Moore
Photography: Benny Chan

2
**ECOLAB EXTERIOR**
Steel/aluminum trailer, plastic,
wood, recycled building elements, 1998
Design team: Jennifer Siegal, Ausencio Ariza, Larry Cheung, Thomas Cohen, Tinifuloa Grey, Chayanon Jomvinya, Jody Segraves
Manufacturer: Woodbury University, Los Angeles, Design/Build Studio
Photography: Benny Chan

3
**PORTABLE HOUSE**
Steel, insulated panels, polygal, homasote, metal siding, 2001
Design team: Jennifer Siegal, Elmer Barco, Thao Nguyen, Jon Racek
Photography: Office of Mobile Design

4, 5
**STOREHOUSE**
Mobile book kiosk
Concept rendering for installation, 2002
Designers: Jennifer Siegal, Kelly Bair
Commissioned by Cooper-Hewitt, National Design Museum
Renderings: Office of Mobile Design

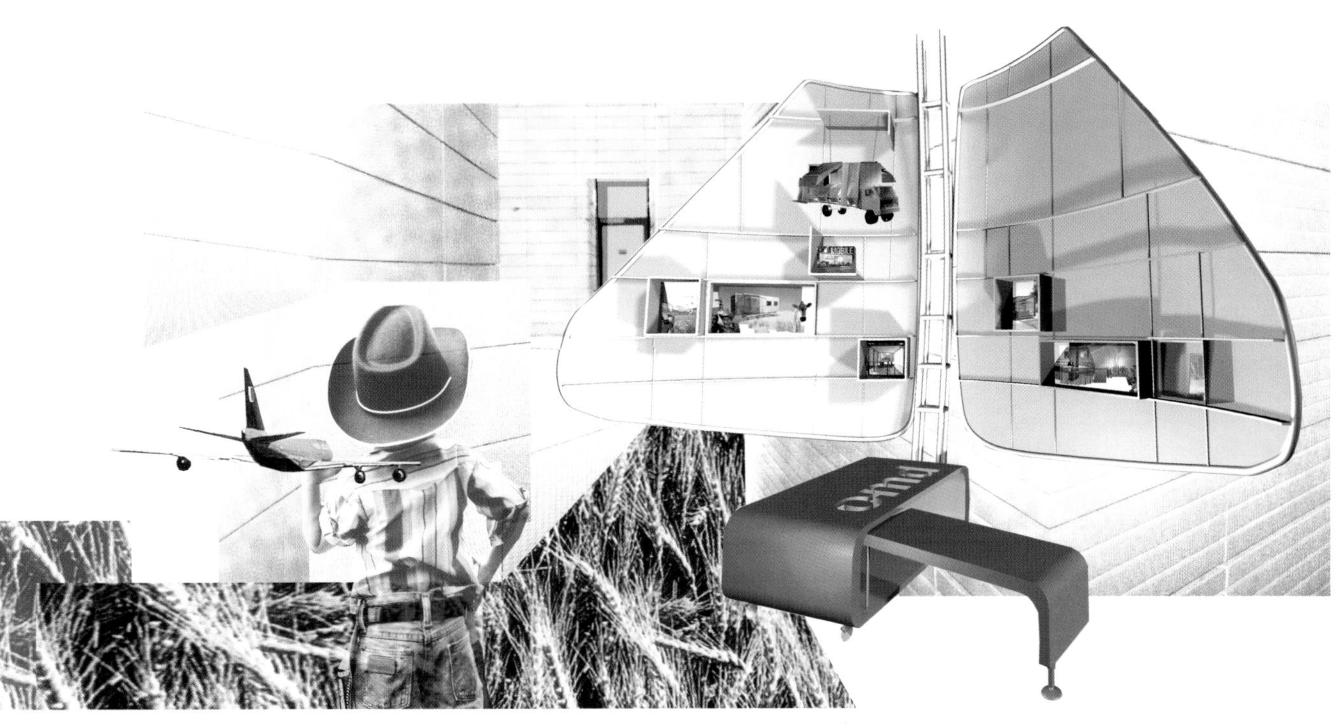

**4, 5**

## SMART DESIGN

*New York City and San Francisco*

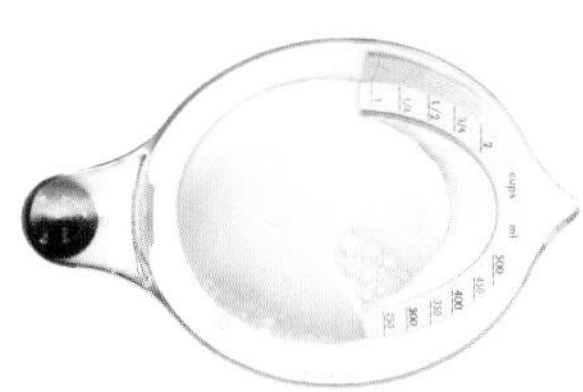

1

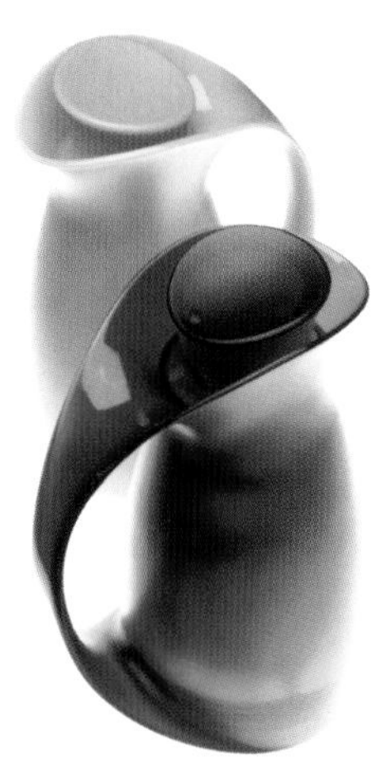

2

Simplicity of purpose plus a nuanced attitude equals designs that have changed the way we live. And what better creative team to accomplish this than one called Smart Design? Founded in 1979 by Davin Stowell, this bicoastal design consultancy—its offices are in New York City and San Francisco—has affected society in the most profound of ways. And for most of us, Smart Designs have become part of our everyday domestic landscape. They are discreet, enjoyable, user-friendly, and, in a curiously backhanded compliment, overlooked. Plaque-seeking toothbrushes that fit the curve of the user's hand, easy-to-operate juicers, ergonomic kitchen tools with soft-rubber grips: Smart Design's creations are precisely what's advertised—design that is intelligent, conscientious, democratic, stylish.

Among the firm's latest creations is an angled measuring cup for Smart Design's award-winning Good Grips collection for OXO International. Typical measuring cups require eye-level accuracy, but the version created by Smart Design members Goeran Jerstroem and Mark Prommel allows precise liquid measurements to be determined by looking into the cup rather than at the markings on its side. Designer Scott Henderson recently created a colorful plastic thermal carafe, part of a collection of industrial-strength serveware commissioned by WOVO. And Smart Design's transparent blue plastic soap dish for OXO can be mounted wherever you like, thanks to a tough suction-cup attachment that eliminates the need for frustrating and invasive tools.

Rounded, sensual, and practically unbreakable, Smart Design's products bring suave elegance to our homes. But reading too much into any company's work is a constant danger. Sometimes a coffeemaker is just a coffeemaker. As Smart Design founder Davin Stowell has repeatedly said, "A great design has nothing more than it needs to do the job." **MO**

1

**OXO ANGLED MEASURING CUP**
Injection-molded SAN, injection-molded santoprene, 2001
Designers: Goeran Jerstroem, Mark Prommel, Bang Zoom Design
Photography: Nao Tamura

2

**WOVO THERMAL CARAFES**
Injection-molded SAN, injection-molded clear ABS, 2001
Designer: Scott Henderson
Photography: Scott Henderson

3

**CUISINART COLLECTION**
Coffeemaker, tea steeper, hand blender, 1999
Injection-molded polypropylene, ABS, kyton, glass
Designers: Scott Henderson, Tucker Viemeister, Steve Vordenberg

4

**HEWLETT-PACKARD 3400C SCANNER**
Injection-molded polypropylene, injection-molded ABS, glass, thermoplastic, 2000
Designers: Scott Henderson, Allen Zadeh

5

**OXO SUCTION-CUP SOAP DISH**
Injection-molded PVC, 2001
Designer: Scott Henderson

Photography: Michel Gastl except as noted

Cuisinart
Cuisinart
Cuisinart
Perfect Tea™
Steeper

3

4

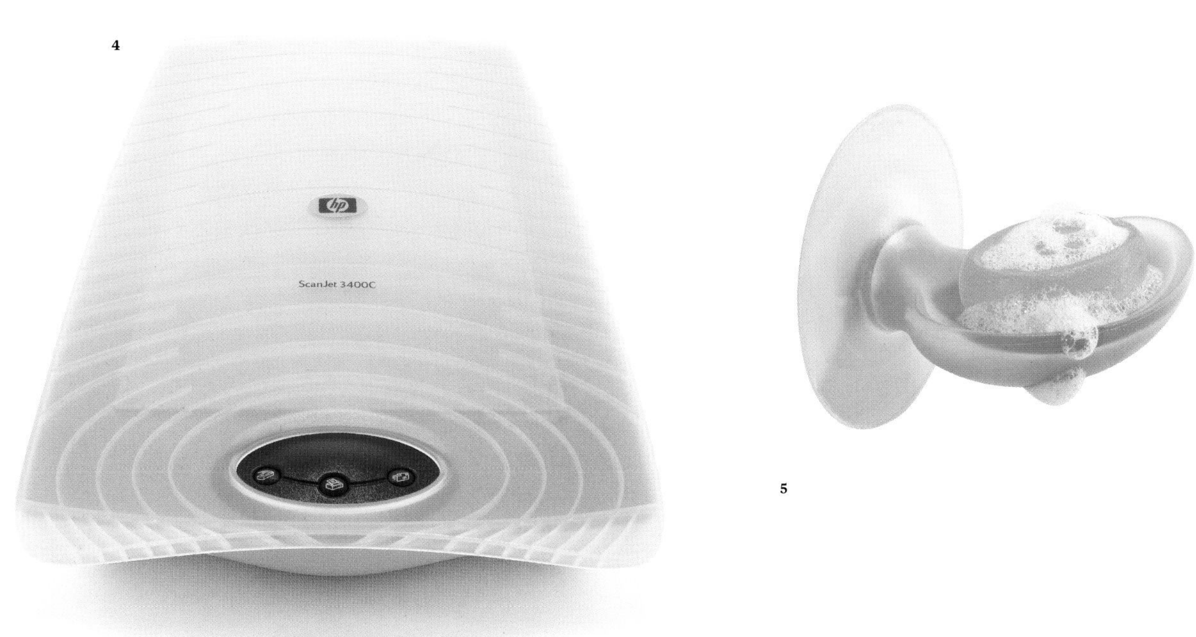
hp
ScanJet 3400C

5

## PAIGE STAHL b. 1975

HOME COOKED DESIGN

*Gloucester, Massachusetts*

1

Social consciousness and the creative spirit don't often combine wit with elegance. But designer Paige Stahl has managed that feat with the kind of aplomb that can elude talents twice her age.

Her 2001 graduation project for the Parsons School of Design is quite literally one of the brightest ideas in recent years: a floor lamp that is suavely conceived, amusing to look at, and environmentally sensitive. Called Lumenair, it is composed of a smoothly finished, attentuated raw-wood base topped with a large frosted polycarbonate planter. Nestled between the legs of the lamp is a glass vial of water, the lifegiving liquid carried to the roots of the plants via a hydroponic wick that also doubles as an on-off cord. Turn the lamp on, and you can bask in a dappled, meditative light inspired by the sun filtering through leaves. Turn the lamp off, and the plant continues to nourish itself, requiring only a periodic refilling of the vial. It is low-anxiety, high-performance gardening at its finest. But best of all is the lamp's built-in beneficial science: The plant's natural respiratory system traps and filters airborne impurities, leaving the air in the room more healthy to breathe than before Lumenair's introduction into the environment.

Stahl's creation may seem impossibly simplistic to some observers, little more than a naive parlor trick or a collegian's amusing conceit. But Lumenair's power lies in its perfect logic, a thoughtful sensibility that infuses Stahl's cork-stoppered, minimalist ceramic vessels that reflect purity of form and joy of use—values that likewise inform her paper-thin Fiberlites votives, candleholders that look like woven fabric but are actually cunningly textured porcelain. **MO**

**1, 3**
**FIBERLITES**
Porcelain votives, 2002
Designer: Paige Stahl
Photography: David Rye

**2**
**LUMENAIR**
Lighting, 2001
Bleached mahogany, polycarbonate, rubber, living plant
Designer: Paige Stahl
Photography: David Rye

2

3

## CHRISTOPHER STRENG b. 1971

*Sheboygan Falls, Wisconsin*

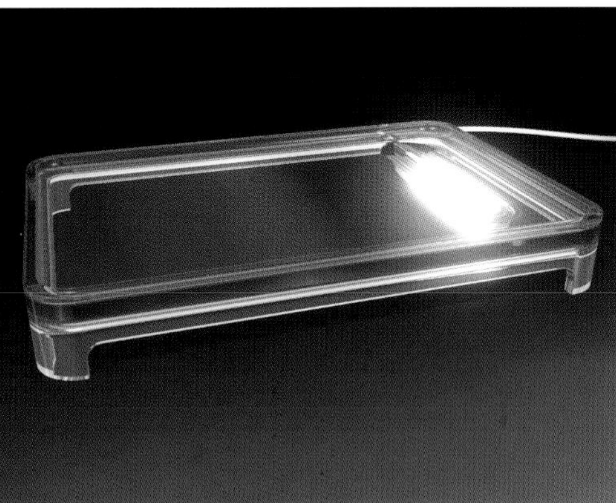

1, 2

In a letter to a friend, the great German playwright and philosopher Johann Wolfgang von Goethe once declared that architecture was frozen music. American designer Christopher Streng, plainly on the same wavelength nearly two centuries later, has called his creations "frozen emotion." Not frigidity, mind you, but emotion arrested, captured in an eternal instant, preserved forever, inviolate. Pressing that point, Streng—a graduate of the Milwaukee Institute of Art & Design and a design consultant for Kohler, the Wisconsin plumbing and furniture manufacturer, and Magis—has long imbued his products with anthropomorphic missions: a chair that basks in "pride and dedication"; a chandelier that "gives you her soul"; a clock described as, among other things, "loving, sinister, encompassing, unforgiving, healing."

Behind Streng's mystical narratives, however, is an increasing array of startlingly beautiful examples of futuristic furniture and accessories. The most recent are arguably Aristotelian in their logic and simplicity. A minimalist wall light made of a slab of clear cast resin that encases a single fluorescent circlet suggests an illuminated block of ice. An even thinner slab of clear resin, also embedded with a fluorescent light source, is molded into a footed tray with vaguely Asian overtones. The LoLa lounge and ottoman, in reinforced plastic, complement the cultural dominance of brilliant transparency in the home-electronics industry, their opaque white surfaces and carnal-pink underbellies as alluring as the latest laptop and as smoothly crafted as a bit of Fabergé enamel. And Streng's Ubu stool is an icon in waiting, a hollowed chunk of sturdy colorful foam or composite plastic that can be used as a seat, a table, or a totem, its open center serving, perhaps, as a portal to some imagined beyond. **MO**

1
**TRAY LIGHT**
Cast resin, compact fluorescent light source, 2001
Designer: Christopher Streng
Photography: Courtesy Streng Studio

2
**WALL LIGHT**
Cast resin, compact fluorescent light source, 2001
Designer: Christopher Streng
Photography: Courtesy Streng Studio

3
**UBU STOOLS**
Composite plastic or flexible foam, 2001
Designer: Christopher Streng
Photography: Blue Moon Studios

4
**LOLA LOUNGE AND OTTOMAN**
Reinforced plastic, 2001
Designer: Christopher Streng
Photography: Streng Studio

3

4

## DANIEL STRENG b. 1968

*Oak Park, Illinois*

1, 2

The brother and sometime design partner of Christopher Streng, Daniel Streng has a vision that is similar but different. Both are drawn to biomorphic design, but whereas his younger sibling's creations openly ride an emotional current, Streng the elder talks persuasively of the interaction between man and object. "Products must be made of love and reason, unique but not extreme, textural and contextual, mythical and logical," he recently explained on a Japanese Website. A graduate of the Milwaukee Institute of Art & Design and a cofounder of Mobas—an international design collaborative—Daniel Streng transforms the merely useful into sublime experiences.

His dazzling Airlight would do any Surrealist proud, a ceiling fixture composed of a single bulb suspended inside a clear polypropelene bag, a veritable lung of luminosity dangling from a polycarbonate tube or a precious treasure secured in a protective bubble. The spreading, comforting seat of the designer's Satellite barstool curves gently and insinuatingly around the sitter's thighs and buttocks, holding him aloft like a kind of offering atop an ultraslim tower of cast aluminum and molded plastic. Streng's plainly titled Low Chair, on the other hand, contains the restless energy of a pup in its tense, anticipatory legs and the aerodynamic attitude of a race car in its angled back. Surprisingly, all that personality is packed into a minimum of design. The Low's silhouette is nothing more than a wafer-thin cutout of composite resins casually shaped into an object for daily living. **MO**

1, 2
**AIRLIGHTS**
Lighting fixtures, 1999
Polypropolene bag, polycarbonate tube
Designer: Daniel Streng
Photography: Douglas Fogelson

3
**SATELLITE BARSTOOLS**
Digital rendering, 1998
Cast aluminum, composite tube, molded plastic
Designer: Daniel Streng
Rendering: Streng Design

4
**LOW CHAIR**
Composite resins, 2001
Designer: Daniel Streng
Photography: Nate Estanson

3

4

GABRIEL CARLSON b. 1975

DEETTE DEVILLE, M.D. b. 1972

BART HANEY b. 1975

SHARON ROSENFELD b. 1975

EDWIN ROSES b. 1974

DAVE SHERMAN b. 1973

HAYES URBAN b. 1974

## SUPERHAPPYBUNNY

*Los Angeles*

Is there anything SuperHappyBunny doesn't do or want to do? Espousing a modest, cheerful goal to take "routine activities," in the words of co-founder Bart Haney, and "brighten them up a bit," this seven-person collective keeps piling on members, design disciplines, and business strategies. Five graduates of Pasadena's Art Center College of Design started the self-described "idea foundry" in 2000. Today, SuperHappyBunny's enterprises include products such as furniture, clothing, and media.

The group's irreverent style-on-a-shoestring sensibility is exemplified by Haney's simple and economical Neo-Amish line of chairs and sofas. Two chairs can be produced from a single 4 x 8–foot sheet of birch plywood with only 7 percent wasted material. Shipped flat, the furniture can be assembled by the consumer without nails, screws, or glue. The purchaser fits the chairs together with a "bunny banger," a plywood clamp that wraps around a Campbell's soup can (not included) to form a toylike hammer. In another project, the Bunnies do Campbell's one better with their self-heating can. A surrounding liquid-filled insulating layer heats the soup with the push of a button.

Disposable food containers also inspire furniture. For the Special #8 table—an oversized, illuminated, acrylic Chinese food takeout box—SuperHappyBunny developed a strategy they plan to extend to other products. The group licensed the Special #8 table from designer Dino Alzadon, engineered the product for production, generated its marketing strategy, and designed sophisticated graphics and instructions. Although SuperHappyBunny operates on artists' budgets, the collective, like its forever-propagating namesake, aims to relentlessly introduce new design objects to the world. "We're like comfort food," Bunny Hayes Urban says, "for those people lucky enough to have horrible jobs." **DA**

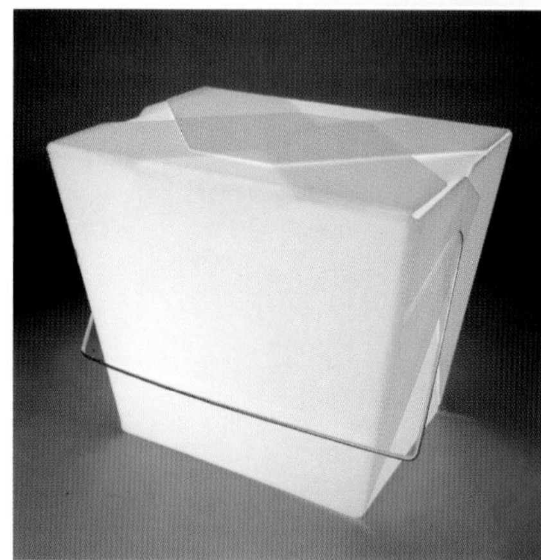

**1, 2**

1
**SELF-HEATING CANS OF SOUP: 3 PACK**
Packaging prototype, 1999
Steel, melamine, tomato soup
Designer: Bart Haney
Photography: Bart Haney

2
**SPECIAL #8**
Lighting/table, 2001
Milk acrylic, stainless steel, lightbulb
Designers: SuperHappyBunny with Dino Alzadon
Manufacturer: SuperHappyBunny
Photography: SuperHappyBunny

3
**NEO-AMISH CHAIR INSTRUCTIONS**
Diagram describing assembly of furniture system, 2000
Designers: SuperHappyBunny with Greg Chapuisat
Photography: SuperHappyBunny

3

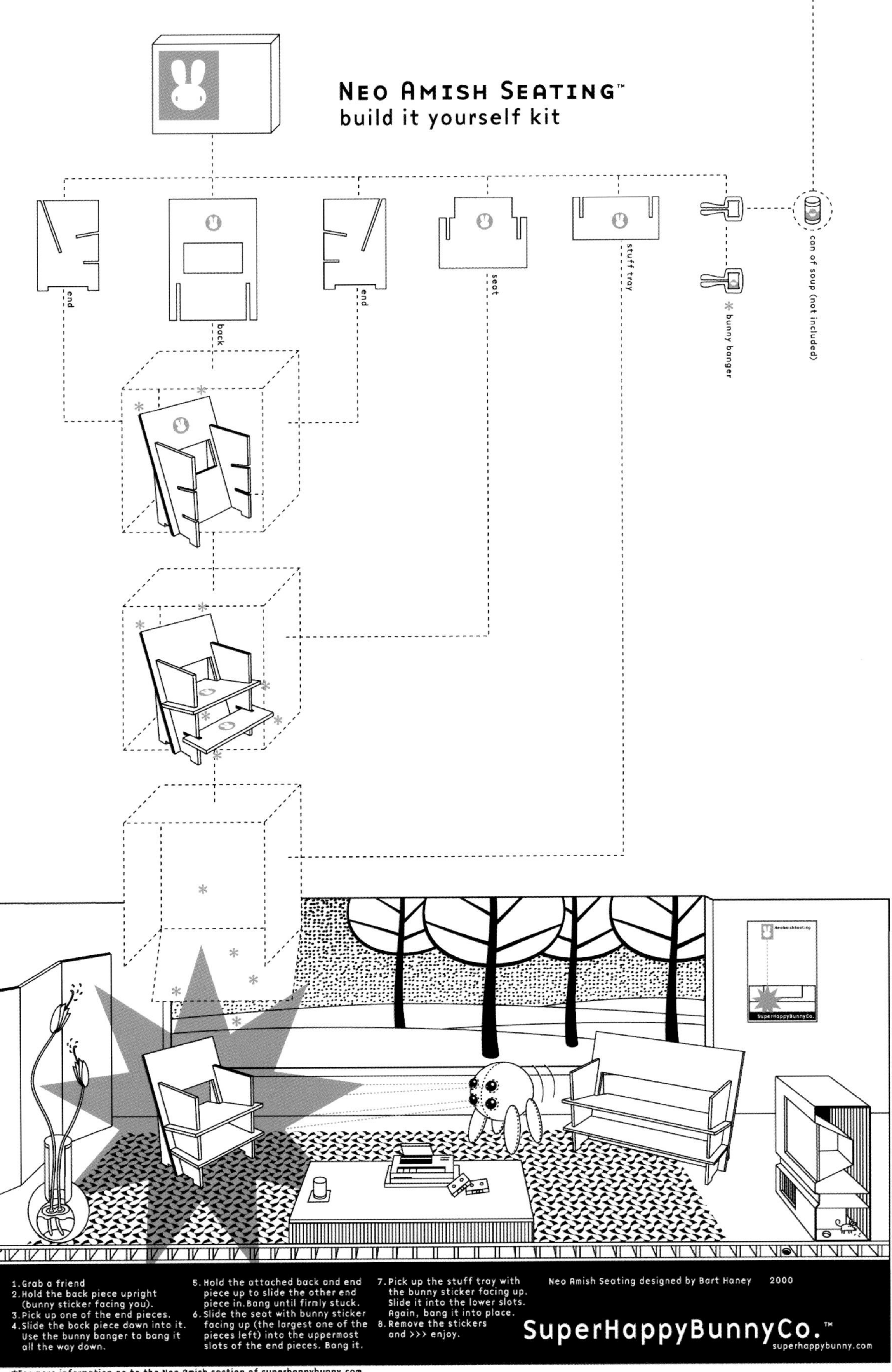
Neo Amish Seating™
build it yourself kit
end
back
end
seat
stuff tray
* bunny banger
can of soup (not included)
1. Grab a friend
2. Hold the back piece upright (bunny sticker facing you).
3. Pick up one of the end pieces.
4. Slide the back piece down into it. Use the bunny banger to bang it all the way down.
5. Hold the attached back and end piece up to slide the other end piece in. Bang until firmly stuck.
6. Slide the seat with bunny sticker facing up (the largest one of the pieces left) into the uppermost slots of the end pieces. Bang it.
7. Pick up the stuff tray with the bunny sticker facing up. Slide it into the lower slots. Again, bang it into place.
8. Remove the stickers and >>> enjoy.
Neo Amish Seating designed by Bart Haney 2000
SuperHappyBunnyCo.™
superhappybunny.com
*For more information go to the Neo Amish section of superhappybunny.com

## TARGET CORPORATION

*Minneapolis*

1, 2

In Target's print and television advertising campaigns, ordinary objects and familiar consumer brands become icons of a hip consumer paradise.

It all began with the campaign "Sign of the Times," launched in 1999 and conceived by the ad agency Peterson Milla Hooks, located in Minneapolis, Target's corporate hometown. The agency saw Target's bull's-eye logo as a simple, powerful form that could define the store's advertising. In the campaign, the symbol overtakes every conceivable surface, from wallpaper and clothing to the eye of a bull terrier.

One ad converts a suburban backyard into a red and white stage where sleek, bottle-blond models pose as members of a simulated family. The grass isn't greener here—it's red. A little boy kicks a (red) ball through the (red) circle of a garden hose, the objects forming a giant target. Nobody in this Photoshop montage is touching, or even looking at one another. What holds their world together is the brand. The ad pokes fun at the idealized American marketing images of the 1950s and 1960s, whose depictions of happy families enjoying the mass-produced bounty of consumerism were equally false, but without the sense of irony.

Target Corporation has a house advertising agency that coordinates the work of independent agencies located around the country. One campaign promotes Target's sense of style alongside its low prices by clothing elegant figures in domestic objects—a lampshade becomes a pleated skirt. In "Blue," Target joins forces with Charmin, Scope, and other manufacturers whose goods or packaging feature a deep sky blue. A coiffed male model gazes lovingly at his own reflection, shooting himself with a bottle of Windex. Branding itself emerges as the star of this bright and shiny universe. **EL**

1
**SIGN OF THE TIMES: SKIER**
Advertisement, 2002
Agency: Peterson Milla Hooks
Art director: Carl Byrd
Creative director: Dave Peterson
Photography: Kenneth Willardt
Art director and creative director (at Target): Minda Gralnek

2
**FASHION AND HOUSEWARES: LAMPSHADE**
Advertisement, 1997
Agency: Kirshenbaum Bond + Partners
Art director: Scott McDonald
Creative director: James Hickcock
Photography: Dewy Nicks



3
**COLOR YOUR WORLD: BLUE**
Advertisement, 2001
Agency: Peterson Milla Hooks
Art/creative director: Dave Peterson
Associate creative director: Amie Valentine
Photography: Myers Robertson
Product photography: Jake Armour
Art director and creative director (at Target): Minda Gralnek

4
**SIGN OF THE TIMES: BARBECUE COUPLE**
Advertisement, 2000
Agency: Peterson Milla Hooks
Art/creative director: Dave Peterson
Associate creative director: Amie Valentine
Photography: Myers Robertson
Art director and creative director (at Target): Minda Gralnek

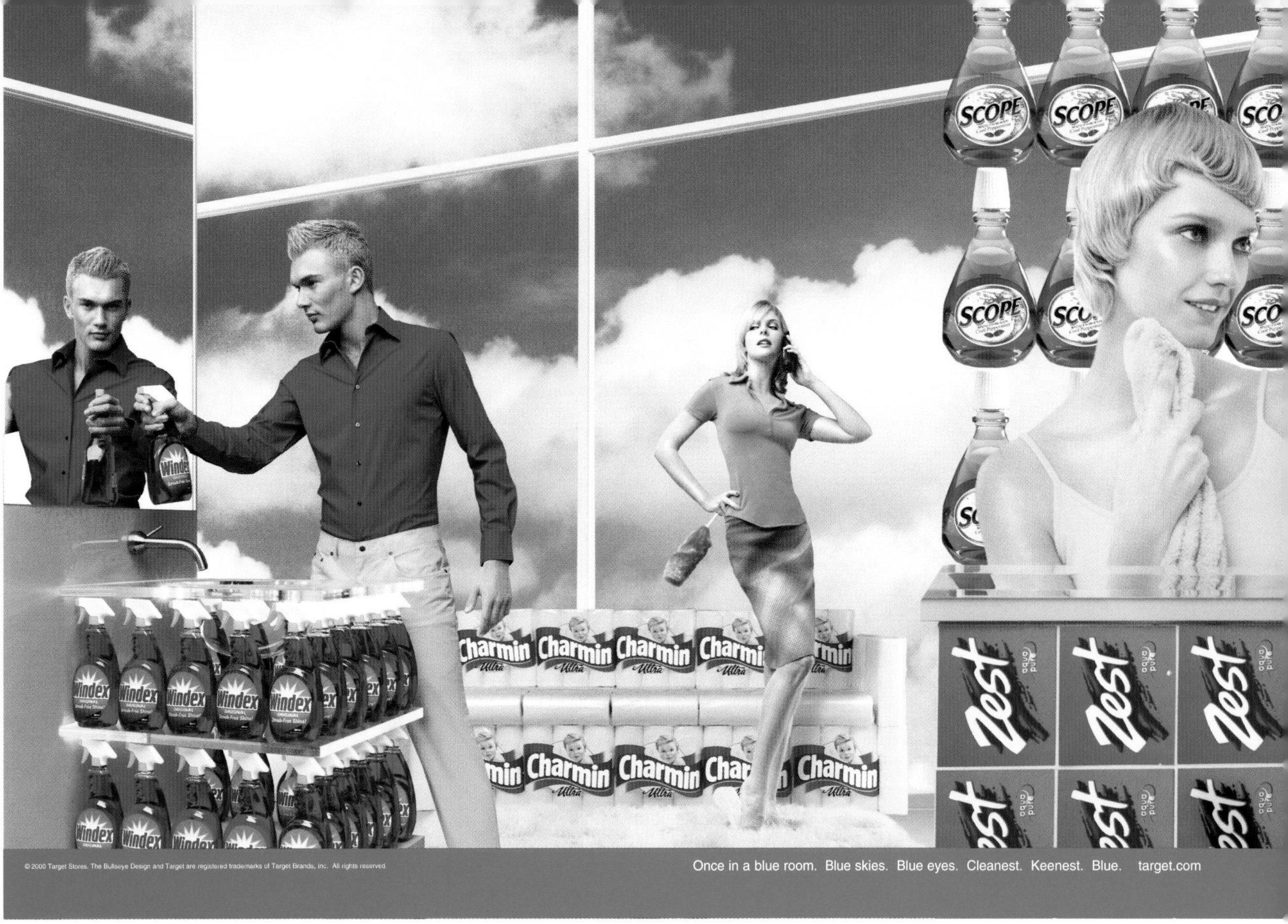
SCOPE
Windex
Charmin
Ultra
Zest
© 2000 Target Stores. The Bullseye Design and Target are registered trademarks of Target Brands, Inc. All rights reserved.
Once in a blue room. Blue skies. Blue eyes. Cleanest. Keenest. Blue. target.com

3

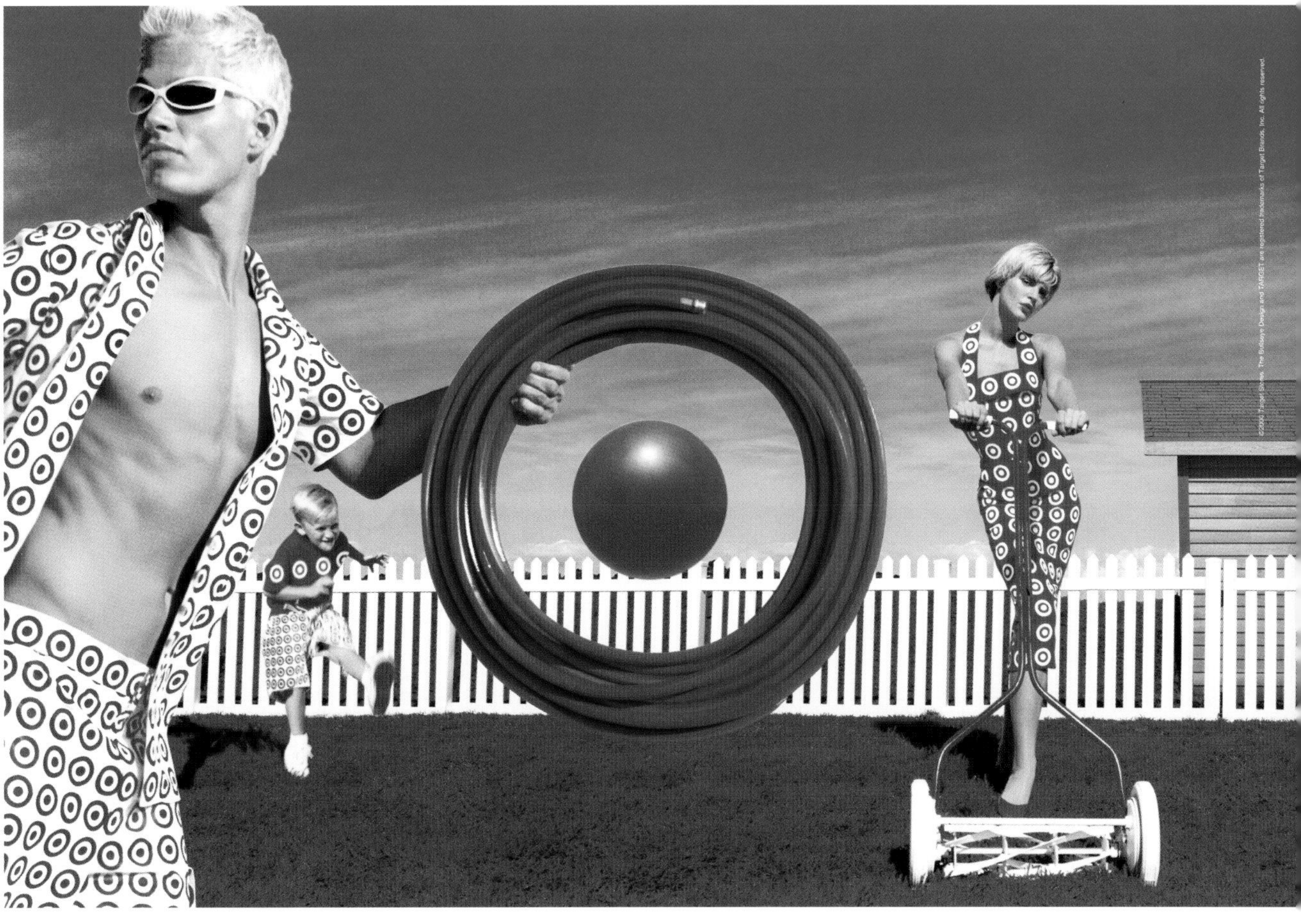
©2000 Target Stores. The Bullseye Design and TARGET are registered trademarks of Target Brands, Inc. All rights reserved.

4

JENNIFER TIPTON b. 1937

*New York City*

1

Darkness is rarely far away in Jennifer Tipton's lighting. In three decades of working in theater, dance, ballet, and opera, today's preeminent lighting designer shapes chiaroscuro effects that punctuate and move dramatic action, but that also suggest, as critic Adam Gopnik has noted, the metaphoric power of art to illuminate the human condition. "Through the formal use of light," Tipton believes, "we can shape the way that we see the world and therefore the way we think about that world."

Light itself is the subject of one of Tipton's most stunning endeavors for New York City's avant-garde Wooster Group. One element in *House/Lights* retells the story of Gertrude Stein's 1938 play *Doctor Faustus Lights the Lights*, in which Faust sells his soul to the devil to give the world electric light. "We've destroyed the night with the invention of electricity," Tipton says, "and it is a sin." Expressing the centrality of light to the story, Tipton's design comprises a wide array of on-stage fixtures, from videos to long fluorescent light boxes and blazing incandescent bulbs hanging from a metal bar. In the pivotal light-begetting scene, one of the characters reaches out for one of these mammoth, blinding globes, like the tantalizing apple in the Garden of Eden.

Tipton often rejects color as a too-easy way to achieve dramatic effects, focusing instead on the purity of light and dark. From the icy pale-blue light of the somber jail in *Richard III* (Yale Repertory Theater) to the opulent white glow of a dining room in *Hansel and Gretel* (Lyric Opera of Chicago) and the shimmering, complex mirror-and-frame effects in *To You, the Birdie* (Wooster Group), Jennifer Tipton demonstrates the expressive range of light, the medium she describes as "this extraordinary stuff of no substance that 'dreams are made on.'" **DA**

1
**HOUSE/LIGHTS**
Theater production, 1999
Wooster Group, New York City
Lighting designer: Jennifer Tipton
Director: Elizabeth LeCompte
Photography: Mary Gearheart

2
**TO YOU, THE BIRDIE**
Theater production, 2002
Wooster Group, New York City
Lighting designer: Jennifer Tipton
Director: Elizabeth LeCompte
Photography: Mary Gearheart

3
**HANSEL AND GRETEL**
Opera production, 2001
Lyric Opera of Chicago
Lighting designer: Jennifer Tipton
Director: Richard Jones
Photography: Robert Kusel

4
**RICHARD III**
Theater production, 2000
Yale Repertory Theater, New Haven
Lighting designer: Jennifer Tipton
Director: Stan Wojewodski, Jr.
Photography: Charles Erickson

2

3

4

## ISABEL TOLEDO b. 1960

TOLEDOTOLEDO

*New York City*

1

Isabel Toledo is a radical classicist. Continuously extrapolating from a strikingly original core of ideas, her clothes are mathematical hybrids executed in endless permutations of circles and triangles. Her earliest pieces were explicitly architectonic, made of full-bodied fabrics that created space around the body. When she introduced jersey into her work in 1989, using the very same patterns, that geometry collapsed into a new way of draping.

In her volumetric work, Toledo creates what she calls “air play” around the body to make the wearer *feel* sexy. The jersey pieces are intended to make the wearer *look* sexy. Toledo continues to play off these two poles. Her Hermaphrodite dress brings two notions of sexuality—the hard and the soft—into closer harmony. Fabric is gathered at the seams, alternately grazing the body and expanding into sculptural volumes; “breasts” are added and legs disappear. However, Toledo is not writing feminist tracts in cloth as much as reveling in the sensual possibilities of her medium. Indeed, her work has a generous pragmatism to it. Her knit T-Shirt Wedding Gown has the capacity to conform to any body type—let it be known that Toledo likes tummies—without sacrificing a whit of elegance.

Just as most of design is the product of epiphanies that launch the constant work of refinement, Toledo’s collections don’t change as much as they mature. She refuses to be held hostage to the seasons and the accompanying ritual of shows. Toledo has been sewing since she was eight years old in Cuba. She has been in the fashion business since 1985 when she and her husband, artist Ruben Toledo, began selling her work out of their Hell’s Kitchen apartment through his signature watercolors. But Isabel Toledo has always been a designer. **SY**

1
**T-SHIRT WEDDING GOWN**
Fabric detail, 2000
Cotton lisle
Designer: Isabel Toledo
Photography: Goran Vejvoda

2, 3
**HERMAPHRODITE DRESS**
**BACK AND FRONT VIEWS**
Silk, 2002
Designer: Isabel Toledo
Photography: William Palmer

2, 3

DALE EVERETT b. 1956

MATTHIEU LEBLAN b. 1969

DAN PAPPALARDO b. 1960

## TROIKA DESIGN GROUP

*Los Angeles*

1

The logo for ABC television, consisting of rounded, Bauhaus-inspired letters framed in a circle, was created by Paul Rand in 1962. At that time, modernist designers used geometric forms to convey a sense of universal, omniscient power. Now, the goal of broadcast design is to stay fresh and relevant in a market no longer dominated by three big networks.

Rand's original logo still lives on-screen today, occupying a dynamic environment of animated dots that can function as arrows, punctuation, spotlights, abstract patterns, or connect-the-dot portraits. Rows of dots rush onto the screen, forming a simple illusion of deep space; two circles meet up with a triangle to become a movie projector. All graphics are rendered in a minimal palette of black, white, and golden yellow. Flat fields of color are paired with black-and-white still photographs, which make the network's stars seem genuine and accessible.

The ABC 2001–2002 Primetime identity was designed and produced at Troika Design Group in conjunction with the production company Wall/Everett.* Troika's other projects include the on-screen identity for VH1's *Late World with Zach*, a music-centered talk show whose blunt, low-tech titles and promotional spots reinforce host Zach Galafianakis's slouchy, nerdy persona. The show's Hollywood location is filmed as a gritty, urban area filled with harshly-lit billboards and all-night diners. In one spot, Zach sneaks into a parking garage and jumps up and down in front of the camera. A yellow stripe painted on the wall matches a stripe on his shirt. In this deadpan, delightfully dumb sight gag, a modernist design element—the stripe—is wielded for comic effect.

Troika's *Late World* identity uses no-nonsense humor and style to attract the younger viewers coveted by advertisers. The ABC identity attempts to deliver that same audience to a network giant. **EL**

1
**LATE WORLD WITH ZACH**
Television graphics, 2002
Design company: Troika Design Group
Creative director: Dan Pappalardo
Designer: Matthieu LeBlan
Executive producer: Chuck Carey
Producer: Holly Bakarich
Associate/line producer: Steiner Kierce
Editor: John Burridge
Photographer: Beth Herzhaft
Client: VH1, Hollywood, California

2
**ABC PRIMETIME**
Television graphics, 2001–2002
Design company: Troika Design Group
Creative director: Dan Pappalardo
Designer: Matthieu LeBlan
Producer: Debra Kaufman
Animators: Jeremy Alcock, Jens Mebes
Editor: John Burridge
Music: Mad Bus Music
Production company: Wall/Everett; Dale Everett, creative director, Marty Wall, executive producer
Live action production company: Johnson Burnett
Client: ABC Entertainment Television Group
Photography: Norman Jean Roy

* Previous seasons were designed and produced at Pittard Sullivan with the leadership of Dan Pappalardo (now at Troika) with Dale Everett and Marty Wall (now at Wall/Everett). The color palette and casual, humorous tone of the current identity builds upon the 1998 advertising campaign "TV is Good," created by Chiat/Day.

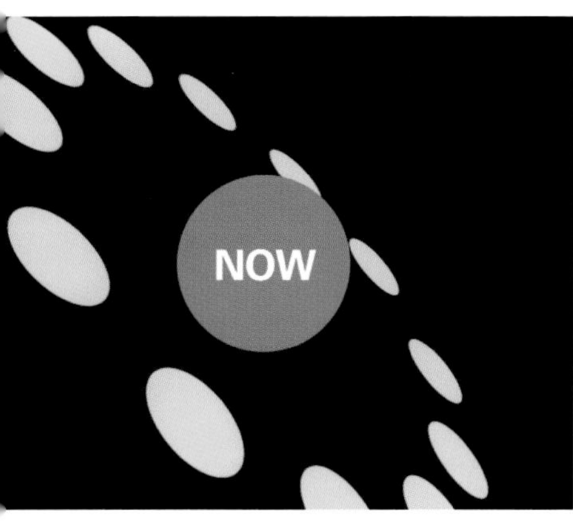
NOW

abc

abc

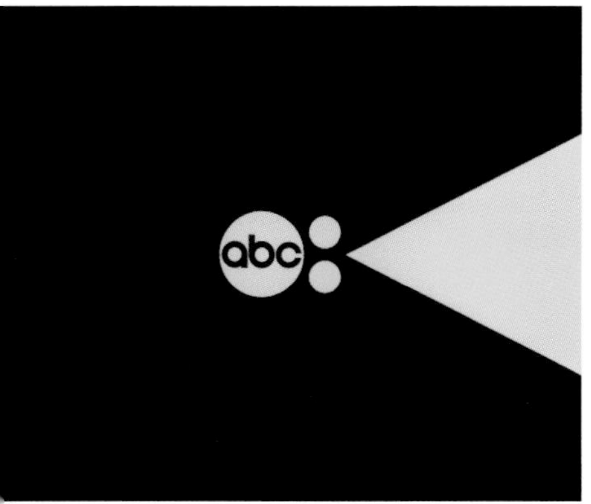
abc

Dharma
& Greg
Now
abc

Exhale.
The Practice
abc

abc

Thieves
abc

NOW
abc

2

abc

Next
abc

## ANDREA VALENTINI b. 1961

*Cranston, Rhode Island*

1, 2

The promise and potential of modern technology, modern materials, and modern movements are undeniable. But these advances can often be troublesome to latter-day Luddites—and basically to just about anyone else who craves futurism with a human touch. Andrea Valentini has made this handshake of disparate philosophies an essential component of her mission as an industrial designer. She effects this union of opposites with flair, insightfulness, and an admirable amount of sparky savoir faire.

Consider the Rhode Island designer's Egg Chair, for example. A large chaise longue made of polyurethane foam, it sports a friendly, tactile corrugated surface. So far, so good: comfort with quirky cachet. But look more closely and Valentini's genius becomes radiantly clear. The Egg can turn in on itself like Pac-Man, the footrest folding back into the seat, the corrugated ridges all nestling together to form a giant and rather friendly looking ball.

Another project involved creating a bowl out of polyethylene foam. Again, Valentini relied on tactile ridges, this time spreading them out loosely to create a soft, asymmetrical container called the Shell Bowl. It looks like it sounds: a conch-like vessel with a beckoning depression at the center to hold fruit, nuts, whatever. Even empty, it invites a relationship, a stroke, a pat, even, oddly enough, a surreptitious grope. And the designer's sculpted Cocoon Chair, another polyethylene production, resembles a giant washcloth or packing blanket casually thrown to the ground in loose folds, patiently awaiting the moment it can cuddle you, satisfying its primary passion. That sense of connection, that belief in objects that encourage physical attraction rather than abstract admiration, makes Valentini's work endlessly enthralling. **MO**

1, 2
**EGG CHAIR**
**CLOSED AND OPEN VIEWS**
High-density polyurethane foam, 2001
Designer: Andrea Valentini
Manufacturer: Coosh, Rhode Island

3
**SHELL BOWL**
Cross-link polyethylene,
aluminum base, 2001
Designer: Andrea Valentini

4
**COCOON LAMP**
Cross-link polyethylene, aluminum
base, 2002
Designer: Andrea Valentini

5
**COCOON CHAIR**
Stamped cross-link polyethylene,
PVC, fleece, 2002
Designer: Andrea Valentini

Photography: Andrea Valentini

4

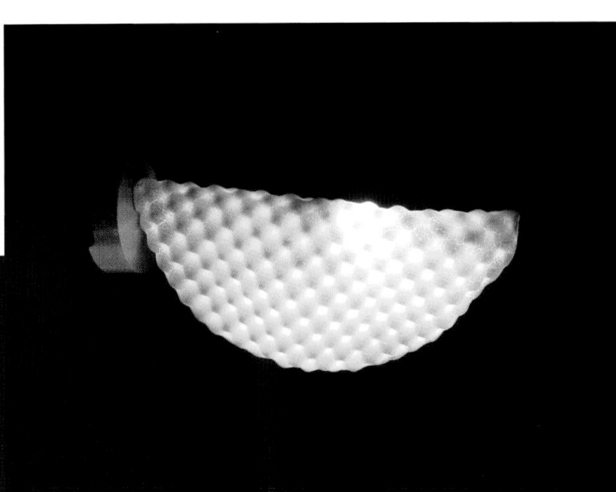

3

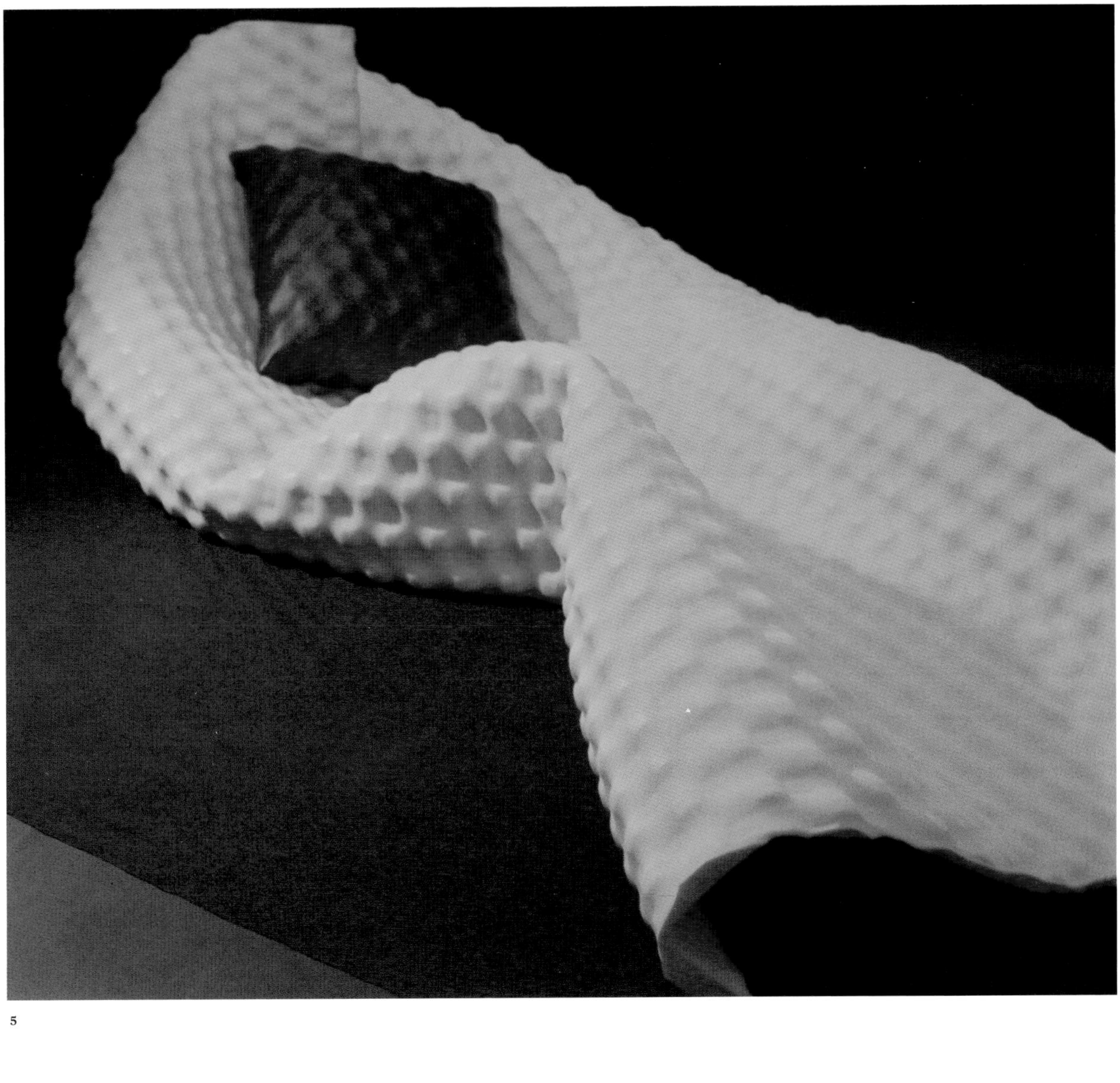

5

## GABRIELA VALENZUELA-HIRSCH b. 1960

*Southampton, New York*

1, 2

As the founder, president, and chief designer of Heartwood, a home-accessories company launched in 1996, artist and former fashion designer Gabriela Valenzuela-Hirsch takes a rigorously environmentally conscious attitude to home products. Driftwood, dead limbs and branches, tree stumps left behind by loggers in the 1940s and 1950s, and naturally fallen trees harvested from the rain forests of Valenzuela's native country, Costa Rica, are recycled into a multitude of affordable but soigné objects for everyday use: platters, mugs, saucers, plates, limited-edition chairs, benches, tables, checkerboard placemats composed of dozens of square scraps of burnished wood. The items are utilitarian and the woods exotic—among them, lignum vitae, corteza, balsamo, and cocobolo—but the guiding principle behind each of these creations is transcendant. Her goal is to utilize every piece of wood gathered and every byproduct that results from the creative process, in its entirety. Post-production wood scraps are transformed into furniture for rural classrooms, Valenzuela-Hirsch explains, while sawdust and wood shavings find their way into the plywood manufactured for the same schools' desks.

This whole-earth thoroughness of purpose extends beyond Valenzuela-Hirsch's near-holistic use of raw materials. She has become a major mover-and-shaker in the Central American conservation movement, encouraging the Costa Rican government to place tighter restrictions on logging, promote preservation of the country's primordial forests, and encourage reforestation of previously denuded tracts of land. And taking the philanthropic efforts one step further, many of Heartwood's products are handmade by a cooperative of Costa Rican craftspeople, primarily women in rural areas, which provides regular employment, educates children, supports healthcare, and builds stronger communities. **MO**

1
**COASTER AND NAPKIN RING**
Cocobola wood, 2000
Designer: Gabriela Valenzuela-Hirsch
Manufacturer: Heartwood, Costa Rica
Photography: Jonathan Kantor

2
**SHELL-SHAPE SMALL BOWL**
Corteza wood, 2000
Designer: Gabriela Valenzuela-Hirsch
Manufacturer: Heartwood, Costa Rica
Photography: Jonathan Kantor

3
**DRUNKEN SET**
Barware and table, 2000
Corteza wood, blown glass
Designer: Gabriela Valenzuela-Hirsch
Manufacturers: Artes y Oficios, Mortensen Ltda. (for glass decanter)
Photography: Jerry Hirsch

4
**APAREJO COUPLETS/SCULPTURES**
Golden genisaro wood, 2001
Designer: Gabriela Valenzuela-Hirsch
Manufacturer: Chavsalazar
Photography: Melvin Estrella

3

4

## JHONEN VASQUEZ b. 1974

*San Jose, California*

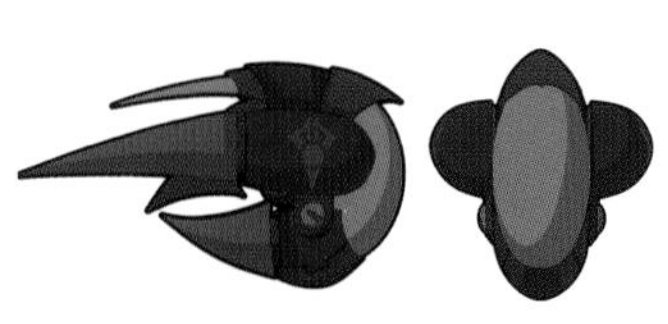


1–4

A galactic trespasser intent on destroying the Earth—if he can just manage not to bungle the job—Zim is the anarchic but strangely appealing cartoon menace at the center of the series *Invader Zim*. His eyes bulge, his voice is metallically shrill, and he hides his hideous alien form within the unassuming shell of a fairly irritating, know-it-all elementary-school student. Oh, and then there's his robot sidekick, Gir, who sports an assumed canine exterior. When the destruction of the globe is within reach, Gir can be tempted from that goal by a friendly pat on the head or the toss of a rubber ball. It's a tough life for a villain. Especially for Zim, a pint-size bad guy who doesn't realize that his superiors came up with his world-destroying mission simply to get him off his home planet, Irk.

Created by writer and artist Jhonen Vasquez (author of the comic book serials "Johnny the Homicidal Maniac," about an oddly appealing serial killer, and "Squee!," the story of a boy frightened of literally everything) and brilliantly brought to life by the artists of Viacom's Nickelodeon (which briefly broadcast an animated series based on Vasquez's 'toon), *Invader Zim* is a dark perversity of the cartoon world, a black mamba slithering through the garden of childish delights. More superklutz than supervillain, though, Zim occupies a middle ground and none too steadily. His grotesque appetites and poisonous plots are infused with the DNA of Stan Laurel and Oliver Hardy.

"I love the idea of anything that's considered to be a superior being—they've got all this amazing technology—and yet ultimately they're still just idiots," Jhonen Vasquez explained in an interview with *Animation World Magazine*. "[Zim has] this incredible arsenal at his hand and the only thing that's stopping him from destroying Earth is the fact that he's a moron." **MO**

1–4
**INVADER ZIM: SPACE SHIP DESIGNS**
Digital animation, 2001
Designer: Jhonen Vasquez
Client: Nickelodeon
Imagery: © 2002
Viacom International Inc.

5–7
**INVADER ZIM**
Stills from animated series, 2001
Designer: Jhonen Vasquez
Client: Nickelodeon
Imagery: © 2002
Viacom International Inc.

5

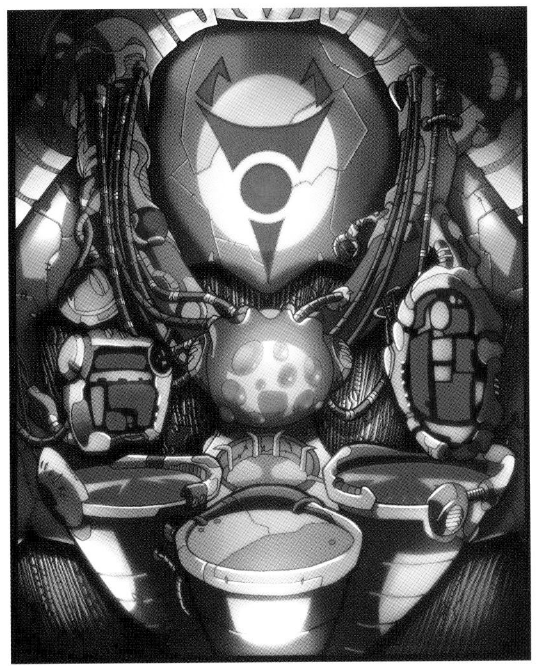

6

7

## CESAR VERGARA b. 1956

*Ridgefield, Connecticut*

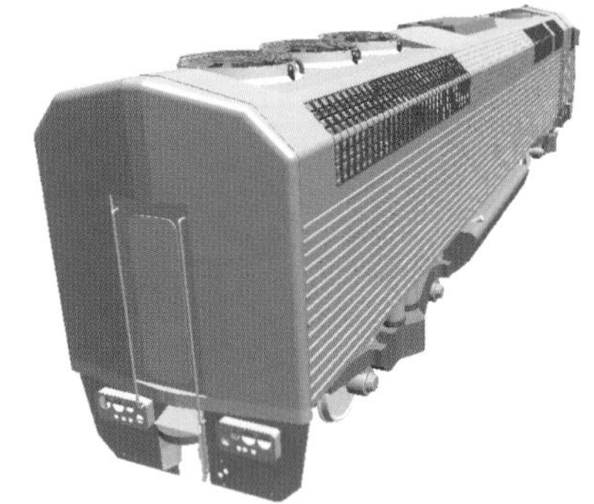

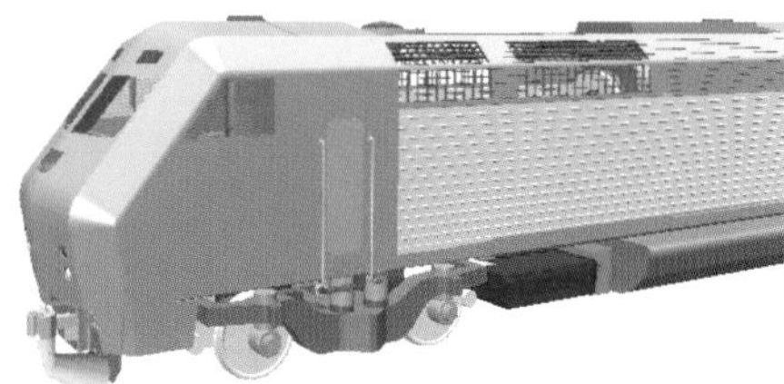

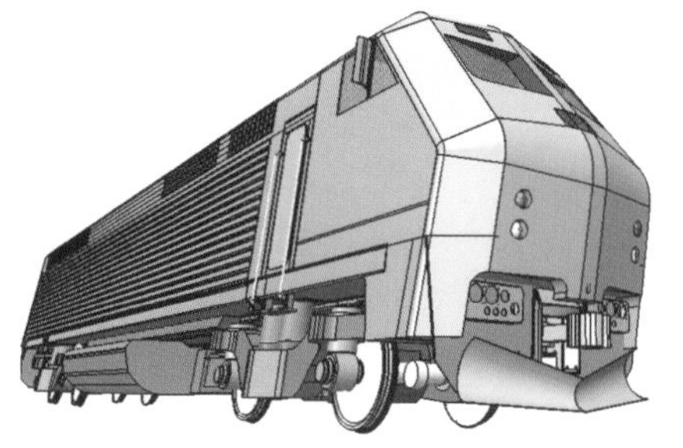

1–3

Cesar Vergara has loved trains since childhood. But this energetic industrial designer, born in Mexico City and presently the chief designer of the New Jersey Transit Corporation, is well aware that trains remain misunderstood vehicles in the autocentric United States. But Vergara has a solution: the power of positive tinkering.

In Vergara's Cascades Talgo and Las Vegas Talgo, 600-foot-long passenger trains that were manufactured in conjuction with the Spanish train giant Talgo and the Electro-Motive Division of General Motors (EMD), what could have been yet more anonymous people movers have become compelling fantasies of the rails. With the simple addition of a pair of seven-foot-tall, hollow fiberglass fins placed at the top rear of the locomotive and matching fins installed at either end of the full length of passenger cars, the silver-and-blue Las Vegas Talgo and its sister, the Cascades Talgo—created by Vergara for the Washington State Department of Transportation—resemble industrial-strength Chinese dragons. Rather than merely chugging from point A to point B, they seem to hurtle down the tracks with anthropomorphic glee. As Vergara explains, "The fins don't provide any aerodynamic effect, but they do provide a spiritual lift."

Inside is more design for delight's sake. The Las Vegas Talgo's bistro car, for instance, has an old-time glamour unimagined since the days of Henry Dreyfuss's 1938 design for the 20th Century Limited. Vergara paved its vast ceiling with a 3M Scotchprint of outer-space galaxies, the stars powered by 1,200 fiber-optic lights.

The result? Statistics indicate that ridership in the Cascades corridor, where both trains currently run, has increased significantly since their introduction, proof that if you build it, they will come. **MO**

1–3
**NEW JERSEY TRANSIT PL 42-AC**
Digital renderings of locomotive, 2002
Designer: Cesar Vergara
Manufacturers: Alstom, EMD General Motors
Renderings: Jorge Vara Alstom, Cesar Vergara

4
**CASCADES TALGO**
Train exterior, 2001
Designer: Cesar Vergara
Manufacturers: Talgo, EMD General Motors
Photography: Steven Brown

5
**LAS VEGAS TALGO**
Train interior, 2001
Designer: Cesar Vergara
Manufacturer: Talgo; ceiling decals by Reidler Decal
Client: Washington State Department of Transportation, Amtrak
Photography: Steven Brown

4

5

## KIKI WALLACE b. 1956
## MARK SOFIELD b. 1959

### PROSPECT NEW TOWN

*Longmont, Colorado*

1

Prospect could not be more different from any other commercial housing development in the United States. Imagine a modernist sudivision—even the two words cause friction—and you have Prospect.

The brainchild of developer Kiki Wallace, Prospect first came into existence as another manifestation of New Urbanism with a land plan and neotraditional design code by the firm Duany Plater-Zyberk. Enter architect Mark Sofield. Hired by Wallace to design and review plans for the builders of Prospect, Sofield cut his teeth on the Queen Anne, Tudor, and Craftsman bungalow houses originally encouraged.

Buoyed with confidence at the success of phase one, Wallace let on that he had more radical intentions and found he had a sympathetic soul in his architect. In a remarkable shift of events in the spec housing business, Wallace and Sofield turned Prospect into a beacon of modernism. Here, the Bauhaus meets the vernacular of Colorado farming and mining structures. Add to that a predilection for stucco—a material ideally suited to the baking light of the West—and you have a veritable Venice-on-the-prairie of hot colored boxes. The palette is by Kelly Feeney, the third member of Prospect's architectural review committee.

Wallace and Sofield—along with their builders, neighbors, and associated architects—have embarked on an experiment that hums with the echoed ideals of American utopian communities, from the Shakers to 1960s communes. Only this time, the ambition is even grander. Prospect's founder and designer are creating a community that is diverse in every sense of the word, but they are doing it within the capitalist system of home ownership. Wallace and Sofield have found that if you build a brave new world, the folks drawn to it will be different—less dependent on received notions of what makes a house and who makes up a town. **SY**

1
**PROSPECT STREETSCAPE**
2002
Design team: Mark Sofield, designer; Kiki Wallace, developer; Kelly Feeney, colorist

2–5
**PROSPECT HOUSES**
1997–2002
Details of homes in housing development
Design: Leroy Street Studio (2); Mark Sofield (3, 4); Gray Organschi Architecture (5)

Photography: Jeff Minton for *dwell magazine*

3

2

5

4

DAVID WASCO b. 1954

SANDY WASCO b. 1954

*Los Angeles*

For David Wasco and Sandy Reynolds-Wasco, God is truly in the details. A production designer for Hollywood films, David Wasco has visualized scripts for such leading independent directors as Quentin Tarantino, David Mamet, and Wes Anderson, usually collaborating with his wife, set decorator Sandy Reynolds-Wasco, who selects furnishings and objects with an equally unerring eye. Together the Wascos create spheres of significant details that embody the lives of their films' fictional characters.

Typically called upon to depict society's fringe, David Wasco has developed an American Eccentric style using combinations of existing sites and new sets. To fashion the ancestral home of the regally weird family in *The Royal Tenenbaums* (2001), Wasco and director Wes Anderson selected a derelict Harlem brownstone that the Wascos restored and redressed. The result was a contemporary yet anachronistic world filled with the detritus of Etheline Tenenbaum, an anthropologist, and her precocious children, all marooned in emotional adolescence. The children's spaces are collages of their quirky interests. The daughter's bedroom, an elegant collection of masks, ballet slippers, and a single bed curtained off like a stage, displays traces of her youthful career as a playwright. The two sons' rooms are a compendium of scientific contraptions, from microscopes and mice cages to antique anatomical models. One son retreats to an indoor tent that offers both a protective, maternal environment and the potential for secret adventure. Throughout the house, layers of mismatched patterns suggest that the Tenenbaums are a family of misfits—both with each other and with the world outside. The Wascos' sets for *The Royal Tenenbaums* go beyond mere decor to become tableaux whose meanings derive from the things they contain—cabinets of curiosities from an odd and magical kingdom. **DA**

**THE ROYAL TENENBAUMS**
Sets from feature film, 2001
Production designer: David Wasco
Set decorator: Sandy Reynolds-Wasco
Director: Wes Anderson
Client: Touchstone Pictures, Los Angeles
Photography: James Hamilton

## DENNIS WEDLICK b. 1959

*New York City*

1, 2

In this age of increasingly Brobdingnagian suburban houses, where extravagant square footage often can mean the death of artistry, Dennis Wedlick is an anomaly: a modern-minded, history-inspired architect whose spatial philosophy continues to be that less truly is more.

Trained in the office of Philip Johnson, *eminence grise* of modernism, Wedlick is the master of a magical portfolio of no-waste, high-style, neo-traditional domestic buildings constructed from utterly mundane materials: standard-issue windows, off-the-rack columns, lowly asphalt shingles, prefabricated metal fireboxes, millwork bought by the linear yard. By processing these typically uninspiring ingredients in a strategic, inventive, and cost-effective manner, Wedlick creates homes whose deceptively small spaces recall the footprint-defying buildings seen in *Tom and Jerry* cartoons, where cat chases mouse into a cottage that conceals an impossible multitude of vast rooms. Upon seeing Wedlick's own house in Kinderhook, New York, an observer once called the architect's buildings "as frugal as a Shaker sanctum and playful as a possum."

Outside, roofs are dramatically broad and steep, minimizing the need for costly external finishing while allowing for peaked silhouettes that recall everything from Gunnar Asplund to nineteenth-century Russian dachas. Inside, ceilings alternate between high and low, creating a telescoping sense of luxurious space—even in a house as small as 22-1/2 feet long by 20 feet wide, like the one Wedlick designed for clients in the Catskill Mountains.

Despite the fairytale silhouettes and curious footprints that have become leitmotivs of his work—among them, houses shaped like stars or recalling upended Viking ships—a Wedlick house contains little wasted space but extraordinary amounts of poetry. **MO**

**1, 2**
**SAGAPONACK ARC HOUSE**
Sagaponack, New York, 1998
Exterior and interior views
Designer: Dennis Wedlick, Dennis Wedlick Architects
Photography: Jeff Goldberg/ESTO

**3, 4**
**MALDEN BRIDGE HOUSE**
Malden Bridge, New York, 1999
Exterior and aerial views
Designer: Dennis Wedlick, Dennis Wedlick Architects
Photography: Jeff Goldberg/ESTO

**5, 6**
**FORESTBURG HOUSE**
Forestburg, New York, 1997
Designer: Dennis Wedlick, Dennis Wedlick Architect
Photography: Jeff Goldberg/ESTO

3, 4

5, 6

DAVID WEEKS b. 1968

LINDSEY ADELMAN b. 1968

## DAVID WEEKS LIGHTING + BUTTER

*New York City*

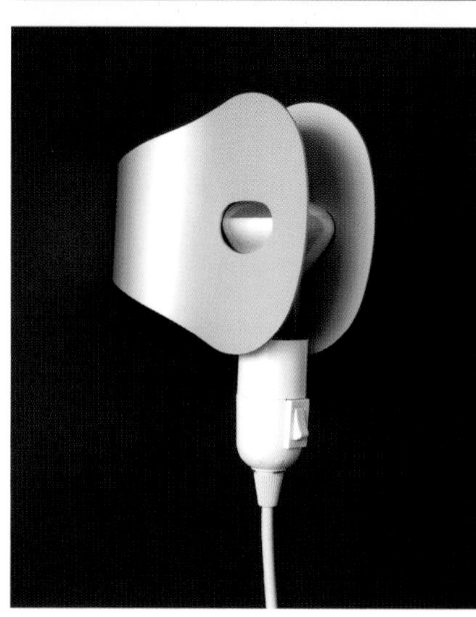

1–3

David Weeks has figured out how to have his cake and eat it—with Butter. Weeks functions both as an independent studio designer under David Weeks Lighting (DWL) and as Lindsey Adelman's partner in Butter, which specializes in mass-produced and eminently affordable lighting. Between the two, he has managed to achieve an elusive balance between the rawness of the specific and the smoothness of the general.

The lamps, wall sconces, and chandeliers that have their provenance with DWL are essentially limited editions produced by hand in a system that medieval guilds would recognize. The work reflects a historically informed aesthetic, albeit more contemporary, evoking the sculptural sensibility of Alexander Calder's mobiles and the organic modernism of Charles and Ray Eames's furniture. Lamp shades are variously made of hand-finished steel and aluminum, fiberglass, plastic, paper, and wood veneer with an exactitude not possible with high volume. Armatures are soldered in the studio. Details such as silk-covered electrical cords and turned wood knobs are essential to his finely honed design.

Such obsessions are not for Lindsey Adelman. After working together at DWL, she and David decided to take the opposite tack: selling designs not lamps. With bare bulbs, wire, sockets, cords, and paper, they design the simplest (and most satisfying) of lighting fixtures and hand them off to commercial producers who can sell most of them for less than an average monthly electrical bill. Butter now not only creates the disarmingly direct Dumpling pendant lamp, the Daisy Chain, and the Tong wall sconce, but has recently expanded to pursue collaborations with other designers in other disciplines.

Weeks's practice may be bifurcated, but that's because he doesn't see access to aesthetics as a choice. He's an equal opportunity designer. **SY**

1
**DAISY CHAIN PENDANT**
Lighting, 2001
Steel wire, electrical parts
Designers: Lindsey Adelman and David Weeks, Butter
Photography: Courtesy Butter

2
**DUMPLING PENDANT**
Lighting, 2001
Fiberglass paper, nylon thread, steel, electrical parts
Designers: Lindsey Adelman and David Weeks, Butter
Photography: Courtesy Butter

3
**TONG WALL LIGHT**
Anodized aluminum, electrical parts, 2001
Designers: Lindsey Adelman and David Weeks, Butter
Photography: Courtesy Butter

4
**HANGING MOBILE**
Aluminum, nickel plated steel, 1998
Designer: David Weeks
Photography: Antoine Bootz

5
**ALUMINUM BULLET CHANDELIER**
Aluminum, blackened steel, 1998
Designer: David Weeks
Photography: Antoine Bootz

4

5

# LORRAINE WILD b. 1953

LORRAINE WILD STUDIO

*Los Angeles*

1–4

5–7

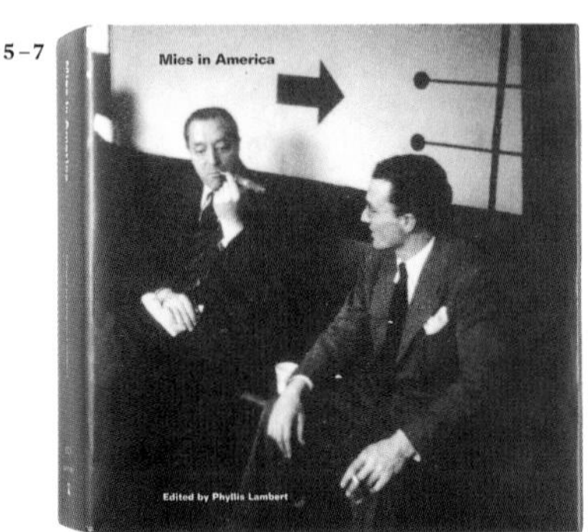


9–11

12–15

Lorraine Wild works from the word. She takes her design cues from content, sequencing the information in a web of visual puns and parallel moves. In *The World from Here*, an exhibition catalog of rare books, she excels as both editorial diplomat and auteur. The books appear on a neutral white ground in accordance with curatorial wishes; the essays appear on separate pages, superimposed over flat planes of color shaped like the books they describe. The silhouette becomes a mnemonic device for the previous page, the subtle palette, a form of structural punctuation.

*Mies in America*, a book dedicated to the details of spatial relationships, drew on Wild's generational advantage. Trained as a graphic designer when galleys of type were pasted on gridded boards, she bridges the conceptual gap between the unstructured space of the computer screen and the tangible dimensions of the page. Her systems of proportion are anchored in the physical process of printing. With the *Michal Rovner* catalog, Wild shifts her frame of reference. Choreographed video sequences float on saturated fields of black, alluding to the immersive quality of art seen in the dark.

The epitome of collaborative authorship, *L.A. Now* has a list of credits more akin to a Hollywood movie than a book. Instigated by architect Thom Mayne and educator Richard Koshalek, it involved, among others, UCLA, Arts Center, and Wild's own students and colleagues at California Institute of the Arts. Never shy of complexity, Wild codeveloped and art-directed a wholly new kind of photographic and statistical atlas of Los Angeles, drawing a nuanced portrait of a city that is often cast as a set of clichés. Like all Wild's work, *L.A. Now* is the product of a collaboration in which the designer is allowed to interpret the conversation. **SY**

1–4
**MICHAL ROVNER: THE SPACE BETWEEN**
Illustrated book, 2002, offset lithography
Designer: Lorraine Wild with Robert Ruehlman and Jessica Fleischmann
Photography: Michal Rovner et al.
Publisher: Whitney Museum of Art, New York, and Steidl, Göttingen

5–7
**MIES IN AMERICA**
Illustrated book, 2001, offset lithography
Designer: Lorraine Wild
Publisher: Canadian Centre for Architecture, Montréal, and Harry N. Abrams, New York

9–11
**L.A. NOW**
Illustrated book, 2001, offset lithography
Art direction: Lorraine Wild and Scott Zukowski
Design: Jessica Fleischmann, Stuart Smith, and Jon Sueda, California Institute for the Arts
Photography: Mark Lipson, Karin Apollnia Müller, Erik Hillard et al.
Publisher: Art Center College of Design, Pasadena, and University of California Press, Berkeley

12–15
**THE WORLD FROM HERE**
Illustrated book, 2001, offset lithography
Designer: Lorraine Wild
Photography: Paula Goldman
Publisher: UCLA Grunwald Center for the Graphic Arts and the Armand Hammer Museum of Art and Cultural Center, Los Angeles

l.a. now
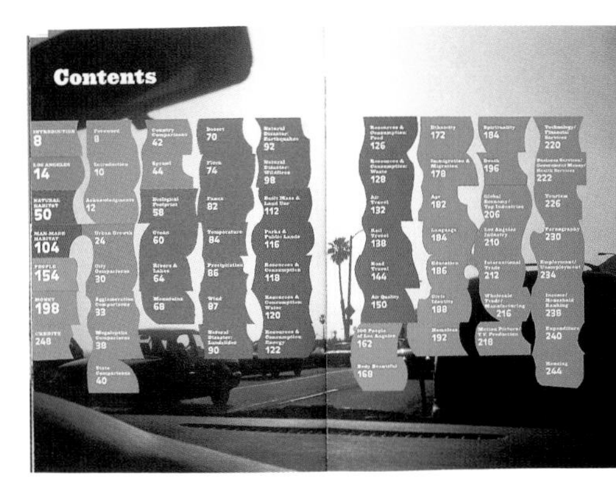
Contents
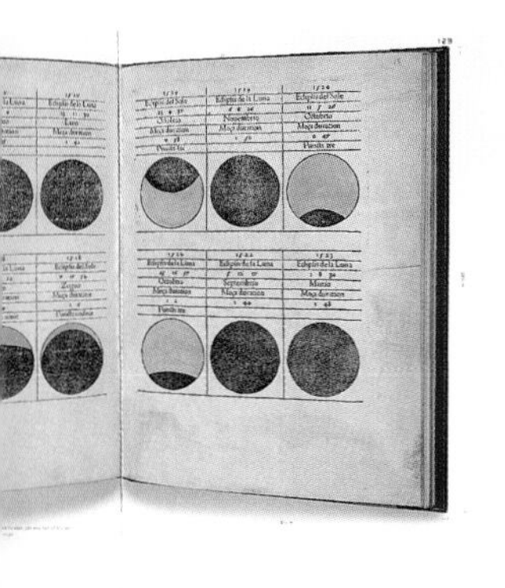

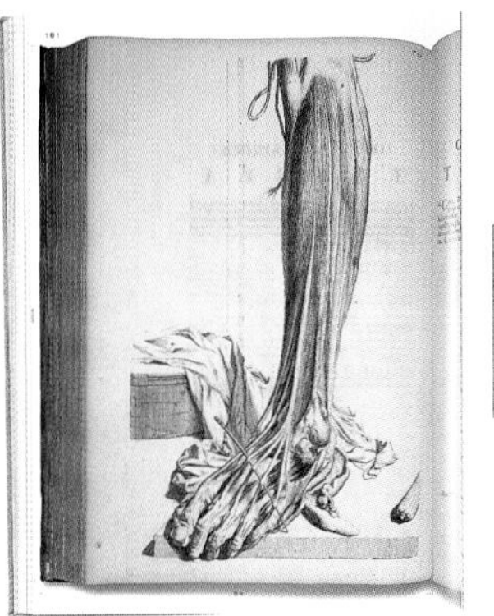
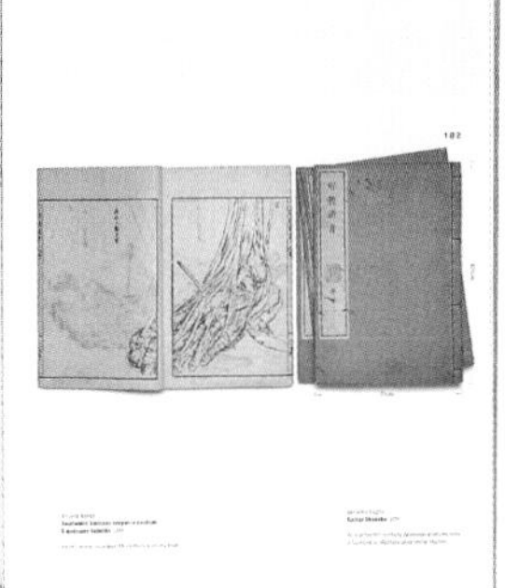

STEPHEN WOLFRAM b. 1959

*Boston, Massachusetts, and Champaign, Illinois*

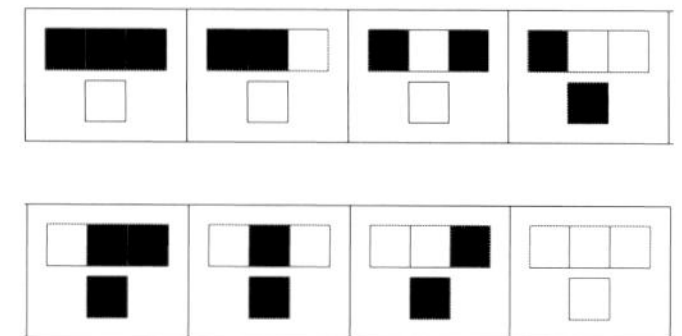

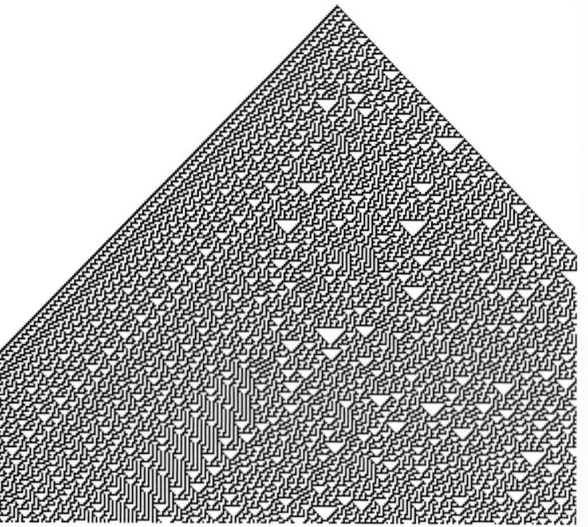

In May 2002 Stephen Wolfram published an enormous book that rethinks nearly every field of analytical thought, from physics, biology, and mathematics to philosophy and theology. *A New Kind of Science*, which is 1,195 pages long and took ten years to write, revolves around the following premise: simple rules can generate immense complexity. Indeed, the most complex behaviors in the physical world—from weather systems to financial markets—can be modeled by a few rules, which, allowed to play out in time, yield intricate and unpredictable patterns.

Wolfram's research uses cellular automata, sets of rules governing a grid of squares. A cell is turned on or off on the basis of the cells preceding it on the grid. Because they simulate patterns of growth and change, cellular automata are considered a form of artificial life—a life materialized in a purely graphic form, on a page or computer screen.

The genesis of Wolfram's theory is Rule 30, a cellular automaton that begins from a single cell, growing line by line into a pyramid with a wildly complex interior surface. Rule 30 is, essentially, a two-color automaton—each cell is either on or off. When automata are built with colors or shades of gray, they are governed by a much larger number of rules and conditions. Although we might expect a system generated from more rules (more colors) to be more complex, Wolfram discovered that this is not, in fact, the case. The level of complexity achieved in the multicolored automata at right is comparable to the complexity generated by Rule 30.

This insight has stunning implications. When systems reach a certain level of complexity, they become equivalent to one another. Human thought, for example, is no more or less complex than the movement of smoke through a room. According to Stephen Wolfram, the workings of the entire universe will ultimately be reduced to several lines of code. **EL**

1–3

1
**RULE 30: RULE SPECIFICATION**
Digital image, 2002
Designer: Stephen Wolfram
Publisher: Wolfram Media, Champaign, Illinois

2
**RULE 30: 25 STEPS**
Digital image, 2002
Designer: Stephen Wolfram
Publisher: Wolfram Media, Champaign, Illinois

3
**RULE 30: 250 STEPS**
Digital image (detail), 2002
Designer: Stephen Wolfram
Publisher: Wolfram Media, Champaign, Illinois

4
**TOTALISTIC CELLULAR AUTOMATA**
Digital image, 2002
Designer: Stephen Wolfram
Publisher: Wolfram Media, Champaign, Illinois

4

## JIM ZIVIC b. 1960

BURNING RELIC

*New York City*

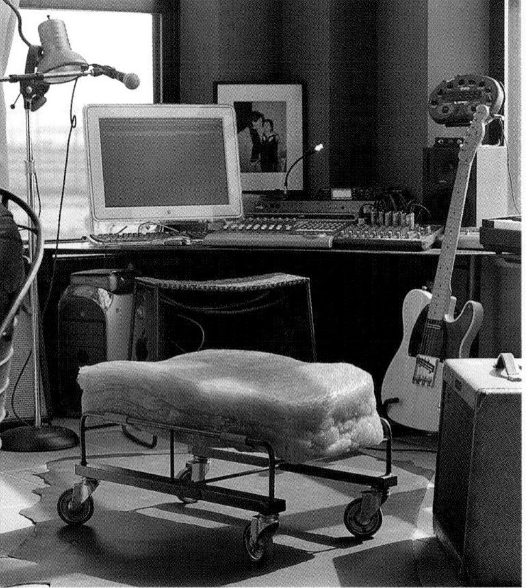

1, 2

The hardest line to walk may be that between craft and design—unless you are Jim Zivic of Burning Relic. Zivic understands craft as a process of making, not an aesthetic, and design as a conceptual framework, not a particular practice. In his case, the framework embraces sources as diverse as Joseph Beuys's sculpture and Civil War campaign furniture.

Spare but not spartan, Zivic's furniture is elemental and sensual at the same time. Coal, rubber, leather, and steel are the palette of raw materials he transforms into functional furnishings with minimal intervention. Anthracite blocks are carved and polished; raw Malaysian rubber is cut and stacked; leather panels are seamed and stapled. The result is a suite of tables, seats, and floor coverings that seem both familiar and new. The typical geography of materials in the domestic setting has been redrawn. In Jim Zivic's world you can find yourself literally sitting on flooring or stacking your books on a big rock.

At his farm in upstate New York, he shapes side tables out of coal monoliths taken from Pennsylvania mines. Zivic carves the anthracite blocks with diamond saws, sanding and finishing them to varying degrees, from matte to mirror. He fabricates stools with seats of linked leather, welding their armatures in delicate lines of steel. The lids of baby pianos are deployed as table tops or loveseats. In a music studio for Lou Reed, Zivic brings all the elements together with off-beat elegance.

Call it post-industrial, call it personal; Zivic's work is rooted in childhood collections of arrowheads and a contemporary do-it-yourself ethos. Absent is the preciousness and pretension of art furniture. Present is a design sensibility that locates luxury in materials but deflects their latent kitsch with a disciplined modesty of form **SY**

1, 2
**STUDIO**
New York City, 2002
Designer: Jim Zivic
Client: Lou Reed

3
**LEATHER LINK STOOL**
Leather, steel, 2001
Designer: Jim Zivic

4
**INGRID**
Side table, 2001
Polished, carved coal
Designer: Jim Zivic

Photography: David Sundberg

3

4

# index

A

**FEARLESS**
Textile pattern design, 2001
Lithograph on nylon
Designer: Geoff McFetridge, Champion Graphics
Client: Stussy, Irvine, California

B

**RED DAWN**
Textile pattern design, 2001
Lithograph on canvas
Designer: Geoff McFetridge, Champion Graphics

C

**STONER FOREST**
Textile pattern design, 2001
Lithograph on canvas
Designer: Geoff McFetridge, Champion Graphics

D

**REPEAT**
Fabric (detail), 2002
Cotton, polyester, rayon
Designer: Hella Jongerius in collaboration with Maharam Design Studio
Manufacturer: Maharam

E

**PRADA WALLPAPER**
New York City, 2002
Digital print on coated fabric
Designers: Karen Hsu and Michael Rock, 2x4 (with OMA/AMO architects: Rem Koolhaas, Ole Scheren, Eric Chang, Tim Archambault)
Client: Prada

F

**CHROMOSOME 22**
Gene map (detail), 2002
Designer: Benjamin Fry, MIT Media Lab

G

**LOOKING CLOSER CONFERENCE**
Poster (detail), 2001
Offset lithograph
Designer: Paul Elliman
Publisher: American Institute of Graphic Arts (AIGA)

H

**WOODGRAIN**
Pattern design, 2001
Designer: Todd St. John, HunterGatherer

I

**TOOTHBRUSH AND TOOTHPASTE**
Endpaper, 2001
Illustrator: Christoph Niemann
Art director: Robert Priest
Publisher: American Illustration Annual

J

**THE UNITED STATES**
Painting, 1999
Acrylic on canvas
Artist: Paula Scher

K

**MODERN CONSTELLATIONS**
Pattern, silkscreened pillow, 2001
Designers: Todd St. John and Gary Benzel, HunterGatherer

L

**THE INNERMOST MINDSCAPE**
Textile design, 2001
Designer: Geoff McFetridge, Champion Graphics

A

B

C

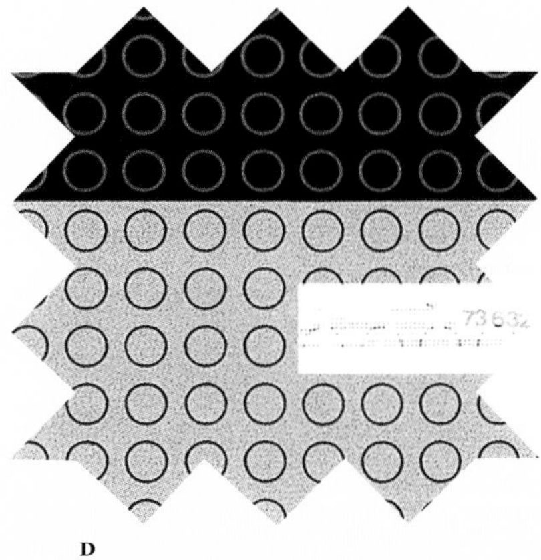
D

E

F

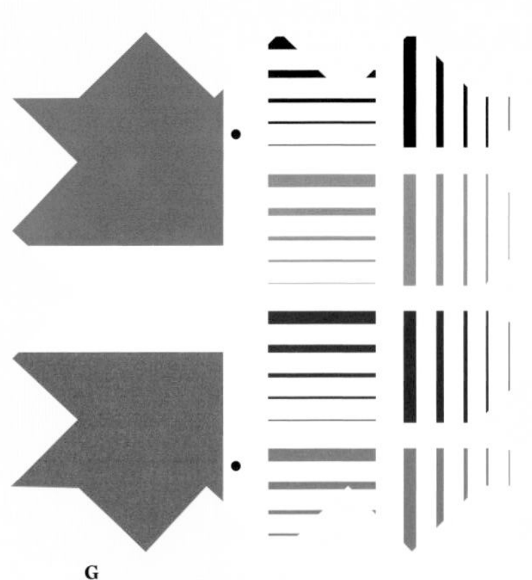
G

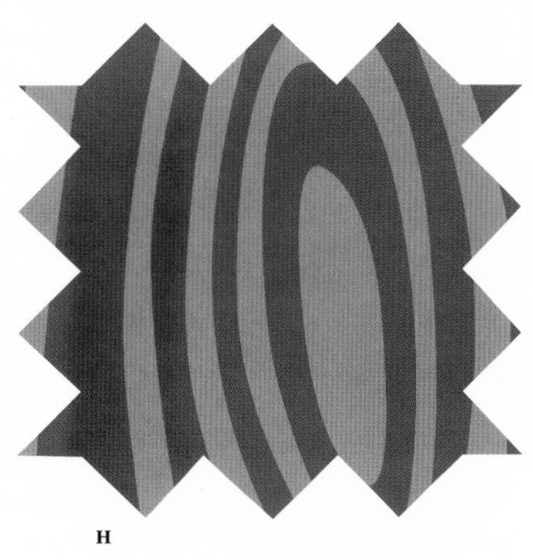
H

I

J

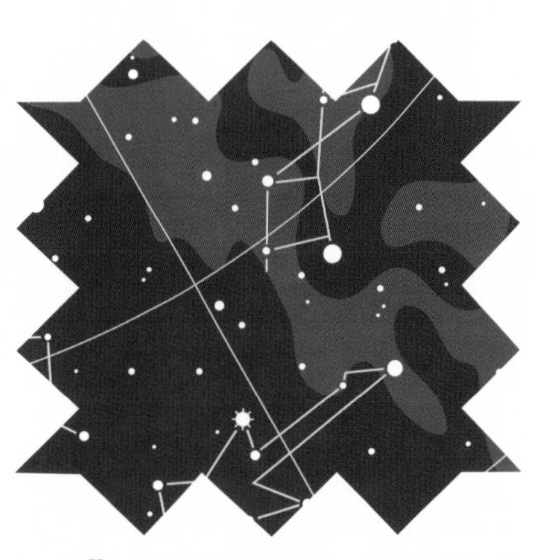
K

L

BOOK DESIGN

*Ellen Lupton*
*Cooper-Hewitt*
*National Design Museum*

COVER ART

*Patterns on cover and endpapers designed by Geoff McFetridge, Champion Graphics*

TYPOGRAPHY

NEUTRA DISPLAY
*House Industries, 2002*

Mercury News
*The Hoefler Type Foundry, 2002*

Retina
*The Hoefler Type Foundry, 2002*

EDITORS

*Elizabeth Johnson*
*Cooper-Hewitt*
*National Design Museum*

*Mark Lamster*
*Princeton Architectural Press*

MANAGING EDITOR

*Allison Henriksen*
*Cooper-Hewitt*
*National Design Museum*

DONALD ALBRECHT is an independent curator, architect, and writer who is Exhibitions Curator at Cooper-Hewitt, National Design Museum. He has curated many exhibitions on twentieth-century architecture and design, including the 2000 *National Design Triennial: Design Culture Now* and *New Hotels for Global Nomads.* He is exhibition director and catalog editor for the international traveling exhibition, *The Work of Charles and Ray Eames: A Legacy of Invention,* organized by the Library of Congress and the Vitra Design Museum.

ELLEN LUPTON is a curator, writer, and graphic designer. She is the Cooper-Hewitt, National Design Museum's Curator for Contemporary Design. She has produced numerous exhibitions and publications, including *Mechanical Brides: Women and Machines from Home to Office,* the 2000 *National Design Triennial: Design Culture Now,* and *Skin: Surface, Substance, and Design.* She is chair of the graphic design programs at the Maryland Institute College of Art in Baltimore.

MITCHELL OWENS is a writer specializing in the field of interior design. Currently Interior Design Director at *Elle Décor,* Owens has written about art, architecture, design, design history, garden design, and numerous other topics. He is a regular contributor to *The New York Times* and *New York Times Magazine.*

SUSAN YELAVICH is the former Assistant Director for Public Programs at Cooper-Hewitt, where she was responsible for the programmatic development of the Museum's exhibitions, education programs, and publications. She curated the Museum's exhibition *Design for Life: A Centennial Celebration,* and is the author of the books, *Design for Life* and *The Edge of the Millennium: An International Critique of Architecture, Urban Planning, Product and Communication Design.* She is now an independent consultant working on a variety of book and exhibition projects.

DUDE!
SHAKA
CHAMPION
DUDE!